About Pfeiffer

Pfeiffer serves the professional development and hands-on resource needs of training and human resource practitioners and gives them products to do their jobs better. We deliver proven ideas and solutions from experts in HR development and HR management, and we offer effective and customizable tools to improve workplace performance. From novice to seasoned professional, Pfeiffer is the source you can trust to make yourself and your organization more successful.

P Essential Knowledge Pfeiffer produces insightful, practical, and comprehensive materials on topics that matter the most to training and HR professionals. Our Essential Knowledge resources translate the expertise of seasoned professionals into practical, how-to guidance on critical workplace issues and problems. These resources are supported by case studies, worksheets, and job aids and are frequently supplemented with CD-ROMs, websites, and other means of making the content easier to read, understand, and use.

P Essential Tools Pfeiffer's Essential Tools resources save time and expense by offering proven, ready-to-use materials—including exercises, activities, games, instruments, and assessments—for use during a training or team-learning event. These resources are frequently offered in looseleaf or CD-ROM format to facilitate copying and customization of the material.

Pfeiffer also recognizes the remarkable power of new technologies in expanding the reach and effectiveness of training. While e-hype has often created whizbang solutions in search of a problem, we are dedicated to bringing convenience and enhancements to proven training solutions. All our e-tools comply with rigorous functionality standards. The most appropriate technology wrapped around essential content yields the perfect solution for today's on-the-go trainers and human resource professionals.

Pfeiffer
www.pfeiffer.com
Essential resources for training and HR professionals

The Pfeiffer Book of Successful Leadership Development Tools

The most enduring, effective, and valuable training
activities for developing leaders

Edited by Jack Gordon

Pfeiffer
A Wiley Imprint
www.pfeiffer.com

How to Use This Resource

This handbook is intended as a working resource for trainers and consultants attempting to encourage and develop better leadership in business and non-profit organizations. It focuses on building leadership skills in the management ranks, from first-level supervisors to top executives. All of the material in the book may be reproduced and used in training sessions and workshops. The presentations, experiential learning activities, and survey instruments are offered as a set of tools to select and employ in a wide range of situations.

It's a top-of-the-line tool kit. The handbook was compiled to represent the best material on leadership development published in the thirty-year history of the Pfeiffer *Annuals*.

Here are two examples suggesting how you might use it.

Situation 1

You're introducing a group of managers to Douglas McGregor's Theory X – Theory Y Model, the goal being to persuade and demonstrate to them that Theory Y assumptions and behaviors are more likely to get subordinates to put forth their best efforts on behalf of the organization. To refresh your memory or improve your own understanding, you might read the article about the model in the book's Presentations section. You also might draw on it for a brief lecture. You may even decide to copy and distribute it as a handout.

To provide participants with insight into the unexamined philosophies that may be guiding their own behavior, you might open the first workshop by having them complete and discuss a survey such as "The Supervisory and Leadership Beliefs Questionnaire," found in the Inventories section.

Then, to bring the lessons home, you might lead them through an exercise in the Experiential Learning Activities section—probably one of those we've classified as dealing with "Style and Approach." Several of those activities touch on McGregor's model, either explicitly or implicitly.

Situation 2

A new CEO has decided that changes in the company's policies or procedures are required if its managers are to lead more effectively. One of the experiential learning activities we've grouped under the heading "Organizations and Systems" might help the CEO—and you—deliver the message to lower-level managers in a visceral way. Check out activities such as "Organizational Structures: A Simulation," or "There's Never Time to Do It Right: A Relay Task."

In addition, questionnaires such as the two versions of Udai Pareek's "Motivational Analysis of Organizations" in the Inventories section could shed needed light on why the organization is stuck in its current operating mode and on the underlying factors that will have to be addressed if real change is to occur.

CHOOSE YOUR TOOLS

Even a quick glance through the Contents will suggest many other situations and needs that these resources could serve. It is up to you to choose the best tools for a given job. There are no "correct" presentations to match with correct activities and correct instruments in any particular circumstance, and we don't mean to suggest that you will want to use items from all three sections for every challenge that comes up. Use an instrument here, an experiential activity there, and a presentation simply for some good background reading.

When faced with any training challenge, it is up to you to learn as much as possible about the situation you're trying to address and the people involved in it before you settle on a strategy and tactics to set things right. These materials won't do your thinking for you, but they can help you solve a lot of problems. As a set, we think they make up the most versatile and useful tool kit you'll find for imparting insight and building skills in an organization's leadership ranks.

About the Editor

Jack Gordon is the former chief editor of *Training* Magazine. His articles and columns on workplace training have appeared in *The Wall Street Journal*, *San Diego Chronicle*, *Minneapolis Star Tribune*, and *Learning & Training Innovations*. He has written on other subjects for numerous publications, including *The Economist*, *The Journal of Law & Politics*, and *Independent Banker*. He has served as editor of numerous books, including *The Pfeiffer Book of Successful Conflict Management Tools* and *The Pfeiffer Book of Successful Communication Skill-Building Tools*.

Contents

Introduction

A book about leadership ought to begin by defining its terms. This puts me in hot water right off the bat because the best definition I have heard of leadership as a distinct phenomenon and a teachable skill is a troublesome one. It came from an Atlanta training consultant named Jim Georges.

If you want to isolate leadership as something different from bossing or managing on the one hand but also different from a collection of virtuous character traits that an individual could possess even if stranded alone on a desert island, then you have to think of it like this, Georges said: Leadership occurs whenever one person persuades one or more others to commit, "head and heart," to a given course of action.

That's all there is to it, he said. If you persuade me, intellectually and emotionally, that we should zig instead of zag, and I proceed to zig willingly, then you have demonstrated leadership in this situation.

That definition has some important virtues. It nicely illustrates the difference between following a leader because you want to and obeying a boss because you have to. It presents leadership as a skill that can be exercised not just by managers but by anyone in an organization, regardless of position authority. And it helps to demystify a subject that too easily can turn into an exercise in fawning idolatry, everyone worshipping at the feet of a golden statue of John F. Kennedy or former General Electric CEO Jack Welch.

But I call it troublesome because it shuts the door to a lot of things we want leadership to mean when we call for politicians to exhibit more of it or when we try to encourage and develop it in our workplaces. The definition insists that leadership, as a discrete skill, is really no more than the art of persuasion. We can say that Adolf Hitler was an evil leader, but we can't deny that he was a skillful and effective one. As soon as we try, we're talking about something other than leadership as a thing unto itself—or as a particular skill that can demonstrated and taught.

I think the point is valid, but as far as this book is concerned, it is also moot. When we set out to train leaders in our organizations, we want Churchills and Roosevelts, not Hitlers, and semantics be damned. The people who ran Enron Corp. were skillful and effective leaders, widely admired in the financial community and the business press, right up until they destroyed the company. That is, they were skillful and effective if leadership means no more than persuasion.

In practice, we cram a great many things besides persuasion skills into leadership-development programs, and well we should. We don't just seek to mold people who can attract followers. We want leaders who will take their followers somewhere worth going—leaders who will elicit employees' best efforts to make our companies successful and who will give us stronger, healthier, better functioning organizations. If, in the process, we blur the distinctions between leadership skills, management skills, organizational insight, and ethics, well . . . so what?

THE BEST OF THIRTY YEARS

This book is a compilation of material chosen from three decades of the Pfeiffer *Annuals* and *Handbooks*. Since 1969, trainers and consultants have found in these volumes a treasure chest of resources for a wide range of training and organization-development needs. They offer not just ideas or educational reading but tools meant to be put to work for training and other purposes.

Like the *Annuals*, the book is organized into three sections: Presentation and Discussion Resources (articles); Experiential Learning Activities; and Inventories, Questionnaires, and Surveys. The selections were picked as the all-time best the *Annuals* and *Handbooks* have to offer on matters pertaining to the topic of leadership development.

We chose the material not only for quality but with an eye toward serving a broad range of objectives. While it's true that leadership skills can be exercised by anyone, organizations are concerned primarily with developing those skills in their management ranks, from first-level supervisors to executives. We picked activities and instruments aimed at all levels of the management hierarchy.

We also tried to include material that addresses leadership from a number of different perspectives. This should increase the likelihood that you'll find an article, an activity, or a questionnaire suited to a particular training situation.

THE SECTIONS

The bias in our selections is toward practicality more than theory. For instance, in the opening article of the Presentations section, "Leadership Is in the Eye of the Follower," James M. Kouzes and Barry Z. Posner cut through a great deal of trait-based research to argue persuasively that the one indispensable factor defining effective leaders is credibility in the eyes of followers. Indeed, that's ultimately what will determine your success at persuading me to zig instead of zag. Almost everything else in this book really has to do in one way or another with how to build and maintain credibility.

The Presentations section does, however, include two pieces that deal directly with theory. One is an overview of management theorists who have shaped modern thought about organizations and leadership. The other is an explanation of Douglas McGregor's Theory X-Theory Y model, which we believe is central to determining which managers will be viewed merely as bosses and which will be seen as leaders.

The Experiential Learning Activities in the second section form the heart of the book. These are complete, ready-made training exercises designed to meet a variety of needs for different audiences. Some deal directly with identifying traits and practicing behaviors associated with effective leaders. Some address organizational factors that will affect or undermine the efforts of managers at all levels to function as leaders instead of just as bosses or mouthpieces for an oppressive regime.

And, yes, some ignore distinctions between "management" skills and "leadership" skills. Why? Because leadership really *is* about credibility. How many managers have you known who were lousy at giving performance feedback, lousy at delegating, lousy at running meetings, and lousy at managing their own time—but whom you nevertheless regarded as effective leaders? Let me guess: None.

The Inventories section contains questionnaires and instruments that help people clarify their own beliefs about leadership, classify their behavior, see themselves as others see them, and gain insight into the prevailing values of their organizations.

A Toolbox

This book is not intended as a potboiler to be read from cover to cover, but as a resource—a collection of working tools. The experiential learning activities and the surveys are complete packages: Duplicate the materials, use them, and adapt them as you see fit for training purposes (the experiential activities all suggest variations, and you can invent your own). You also may duplicate the articles for use as handouts or background reading.

There are just two exceptions to that liberal copyright policy. If noted, reprint permission must be obtained from the primary sources. And if the materials are to be reproduced in publications for sale or are intended for large-scale distribution (more than 100 copies in 12 months), prior written permission is required. Please contact Pfeiffer if you have questions.

This volume contains thirty years of expertise in the teaching of leadership skills. We offer it in the hope that the contents will help build better organizations for working people everywhere.

Jack Gordon
Editor

Part 1
Presentation and
Discussion Resources

Think of the articles in this section as a recommended reading list. They are intended to educate rather than to train. Read them yourself to gain knowledge and insight into the subject of leadership. Use them as handouts in workshops. Slip them quietly to individual supervisors or managers who come to you for advice or aid.

We chose these selections not only as the best discussions of leadership that the Pfeiffer *Annuals* have to offer but also with an eye toward covering several bases and serving a variety of needs. Three of them caution in different ways against too heavy a reliance on theory or on trait-based models of what makes an effective leader. The theme—you can't lead from a textbook —recalls novelist John Barth's observation that "a good teacher will teach well regardless of the [educational] theory he suffers from." But far from taking a deterministic view of leadership skills as something you're either born with or not, these articles offer real insight and excellent practical advice.

On the other hand, two of the selections are included precisely to provide a grounding in classic theories that have shaped the study of leadership and management as distinct and teachable practices. Anyone who proposes to teach the subjects should be familiar with names such as Frederick Taylor and Elton Mayo, if only to avoid potential embarrassment. As for Douglas McGregor's Theory X-Theory Y model, it is arguably the most fundamental

1

statement ever made of the philosophical gap that separates managers who will be obeyed from leaders who will be followed.

The opening article, "Leadership Is in the Eye of the Follower," makes a similarly fundamental point by concluding that the traits and behaviors displayed by successful leaders can be summarized in a single word: credibility.

The last one, "Visionary's Disease and the CEO," dissects a phenomenon that became all too familiar during the dot-com boom and that the entire world economy has lived to regret. Visionary's disease is not limited to high-tech companies, and the article serves as a cautionary tale for any leader who confuses his own passing enthusiasms with "stretch goals" for his followers.

Here are capsule summaries of the presentations.

- Leadership Is in the Eye of the Follower: And what followers demand from a leader boils down to one thing: credibility.

- Leadership as Persuasion and Adaptation: Leaders are defined not so much by any set of traits they possess as by how they adapt to circumstances.

- Leadership from the Gestalt Perspective: To become an effective leader, start with who you are and what you actually believe, not with someone else's theory of who you ought to be.

- An Overview of Ten Management and Organizational Theorists: From the time of Moses, thinkers have grappled with the question of how to organize and lead people. Here is a survey of the answers that have shaped our modern understanding.

- McGregor's Theory X-Theory Y Model: An unsentimental explanation of Douglas McGregor's concept of the two basic philosophies that every manager—and every would-be leader—must choose between.

- Impact at Ground Zero: Where Theory Meets Practice: Most resounding leadership failures result not from faulty theories but from poor execution.

- A Model for the Executive Management of Transformational Change: How HRD professionals can guide executives through a major change in the organization's strategy, methods, or structure.

- Visionary's Disease and the CEO: Prophetic advice from the height of the dot-com boom for leaders who get carried away with "the vision thing."

1

Leadership Is in the Eye of the Follower

James M. Kouzes and Barry Z. Posner

What you have heard about leadership is only half
the story. Leadership is not just about leaders; it is
also about followers. Leadership is a reciprocal process. It occurs between people. It is not done by one
person to another.

Successful leadership depends far more on the follower's *perception* of the leader
than on the leader's abilities. Followers, not the leader, determine when someone possesses the qualities of leadership. In other words, leadership is in the
eye of the follower.

LEADERSHIP CHARACTERISTICS

During a five-year period we investigated the perceptions that followers have of
leaders. We asked more than 10,000 managers nationwide from a wide range
of private and public organizations to tell us what they look for or admire in
their leaders. The results from these surveys have been striking in their regularity. It seems there are several essential tests a leader must pass before we are
willing to grant him or her the title of "leader."

According to our research, the majority of us admire leaders who are
honest, competent, forward-looking, inspiring, and, ultimately, *credible*.

Honesty

In every survey we conducted, honesty was selected more often than any other leadership characteristic. After all, if we are to willingly follow someone, whether into battle or into the boardroom, we first want to assure ourselves that the person is worthy of our trust. We will ask, "Is that person truthful? Ethical? Principled? Of high integrity? Does he or she have character?" These are not simple questions to answer. It is not easy to measure such subjective characteristics. In our discussions with respondents we found that it was the *leader's behavior* that provided the evidence. In other words, regardless of what leaders say about their integrity, followers wait to be shown.

Leaders are considered honest by followers if they do what they say they are going to do. Agreements not followed through, false promises, cover-ups, and inconsistencies between word and deed are all indicators that an ostensible leader is not honest. On the other hand, if a leader behaves in ways consistent with his or her stated values and beliefs, then we can entrust to that person our careers, our security, and ultimately even our lives.

This element of trustworthiness is supported in another study we conducted of leadership practices. In that study we found that of all behaviors describing leadership, the most important single item was the leader's display of trust in others. Irwin Federman, venture capitalist and former president and CEO (chief executive officer) of chip-maker Monolithic Memories, says it best: "Trust is a risk game. The leader must ante up first." If leaders want to be seen as trustworthy, they must first give evidence of their own trust in others.

Sam Walton, founder and chairman of Wal-Mart Stores, Inc., provides an excellent example of trustworthiness and "anteing up first" in leadership: In 1983 Walton—rated by *Forbes* to be the richest man in the United States—made a wager. Concerned that the company might have a disappointing year, he bet Wal-Mart employees that if they achieved a greater profit than in previous years he would don a hula skirt and hula down Wall Street. They did. And he did. He kept his word and did what he said he would do. He showed he had integrity, even if it meant public embarrassment. But imagine what would have happened had Sam not kept his word. You can believe that his employees would not have anted up for the next bet!

Competence

The leadership attribute chosen next most frequently is competence. To enlist in another's cause, we must believe that person knows what he or she is doing. We must see the person as capable and effective. If we doubt the leader's abili-

The Pfeiffer Book of Successful Leadership Development Tools © 2003 John Wiley & Sons, Inc. Published by Pfeiffer.

ties, we are unlikely to enlist in the crusade. Leadership competence does not necessarily refer to the leader's technical abilities. Rather the competence followers look for varies with the leader's position and the condition of the company. For example, the higher the rank of the leader, the more people demand to see demonstrations of abilities in strategic planning and policy making. If a company desperately needs to clarify its corporate strategy, a CEO with savvy in competitive marketing may be seen as a fine leader. But at the line functional level, where subordinates expect guidance in technical areas, these same managerial abilities will not be enough.

We have come to refer to the kind of competence needed by leaders as *value-added competence*. Functional competence may be necessary, but it is insufficient. The leader must bring some *added value* to the position. Tom Melohn, president of North American Tool and Die (NATD) in San Leandro, California, is a good case in point. Tom, along with a partner, bought NATD several years ago. A former consumer-products executive, Tom knows nothing about how to run a drill press or a stamping machine. He claims he cannot even screw the license plates on his car. Yet, in the nine years since he bought the company, NATD has excelled in every possible measure in its industry, whereas under the original founder—an experienced toolmaker—NATD achieved only average or below-average results.

If Tom brings no industry, company, or technical expertise to NATD, what has enabled him to lead the firm to its astounding results? Our answer: Tom added to the firm what it most needed at the time—the abilities to motivate and sell. Tom entrusted the skilled employees with the work they knew well; and for his part, he applied the selling skills he had learned from a quarter-century in marketing consumer products. He also rewarded and recognized the NATD "gang" for their accomplishments, increasing their financial and emotional sense of ownership in the firm.

Being Forward-Looking

Over half of our respondents selected "forward-looking" as their third most sought after leadership trait. We expect our leaders to have a sense of direction and a concern for the future of the company. Some use the word "vision"; others, the word "dream." Still others refer to this sense of direction as a "calling" or "personal agenda." Whatever the word, the message is clear: True leaders must know where they are going.

Two other surveys that we conducted with top executives reinforced the importance of clarity of purpose and direction. In one study, 284 senior executives rated "developing a strategic planning and forecasting capability" as the most critical concern. These same senior managers, when asked to se-lect the most important characteristics in a CEO, cited "a leadership style of honesty and integrity" first, followed by "a long-term vision and direction for the company."

By "forward-looking" we do not mean the magical power of a prescient visionary. The reality is far more down to earth: It is the ability to set or select a desirable destination toward which the organization should head. The vision of a leader is the compass that sets the course of the company. Followers ask that a leader have a well-defined orientation to the future. A leader's "vision" is, in this way, similar to an architect's model of a new building or an engi-neer's prototype of a new product.

Think of it another way. Suppose you wanted to take a trip to a place where you had never been before—say Nairobi, Kenya. What would you do over the next few days if you knew you were going there in six months? Prob-ably get a map, read a book about the city, look at pictures, talk to someone who had been there. You would find out what sights to see, what the weather is like, what to wear, and where to eat, shop, and stay. Followers ask nothing more from a leader than a similar kind of orientation: "What will the com-pany look like, feel like, be like when it arrives at its goal in six months or six years? Describe it to us. Tell us in rich detail so we can select the proper route and know when we have arrived."

Inspiration

We expect our leaders to be enthusiastic, energetic, and positive about the future—a bit like cheerleaders. It is not enough for a leader to have a dream about the future. He or she must be able to communicate the vision in ways that encourage us to sign on for the duration. As Apple Computer manager Dave Paterson puts it, "The leader is the evangelist for the dream."

Some people react with discomfort to the idea that being inspiring is an essential leadership quality. One chief executive officer of a large corpo-ration even told us, "I don't trust people who are inspiring"—no doubt in re-sponse to past crusaders who led their followers to death or destruction. Other executives are skeptical of their ability to inspire others. Both are making a mistake. It is absolutely essential that leaders inspire our confidence in the va-lidity of the goal. Enthusiasm and excitement signal the leader's personal con-viction to pursuing that dream. If a leader displays no passion for a cause, why should others?

Credibility

Three of these four attributes—honesty, competence, and being inspiring—comprise what communications experts refer to as "credibility." We found, quite unexpectedly, in our investigation of admired leadership qualities that more than anything else people want leaders who are *credible*. Credibility is the foundation on which inspiring leadership visions are built. When we believe a leader is credible, then we somehow feel more secure around him or her. This sense of security enables us to let go of our reservations and release enormous personal energy on behalf of the common vision. Credibility and an attractive image of the future are the very essence of leadership.

However, credibility is extremely fragile. It takes years to earn it, an instant to lose it. Credibility grows minute by minute, hour by hour, day by day, through persistent, consistent, and patient demonstration that one is worthy of followers' trust and respect. It is lost with one false step, one thoughtless remark, one inconsistent act, one broken agreement, one lie, one cover-up.

LEADERSHIP PRACTICES

Leaders establish and maintain their credibility by their actions, and in our research we uncovered five fundamental practices that enabled leaders to earn followers' confidence and to get extraordinary things done. When at their best, leaders (1) challenge the process, (2) inspire a shared vision, (3) enable others to act, (4) model the way, and (5) encourage the heart.[1]

Challenging the Process

Leaders are pioneers—people who seek out new opportunities and are willing to change the status quo. They innovate, experiment, and explore ways to improve the organization. They treat mistakes as learning experiences. Leaders also stay prepared to meet whatever challenges may confront them.

Inspiring a Shared Vision

Leaders look toward and beyond the horizon. They envision the future with a positive and hopeful outlook. Leaders are expressive and attract followers through their genuineness and skillful communications. They show others how mutual interests can be met through commitment to a common purpose.

---

1. The *Leadership Practices Inventory* measures these five practices.

Enabling Others to Act

Leaders infuse people with spirit-developing relationships based on mutual trust. They stress collaborative goals. They actively involve others in planning, giving them discretion to make their own decisions. Leaders ensure that people feel strong and capable.

Modeling the Way

Leaders are clear about their business values and beliefs. They keep people and projects on course by behaving consistently with these values and modeling how they expect others to act. Leaders also plan and break projects down into achievable steps, creating opportunities for small wins. They make it easier for others to achieve goals by focusing on key priorities.

Encouraging the Heart

Leaders encourage people to persist in their efforts by linking recognition with accomplishments, visibly recognizing contributions to the common vision. They let others know that their efforts are appreciated and express pride in the team's accomplishments. Leaders also find ways to celebrate achievements. They nurture a team spirit that enables people to sustain continued efforts.

UNIQUE RELATIONSHIP

Leadership is a relationship, a unique and special trust between the leader and followers. The development of this trusting relationship requires our full and caring attention as leaders. Below are five prerequisites to building and maintaining this bond of trust.

1. *Know your followers.* Building any relationship begins with getting to know those we desire to lead. Get to know their hopes, their fears, their values, their biases, their dreams, their nightmares, their aspirations, and their disappointments. Find out what is important to your followers. Come to know what they seek. Only in this way can you show them how their interests can be served by aligning with yours.

2. *Stand up for your beliefs.* People who take a stand are appreciated in U.S. culture. We resolutely refuse to follow people who lack confidence in their

own values and decisions. Confusion among your followers over your stand creates stress; not knowing what you believe leads to conflict, indecision, and political rivalry. There is, however, a danger in always standing on principle; it can make one rigid and insensitive. The key to escaping rigidity is to remain open to others. Listen; understand; empathize. We respect leaders who can listen to and understand our points of view, yet believe in their own hearts that other viewpoints are superior. If your beliefs are strongly held, ethical, and based on sound thinking, followers will find ways to align themselves with you.

3. *Speak with passion.* Managers constantly talk about motivating their people, of lighting a fire under them. If the leader is a wet match, there will be no spark to ignite passion in others. Enthusiasm, energy, and commitment begin with the leader. To gain the commitment of others you must communicate your excitement about the dream. Paint word pictures. Tell stories. Relate anecdotes. Weave metaphors. Enable others to see, hear, taste, smell, and feel what you experience. When the dream lives inside others, it lives forever.

4. *Lead by example.* Leaders are role models. We look to them for clues on how we should behave. We always believe their actions over their words. We will never forget the story told to us by a young manager, John Schultz, about his days as a high-school football player:

> When I played high-school football, I had three coaches. The first two were exactly alike. Each said, "Men, while you are in training I don't want you to smoke, drink, stay up late, or fool around with girls. Got that?" Then we would watch our coaches during the season. They would smoke, drink, stay up late, and fool around with women. So what do you suppose we did? Boys will be boys, after all.
>
> My third coach was the best I ever had. At the beginning of the season we had the same locker-room sermon as with the other coaches. Except this coach just said, "I have only one rule. You can do anything I do. If I smoke, drink, stay up late, or fool around with women, then I would expect you to do the same. But if I don't, you'd better not!"

If leaders ask followers to observe certain standards, then the leaders need to live by the same rules. That is exactly what we were told many times by exemplary leaders. You can only lead by example. Leadership is not a spectator sport. Leaders do not sit in the stands and watch. Hero myths aside, neither are leaders in the game substituting for the players. Leaders coach. They show others how to behave.

5. *Conquer yourself.* Jim Whittaker, the first American to reach the summit of Mt. Everest, learned that he could not conquer a mountain, because mountains cannot be conquered. He had to conquer himself—his hopes, his fears. It might brighten our heroic image of leaders to believe that they conquer organizations, communities, states, nations, the world. It might make good cinema to picture the leader riding into town on a white horse and single-handedly destroying the villains. But this superhero portrait of great leaders only perpetuates a falsehood. The real struggle of leadership is internal. The everyday struggles of leaders include internal questions such as: Do you understand what is going on in the company and the world in which it operates? Are you prepared to handle the problems the company is facing? Did you make the right decision? Did you do the right thing? Where do you think the company should be headed? Are you the right one to lead others there?

This inner struggle places enormous stress on the leader. Followers do not want to see that their leaders lack self-confidence. Certainly they like to know their leaders are human, that they can laugh and cry and have a good time; but followers will not place their confidence in someone who appears weak, uncertain, or lacking in resolve. Followers need to sense that the leader's internal struggle has been fought and won. Conquering yourself begins with determining your value system. Strongly held beliefs compel you to take a stand.

THE EYE OF THE FOLLOWER

These characteristics, these practices, these relationships are tough measures for the leader. It may not seem right to be judged so harshly, but followers perceive leadership in their own terms, and those terms are not always fair. After all, the leader is not a leader unless there are followers; and there are no true followers unless the leader is a leader in the eye of the follower.

Originally published in The 1989 Annual: Developing Human Resources.

Adapted from James M. Kouzes and Barry Z. Posner, "Eye of the Follower" (*Administrative Radiology*, April 1986, pp. 55–56, 58, 63–64); *The Leadership Challenge: How To Get Extraordinary Things Done in Organizations* (San Francisco, CA: Jossey-Bass, 1987); and *The Leadership Practices Inventory* (San Francisco, CA: Pfeiffer, 1988). Used with permission. *The Leadership Challenge* and *The Leadership Practices Inventory* are available from Pfeiffer.

2

Leadership as Persuasion and Adaptation

Julia T. Wood

Group leadership has been of interest to scholars and practitioners in the social sciences since people first began studying their own behaviors. A great deal of attention has been directed toward questions such as "What are the characteristics of task leaders?," "What are the variables that affect the emergence and maintenance of leadership in problem-solving groups?," and "What is the best method of training leaders?" As a result of the many different orientations, however, there is a lack of consistency in research findings about leadership. No one really seems to know what "good leadership" is (Lumsden, 1974). Nevertheless, it is essential to understand the nature of leadership and the ways in which we can improve it.

PREVIOUS APPROACHES TO LEADERSHIP

There are several approaches that have been prominent in research concerned with the determinants of leadership. The "trait approach," the "situational approach," the "follower approach," and the "contingency model" have been proposed as explanations of the factors that determine leadership in small groups.

The Trait Approach

The first concentrated attempt to define the factors that result in leadership was the "trait approach." Enormous amounts of time and effort were devoted to constructing lists of the physical and psychological attributes believed to differentiate leaders from nonleaders. Unfortunately, there was minimal agreement among researchers as to what those distinguishing traits were. The lists of "definitive qualities of leaders" were almost as numerous as the researchers who constructed them. Of several hundred traits studied, only a very few were consistently correlated with leadership (Shaw, 1971). Gouldner (1950) reviewed the empirical investigations related to leadership traits and concluded that "there is no reliable evidence concerning the existence of universal leadership traits" (p. 34). The trait approach is unsatisfactory because it implies that leaders are born, not made.

The Situational Approach

A second perspective on leadership, the "situational approach," holds that it is the social circumstances that command the degree to which any person's leadership potential is exercised. According to this approach, the crucial determinant of leadership is the social environment in which leadership is needed. The major claim of the situational approach is that different leadership skills are required in different situations. The deficiency of this approach, however, is that it implies that leaders are born of situations, not of their own abilities.

The Follower Approach

Although the situational approach is currently endorsed by many researchers, a third orientation to leadership has received some acceptance. The "follower approach" maintains that the most effective leaders are those most able to satisfy the needs or desires of a group of followers (Sanford, 1950; Tannenbaum, Weschler, & Massarik, 1974). The follower approach is inadequate because it implies that the emergence and maintenance of leadership is dependent on followers, not on a leader's own skills.

The Contingency Model

By combining ideas from the situational approach and the study of leadership styles, a fourth approach to leadership was developed (Fiedler, 1964). This model maintains that effective leadership depends not only on a leader's personal style but also on the characteristics of a situation. The contingency model is an exciting step in our understanding of leadership, because it refutes the simplistic and one dimensional explanations of the earlier approaches. Nevertheless, this model, too, is unsatisfying because it ignores the leader's personal ability to control himself or herself and the situation.

Assumptions of Four Approaches

In order to understand more fully these four approaches to small-group leadership, it is helpful to identify the assumptions on which they are based.

1. The trait approach maintains that a person either does or does not possess the particular traits that are considered to be the determinants of leadership.

2. The situational approach assumes that certain situations call for certain types of leadership and that the leaders will be those who best fit the requirements of a situation. The situational characteristics are viewed as the determinants of leadership.

3. The follower approach holds that the needs of group members determine who will lead. Leadership, then, is a coincidence between the needs of a membership and the abilities that a person happens to possess. The members' needs are assumed to be the key determinants of leadership.

4. The contingency model maintains that personal styles and situational characteristics combine to determine leadership. A "proper match" between styles and situations determines who will lead a group.

These assumptions show that each of the four major approaches to leadership shares a basic orientation: each approach maintains, at least implicitly, that there is a static quality to leadership, a quality that can be isolated and described apart from leaders who operate in particular group situations. A leader's active involvement in the small-group process has been overlooked, ruling out the possibility that a leader can, like any other human being, adapt his or her behavior in order to enhance his or her effectiveness.

A static conception of leadership, therefore, is inaccurate. Small groups are characterized by contingencies—by a lack of certainty regarding events that may occur. Once we acknowledge this dynamic nature of small groups, it becomes clear that a useful theory of leadership must be similarly dynamic. By considering a rhetorical perspective on the process of leading, we can focus on the dynamic nature of leadership and the possibilities for human control over contingent situations.

A RHETORICAL PERSPECTIVE ON LEADERSHIP

As a philosophy of human action, beginning with the writings of ancient thinkers such as Aristotle and Cicero, rhetoric is based on the belief that humans can control their effectiveness through the discovery and management of behaviors that take place in relation to other people. Humans are seen as purposeful agents who can consciously control their own actions and, therefore, the ways in which others respond to them.

A rhetorical perspective on small-group leadership rejects claims that there are static determinants of leadership. Leading is a process, a persuasive process in which a leader achieves effectiveness by the careful selection and management of his or her actions within a particular group situation. The leader has the potential to control himself or herself, the situation, and the membership through the use of symbolic behavior. A rhetorical perspective on leadership, then, is characterized by two features: (1) the persuasive nature of the leading process and (2) the recognition that humans can control their environments by adapting to social circumstances.

The Persuasive Process

Leading is an active process that involves making choices regarding behaviors. Presumably, a leader has goals for himself or herself, for the individuals in the group, and for the group as a whole. By selecting and implementing behavioral strategies that are designed to lead to these goals, a leader exerts influence and, therefore, engages in persuasion. The leader of a small group inevitably effects persuasions by the ways in which he or she chooses to present himself or herself, by the methods he or she employs in directing the group's tasks, and by the manner in which he or she relates to the group members. A leader's choices influence the members' evaluation of him or her and they, in turn, influence the group's success in reaching collective goals.

The persuasive nature of the leading process has not always been recognized. Some people, for example, persist in claiming that democratic behaviors are not really influences because they imply a "sharing of control." Yet, in choosing to act democratically and not to dominate actively, a leader is exercising influence: he or she engenders in the group members a certain perception of the leader as a leader and of themselves as members of the leader's group. Even the most democratic behaviors are persuasions that reflect a leader's choice of effective behaviors to guide the group. A leader cannot avoid influencing the group. Therefore, identifying and studying the choices of persuasion that must be made by a leader become important: What types of influence does the leader wish to exert? Whom does he or she need to persuade? How do his or her particular choices affect members' perceptions of him or her and of themselves? How are various persuasive effects achieved by a leader? Leaders should be trained to be *aware* of these choices and to estimate the probable effects of various choices on collective goals.

Control Through Adaptation

A rhetorical perspective on leading also emphasizes the possibility that humans can control their environments through sensitive *adaptation*. People are capable of adjusting themselves in order to be more effective in relation to others. In this orientation, it is assumed that a leader can persuade the group members to need what he or she has to offer, to value the skills that he or she possesses, to perceive their situation as one in which his or her guidance is desirable or necessary, to commit themselves to collective goals, and to work together in a satisfactory manner.

Perhaps an example or two will help to clarify the view that leaders can adjust themselves, their memberships, and their situations in order to lead more effectively. When Gerald Ford first became President, he chose to present himself as a simple, honest man. After the criminal and demoralizing events of Watergate, Ford's apparent honesty and openness were welcomed by a nation weary of deceit and secrecy. However, when Ford's "down-home" presentation became the target of criticism and even ridicule, he began to shift his image. He made more definitive statements and took stronger positions on issues of national policy, altering his self-presentation in ways that he presumably believed to be acceptable or desirable to the voting public.

A newly promoted company president, in taking over a firm that had degenerated into chaos, was at first appreciated and praised for his firmness and positive decision making. When the company was on the road to recovery, however, his tightly controlled, authoritative approach was no longer popular with employees. He had to adjust his leadership so that it was more relaxed and person centered.

These are only two examples of figures whose leadership behaviors are best understood from a rhetorical perspective. We must recognize that leaders, members, and group situations are all flexible and that a rhetorical sensitivity to the methods of persuasion can enhance most people's abilities to lead well. Leaders' capacities for adapting themselves and their situations through the deliberate management of their behaviors toward others should be emphasized. Such adaptation is desirable as long as it neither jeopardizes one's personal integrity nor results in unethical behavior toward others.

VALUE OF A RHETORICAL PERSPECTIVE

A rhetorical perspective on leadership offers a realistic and useful means for understanding how leaders emerge, how they maintain their power, and how they build effective, cohesive groups.

A second value of a rhetorical perspective is its potential as a strategy for training leaders. Unlike previous methods of training, a rhetorical approach does not provide any "recipes" for success. Instead, it offers potential leaders a useful way of thinking about themselves in relation to a group and its task. By viewing themselves from a rhetorical perspective, leaders could analyze their own behaviors and the situations in which they are to lead. Potential leaders would be able to assess the interplay among the forces of themselves, their goals, their group members, and their group situations. Given a rhetorical orientation to their work, leaders would be able to plan actions that would probably be effective in their particular circumstances.

Every group situation is different; the rules must vary according to the situations and the people involved. A rhetorical perspective on leadership, viewed as a process of persuasion and adaptation, offers a useful method of analysis for leaders of problem-solving groups.

References

Fiedler, F.E. (1954). A contingency model of leadership effectiveness. In L. Berkowitz (Ed.), *Advances in experimental social psychology*. New York: Academic Press.

Gouldner, A. (Ed.). (1950). *Studies in leadership*. New York: Harper & Row.

Lumsden, G. (1974, Winter). An experimental study of the effect of verbal agreement on leadership maintenance in problem-solving discussion. *Central States Speech Journal, 25*, 270.

Sanford, F.H. (1950). *Authoritarianism and leadership*. Philadelphia, PA: Institute for Research in Human Relations.

Shaw, M.E. (1971). *Group dynamics: The psychology of small group behavior.* New York: McGraw-Hill.

Tannenbaum, R., Weschler, I.R., & Massarik, F. (1974). Leadership: A frame of reference. In R.S. Cathcart & L.A. Samovar (Eds.), *Small group communication: A reader* (2nd ed.). Dubuque, IA: William C. Brown.

Originally published in The 1976 Annual Handbook for Group Facilitators.

3

Leadership from the Gestalt Perspective

H.B. Karp

Abstract: The current trend in organization development is toward large-system interventions. Although
nothing is wrong with this trend, it is important that
individual growth and effectiveness not be ignored.

This article explores the following definition of
leadership: *Leadership is the art of getting people to perform
a task willingly.* However, two key factors affect leader
effectiveness: competence and comfort. A leader can
achieve maximum effectiveness first by being aware
of what and how he or she thinks and second by considering options for any specific situation. Leadership
then becomes the ability to adapt one's authentic style
to the circumstances of a particular situation.

In recent years, the trend in organization development (OD) has been focused
on large-system interventions. Strategies such as self-directed work teams, right-
sizing, and organizational reengineering are just a few examples of this trend.
Although this direction is not wrong, individual growth and effectiveness may
be downplayed, if not completely lost, in the attempt to evolve larger and more
comprehensive interventions. Whether within the context of a major system-
wide change strategy or cast in an individual's daily work routine, a consistent
and pragmatic means of developing leadership is needed—one that will respond to what is occurring right here, right now.

The one theory base that has consistently responded to this demand is Gestalt. Gestalt originated with Fritz Perls in the field of psychotherapy in the mid-1930s. Described as "therapy for normals," the Gestalt theory base has more recently been used to define an effective and healthy organization, just as it has been used to describe a healthy and functioning individual.

In recent years, Gestalt has provided a unique perspective to organizations while maintaining the prime OD objective of increasing individual and group effectiveness through intervention in group processes.

TERMINOLOGY

Prior to presenting the Gestalt leadership model, it will be helpful to clarify several terms and to show how they relate to leadership and, in some cases, to each other.

Leadership

Leadership is the art of getting people to perform a task, willingly. This definition is clearly different from "management," which can be defined as "the science of the allocation of resources." This definition of leadership has three operative terms: *art, task,* and *willingly.*

Art indicates that leadership is a combination of both talent and skills. Leadership talent is distributed normally throughout the population. Not everyone has the talent to be an effective leader, just as not everyone has the talent to be a concert pianist. The opposite side of the coin also implies that very few people either have no talent or have all the talent.

One way to actualize the talent that exists within an individual is by way of skill development, through training, education, and experience.

Art also implies that each leader performs individually. Just as no two singers sing alike, no two authors write alike, and no two sculptors sculpt alike, no two leaders lead alike. It is impossible to teach people to be good leaders. They can only be taught what leadership is about and then assisted in adapting that knowledge to their own individual styles. In the end, people will be effective leaders only to the extent that their potential for individual creativity and uniqueness of expression will allow.

The second term, *task,* means that leadership does not occur in a vacuum. Two structural elements must exist before a leadership function can occur. First, at least two individuals must be involved: a leader and at least one follower. Second, leadership must have an objective. The task may be work oriented, such as manufacturing a product, solving a problem, or designing a new widget; or it may be socially oriented, such as planning a party. Regardless, leadership is a process that affects how the task finally will be accomplished.

Willingly, the third element, means that leadership precludes the use of threat or coercion as a means of getting the job done. The use of threats, monetary rewards, or promises of future promotion to control another's performance requires neither skill nor talent and is not leadership. *Willingly* implies that another person will perform the task without resenting having to do it or resenting you for having assigned it.

It is safe to say that no one is capable of being a maximally effective leader 100 percent of the time and that sometimes it is a lot easier to be a good leader than it is at other times. In this light, the definition for leadership can be converted into the following pragmatic statement: To whatever extent an individual can get others to perform a task willingly in a given situation, to that extent the person can be judged an effective leader.

Leadership Effectiveness

Leadership effectiveness depends on two basic and essential criteria: *competence* and *comfort.*[1]

Competence, which is the more observable and measurable of the two criteria, refers to the leader's ability to get the work done willingly by others; it can be measured through attitude surveys, critical incident analysis, and, of course, the quality of the work itself.

Comfort refers to a leader's comfort with himself or herself and with his or her individual leadership style. The importance of this criterion is that it clearly implies that *there is no one best way to lead.* For example, any accomplished art student can copy a master effectively. It is not until the student takes that skill and creates *something unique* that he or she is considered to be an artist. As it is with painters, so it is with leaders or anyone else who practices an art for a living.

Therefore, if a leader is judged to be competent by observable measures and is comfortable with his or her leadership style, that person has every right to resist the demands of others to alter *how* he or she leads. Like artists, only they themselves know best how to uniquely express their art.

---

1. Note that the term comfort refers to comfort with self and style and does not refer to what might be called situational discomfort, i.e., the discomfort that arises from dealing with situational ambiguity, tough choices, or painful situations.

If, on the other hand, the person is comfortable but not terribly competent or competent but not very comfortable, it may be wise to consider making a career change to something that will easily provide both comfort and competence. It is here that that person stands to make the greatest contribution and simultaneously gain the most satisfaction and growth from the work.

Boundary

One additional Gestalt term, *boundary*, needs to be surfaced because it also has major impact on the leadership model. The essence of Gestalt theory holds that each human being is separate and distinct from all others. A person's individuality, or *I-Boundary*, is made of many sub-boundaries such as attitudes, values, tastes, assumptions, abilities, and so forth. All of these combine to make each person absolutely unique. In a practical sense, each sub-boundary carries the explicit message, "For me, this far and no farther." Thus, boundaries, as the word implies, define and give each individual his or her identifiable personality characteristics, just as its geographic borders give a nation its identifiable configuration.

Figure 1. The Mistrust-Trust Polarity

Human characteristics can be seen as operating in polarities, such as good-bad, strong-weak, introvert-extrovert, or tough-tender. Each sub-boundary then can be seen as an area that is defined by a range within that polarity. For example, in Figure 1, the polarity ranges from "Mistrust" to "Trust." The range that is indicated between the points labeled "a" and "b" is my sub-boundary on this dimension and defines the extent to which I have the capacity to authentically mistrust and trust others. Note that this makes no statement about how other people are, only my capacity on this dimension. The positions at each extreme represent the maximum potential for human experience for this characteristic, i.e., being as mistrusting and trusting as it is humanly possible to be. The configuration in Figure 1 shows that at point a, I am mistrusting enough to always lock my car, no matter where I am parked; at the other extreme, point b, I am trustful enough to take most people at their word the first time I meet them. My range of effectiveness and self-confidence, in terms of mistrusting and trusting others, lies between points a and b. If I try to operate outside these parameters, chances are that I will be tentative, lacking in confidence, and marginally effective at best. All sub-boundaries operate in this way. A person's sub-boundary can also be thought of as one's "Zone of Present Effectiveness" or "Zone of Comfort."

An individual's I-Boundary can be represented by the pattern intersecting the various sub-boundaries, as shown in Figure 2[2]

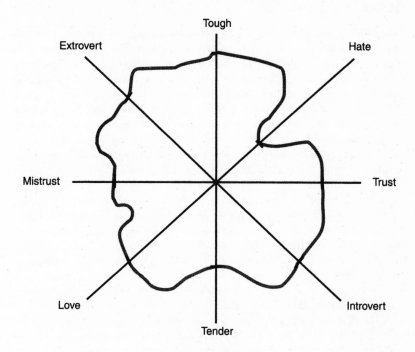

Figure 2. I-Boundry

Each person's I-Boundary is intact. It is essential that each individual recognize, accept, and value his or her personal I-Boundary. The simplest step toward increasing your effectiveness and comfort with self, in leadership or any other area, is to have your *perceived* boundary, (where you think it is or should be) correspond to your *actual* boundary (where it actually is).

---

2. For a more detailed discussion of boundaries and how they work see Polster and Polster (1973), p. 107 or Karp (1995), pp. 9–23.

THE GESTALT LEADERSHIP MODEL

Leadership effectiveness is most influenced by two highly individualistic variables: the need for *congruence* and the need for *integration*.

The Need for Congruence

Congruence, or authenticity, can be viewed as having one's *perceived* boundary correspond to one's *actual* boundary. Regardless of who the person is, a leader will be judged by what he or she *does*. As suggested earlier, leadership effectiveness can only be determined by the appropriateness of the specific actions taken to get others willingly to comply to work.

Because it is highly unlikely that any leader will be able to get willing compliance in every situation, increasing leadership effectiveness becomes a matter of increasing one's "success rate" in choosing the effective and appropriate actions when responding to each new and different situation. It is not so much a matter of *what* the leader elects to do as much as it is a matter of *how* the selection is made.

In Figure 3, the top broken line is designated as "Actions." It represents the nearly infinite range of specific behaviors available to every leader to attempt to get willing compliance to work (planning, supporting, reprimanding, encouraging, training, coaching, and so on).

No specific action, in and of itself, is either good or bad. It is only functional or nonfunctional in getting compliance from another person in a given situation. Again, these actions and their results are the only things that can be observed and judged by anyone else.

Directly below the "Actions" line, however, are three lower levels, all of which are internal to the individual. These levels are not observable or subject to the judgment of others; understanding these levels is clearly the best means by which leaders can increase their own effectiveness.

Boundary

The lowest level, "Boundary," is not only the most general of the three levels, it also is the most basic and important determinant of effective leadership behavior. In this case "Boundary" is synonymous with one's assumptions about people. It refers to how the individual leader experiences self as well as others. Because a leader works exclusively with people, as opposed to cabinet makers who work with wood or masons who work with stone, it is both essential and pri-

Actions	– –
Objectives	————————————————————————
Theory	————————————————————————
Boundary (Assumptions)	————————————————————————

Figure 2. Four Levels of Leadership

mary that leaders be clear about the assumptions they make about people. The single most important question that a leader must answer is "What are people like?"

I would like to point out that the only person I can ever know, to any extent, is myself. My interactions with everyone else, to greater or lesser degree, are based only on my assumptions of how they are. Because I do not share a common nervous system with anyone else, I can never really know how people are merely through observation. Therefore, the more I know about me—who I am and how I see things—the more I am able accurately to check out my assumptions with and about others.

Many theorists, most notably Douglas McGregor (1960), make this point quite strongly. However, the difference between the Gestalt view and other views is that the Gestalt view is much more concerned with *how* the assumptions are made and clarified than it is with *what* the assumptions actually are.

To state the premise simply:

*The more clear and the more confident leaders are about their assumptions concerning people, **regardless of what those assumptions are, the higher the probability that they will be effective leaders.***

Theory

Once leaders are clear and comfortable with the assumptions they hold, the next level to be addressed is "Theory." "Boundary" asks the single question, "What are people like?" In contrast, "Theory" asks the single question, "What is leadership about?" Just as there is an infinite range of assumptions about people, so there is an infinitive range of leadership theories. I would suggest that there are just about as many leadership theories as there are individual leaders and theorists. The real question being asked is, "What is leadership theory about for me?"

Whether an individual ascribes to an established theory, chooses to modify an established theory, or devises an original theory, the important points to remember are as follows:

- The theory must be clear and explicit; and
- The theory must be consonant with the leader's own assumptions about people.

To be explicit, suppose I were to ask a large random sample of people the following question: "Who was the more effective leader—General Douglas MacArthur or Martin Luther King?" My guess would be that most people would judge them as comparable within the contexts of their specific situations. It requires only a passing knowledge of the history of these two men to realize that probably the only thing they had in common was that each held a very clear, defined, and different view of what people were like, themselves included. Not only was each man clear about his assumptions, but each operated out of a style of leadership that was highly consonant with how he saw things. Had MacArthur tried to lead like King or King like MacArthur, neither would have been effective.

Objectives

The third, and last, of the internal levels deals with objectives. This level also addresses a single question: "What do I want?" Objectives can be viewed in two ways. The first and most subjective view relates to personal objectives. Whether these objectives are general and long range ("I want to be successful" or "I want to be highly regarded by my superiors") or short range and specific ("I want a corner office" or "I want the promotion that's coming up"), the more clear and the more concise the individual is about what is wanted, the higher the probability that he or she will succeed.

Secondly, objectives must also be viewed from the organizational perspective. Here the organization's demands become a guideline for the individual's objectives. The more people are clear and comfortable with wanting whatever they want, the higher the probability that they will be able to integrate their personal objectives with the organizational objectives so that pursuing either one will have a positive impact on getting the other. For example, if I am clear about wanting the promotion and clear about what the organizational demand for productivity is, pursuing either one will work toward getting the other. The most important aspects of "Objectives" are the following:

- The individual leader is clear about and "owns" each objective; and
- The "Objectives" are consonant with the leader's "Boundary."

On the surface it would seem that the leader must spend an appreciable amount of time and energy struggling with each of the three lower levels. Paradoxically, this is not the case at all. Actually, the situation simply calls for increasing one's awareness. Clarity on any level is a matter of having one's *perceived* position, i.e., where one thinks one is or should be, accurately reflect one's *actual* position, i.e., where one is.

Actions

The last level literally is where all of the action is. It is here that a leader's effectiveness ultimately is determined. Although no one ever is accountable to anyone else for what happens on any of the three lower levels, a leader is totally accountable for the choices made at the fourth level.

The assumption here is that at any given moment, any one of myriad possible actions are available to attempt to get willing compliance to work from others. The broader the range or the greater the number of authentic choices that fit for the leader at any given moment, the higher the probability that the leader will be able to respond appropriately.

In this case, increasing leadership effectiveness is only a matter of answering the following question: "Given an almost infinite number of choices, how do I select an action that will work best for me in getting willing compliance in this situation, versus selecting one that just barely makes it or doesn't make it at all?"

Most people attempt to answer this question by going outside of themselves (asking a colleague, reading a book, or attending a seminar). There is nothing wrong with this approach; however, I suggest that there is a better place to go, at least at first: Go inside. Herein lies the Gestalt perspective to leadership.

Having worked with this model for a number of years, I see that the clearer the individual is about his or her assumptions concerning self and others, the higher the probability that it will be easy to develop a theory of leadership and a set of objectives that are consistent with and clearly reflect those assumptions. Most important, it is from this position that the leader will be able, with confidence, to select the leadership actions that will enable him or her to deal easily and effectively with most situations.

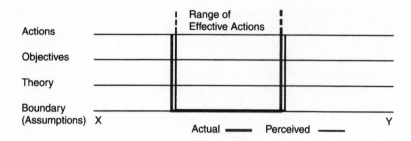

Figure 4a. Manager "A"–Congruence

Using Theory X / Theory Y as a convenient set of assumptions to illustrate the premise in Figure 4a, "A" is clear about how she sees herself, others, and the work setting.[3]

From this point of clarity and comfort, she is more able to develop ways in which to work more confidently and comfortably and she is more able to surface and state clear long- and short-term objectives that are important for her. She is clearer about what is important to her, freer to give her commitments openly and unhesitatingly, more willing to state disagreement with things that are dissonant for her, and much more available for effective collaboration when that is what is called for in the situation (Karp, 1976).

Leader "B," on the other hand, is unclear about his assumptions. For him there is little or no awareness of what people are like, including himself. His tendency is to confuse a changing situation with the notion that the characteristics of people are changing on a moment-by-moment basis. Therefore, no theory ever fits well, no objectives are ever tested, and, more to the point, very few actions are ever wholly trusted by him. Simply stated, nothing ever fits for "B." His purgatory is one of constantly plaguing himself with questions such as, "What will my boss think?" "What should I do next?" "What would my predecessor do in this situation?" and "Is it fair for me to ask for this?"

---

3. The focus of this piece is not yet another reworking of Theory X/Theory Y. "X" and "Y" are being used solely because they represent one very familiar and clear example of a relevant sub-boundary. Equally relevant, but less workable, would be the sub-boundary of mistrust/trust of others. In this case, the "growing edge" of the cynic would be to learn to trust others more appropriately; the "growing edge" for the naive individual would be to learn to mistrust others to the point that that response would be appropriate. Growth can occur in either direction, as opposed to the more conventional view that growth only occurs toward the right or "trust" (Theory Y) end of the continuum. Gestalt theory does not imply that one "should" move toward either pole, that is, that the capacity for trusting is any more valuable than the capacity for mistrusting. The thrust of Gestalt theory is on the individual's being clear about where he or she is on this dimension right now and then being able to move in the direction that is most responsive to getting what is wanted.

Because "B" has no clear sense of what he wants, how he sees things, what is or is not important for him, and little ability to support himself, he has no choice but to rely heavily on other people's views, judgments, and suggestions. This does not provide a healthy prescription for increasing leadership effectiveness.

In Figure 4b, leader "B" actually is somewhere nearer the "X" side of the continuum; however, because of his lack of awareness of this or the social unacceptability of being seen as an "X" type, a surface conversion to human-relations training has occurred, and he perceives himself as being much more toward the "Y" side. This usually takes the form of such thoughts as, "I should be more open (or participative or collaborative or caring)." His assumptions generally are derived from theorists, bosses, and consultants who tell him how he should see other people. From this position, both his theory and objectives are cast in terms of others' views and values.

The result is that his *actions,* although usually adequate, are rarely creative and rarely fully responsive to the situation; frequently, these actions are low risk. The actions he allows himself, that is, those arising from the perceived boundary, are not compatible with who he really is and how he sees things. Those actions that would fit for him and be responsive to the present challenging conditions he rejects for fear of being seen as an autocrat, or Theory X type leader.

As opposed to leader "A," who brings all she has to the work situation, leader "B" brings only the shadow of others. As long as this condition exists, he will never be able to fully maximize his potential for personal growth and creativity, nor will the organization be able to realize the full extent of his ability to contribute effectively. Even more damaging, although more subtle, is that by being incongruent, he models incongruity as his leadership style to

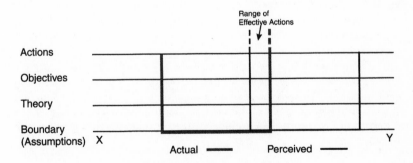

Figure 4b. Manager "B"—Incongruence

those he is attempting to influence. This sets a bad example and tends to increase the probability that the next "generation" of leaders will be even more likely to look to others for guidance and direction first, before attempting to rely on their own knowledge, internal strength, and sense of what is appropriate. His only area for real, effective action is the small area in "Actions" where his actual and his perceived capacities overlap.

The key to increased leadership effectiveness is first to get as much overlap as possible between where you are and where you think you are. The greater the amount of overlap on the "Boundary" level, the more congruence and choices that fit on all other levels, particularly on the "Actions" line.

The Need for Integration

Gestalt theory maintains that every human being is born with the capacity to experience his or her full range of human characteristics. Furthermore, competence and effectiveness are held to be the natural state. What has occurred in most cases is that, because of societal norms, parenting, education, or religious guidance, we have learned to disvalue certain parts of ourselves. With much help from others, we even have attempted to amputate many of these parts. This can have a strong negative impact on leadership behaviors later on in life. For example, suppose that as a young child I was taught never to speak ill of others. Although the value may be a fine one, believing it completely as a child could result in my being a supervisor who is unwilling or unable to give my direct reports clear, corrective feedback on the job.

Integration is the process through which we begin to regain and re-own these lost parts. Integration also serves the function of effectively expanding one's I-Boundary. Casting this into the organizational setting, the premise is as follows:

> The more effective leader will be the one who can generate the most alternatives in any given situation.

Each and every leadership situation that one encounters is, to some degree, unique. A leader's effectiveness will be increased to the extent that he or she can (1) be fully aware of the uniqueness of this particular situation and (2) be able to respond to the situation authentically. This implies that a leader must have more than a single way of approaching and dealing with contingencies.

For example, suppose that I describe and experience myself as being "easygoing" and "thoughtful." Furthermore, suppose that I have been fairly effective overall in consistently coming from this position. People like me this way and reinforce my behavior. However, what happens when there is a crisis or I am attacked in some way? Because over time I have eliminated the tougher, more aggressive parts of myself in order to please others, where do I find the toughness needed to respond to the present situation? In the absence of toughness, I find myself with one of two possible alternatives. I could attempt to restructure the situation so that I could somehow respond to the situation from my comfort zone (attempt to reason with a bully) or I could choose simply not to respond. However, the more authentic ways I have to be—easygoing, tough, thoughtful, aggressive, supportive, angry, humorous, or logical—the more responsive I can be to any ongoing situation.

Note that this does not preclude the reality and the rightness of choosing to spend the greatest majority of my time in my most comfortable stance. It does mean that I can readily leave this stance when the situation calls for it and be just as comfortable for as long as it takes to accomplish what needs to be accomplished from a different position. If leaders would give up their self-demand to be consistent and replace it with a self-demand to be optimally effective, they would be better leaders.

One way of defining alternatives is "ways of being." A second, and equally important, definition refers to the ability to create choices of action before committing to a specific course of action. Managers frequently limit the generation of workable alternatives because of fear of negative reactions from others or a fear of being seen as unfair. When first viewing the situation, responding to these concerns is definitely counterproductive. However, when it is time to make the conscious choice of what to do, then it is appropriate to consider these restrictions.

For example, I can choose not to implement a certain alternative because it would be unfair to another person. However, unless I am free enough to generate that alternative and am willing to consider it, I have consciously denied myself the option of choosing for or against it. In addition, this particular alternative, although unfair to a single individual, might be the best way to avert an overall crisis.

This view of alternatives underscores the premise that there is no one best way to be. It also suggests that, in most cases, there are several potentially effective ways to attack most problems and pursue most objectives. Each effective leader brings a totally unique being (himself or herself) to each organizational decision point, and the most valuable contribution made is his or her unique perspective.

In attaining organizational objectives, the more diverse the originating pool of opinion, the higher the probability that an optimally effective choice will emerge. Anything that discourages a broader range of alternatives limits the potential for a successful outcome. Once again, using Theory X/Theory Y as a convenient reference point, integration can be viewed in terms of how the four levels of leadership contribute to individual leadership effectiveness.

Much recent literature alleges that organizations that operate from a Theory Y set of assumptions and values are more effective than those that operate from a Theory X set. Certainly self-directed work teams and total quality management programs rest solidly in the Theory Y assumptions about people. Although this allegation may be true in many cases, it is not always true. Many organizations are maximally effective operating from a clear set of Theory X assumptions, such as Marine Corps boot camps, certain religious organizations, and almost all penal institutions. The issue is not so much one of *what* the underlying assumptions are, but rather one of *how* clearly those assumptions are stated and owned by the leadership and membership of the respective organizations.

Given, as a necessary precondition, congruence between a leader's actual and perceived boundaries, the more encompassing the boundary, the broader the effective range of "Actions" available.

In Figure 5, leader "A" is operating authentically from the position on the X/Y sub-boundary in Time Period 1 (TP1). She is clear about the assumptions she holds, i.e., that people tend to be lazy, will avoid responsibility, and mostly are not to be trusted. However, she is using that awareness as a means of selecting the appropriate leadership approaches, objectives, and actions that fit best for her.

Assume that she is doing very well and decides that she wants to increase her leadership effectiveness. She attends some workshops in team building and total quality management, does some personal growth work to increase

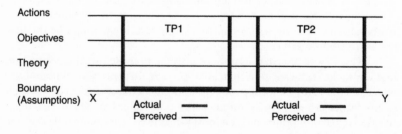

Figure 5. Change

The Pfeiffer Book of Successful Leadership Development Tools © 2003 *John Wiley & Sons, Inc. Published by Pfeiffer.*

her communication and listening skills, and develops a more genuine concern for her people. A year later, at Time Period 2 (TP2), she is holding a more authentic Theory Y set of assumptions at the indicated point in Figure 5. Is this growth? Most people would say that it is; however, I disagree. It is not growth . . . it is change!

At TP1, leader "A" only has the capacity to view people as potentially lazy, unmotivated, and averse to responsibility. At TP2 she only has the capacity to see them as potential opportunities for growth, motivated, and open to responsibility. At TP1, she might have made a good Marine stockade commander but not a very effective supervisor of a social work unit. In TP2, the situation would be reversed. The secret in increasing leadership effectiveness is to be able to do as much of both as you can!

As Figure 5 suggests, growth for "A" in TP1 would be toward the right, or the Theory Y, side of the scale. For whatever reason, she has limited her capacity for supportiveness and trust. Growth for her in TP2 would be toward the left, or Theory X, side of the scale in order to regain her capacity for toughness and mistrust.

Whether speaking of personal growth in the group setting or of leadership effectiveness in the organizational setting, the premise is as follows:

Growth is not changing existing positions but rather expanding them.

Growth, or effectiveness, is best depicted in Figures 6a, 6b, and 6c for leader "B."

Time Period 1 in Figure 6a indicates the starting position, in which the perceived position and actual positions for "B" are congruent. This is the same point that "A" began in Figure 5.

"B" is precisely where he thinks he is. He is clear and unapologetic about where he is and how he sees things and maintains enough flexibility to be willing to learn.

He is now faced with a leadership challenge that requires a more supportive set of assumptions and approaches than he presently possesses. By working out of the extreme congruent position (getting some coaching in communications and listening skills, going to seminars on team building and participative management, and experimenting with some new collaborative techniques that stretch him), he succeeds in overcoming the challenge. Figure 6b, TP2, indicates where he is at the point of successfully responding to the challenge.

He has done such a good job that he is given a promotion to a new location. On his first day at the new location, he discovers to his consternation that each of his new direct reports is either an ex-convict or would like to become one. His growth opportunity now is in the opposite direction. He needs to increase his capacity for mistrust, provide unilateral direction, be willing to discipline, and so forth. These skills are what the new position requires, and growth is now in the opposite direction, toward the X—the more controlling—side of the continuum. "B" loses no capacities in the process. Figure 6c then depicts his capacities after successfully responding to these conditions.

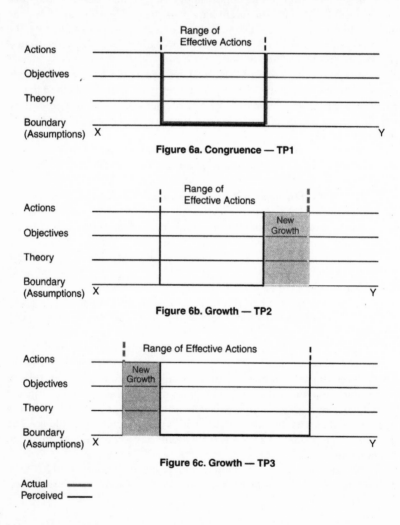

Figure 6a. Congruence — TP1

Figure 6b. Growth — TP2

Figure 6c. Growth — TP3

Actual ▬▬
Perceived ▬

This model suggests three axioms for increasing personal and leadership effectiveness:

1. When growth occurs on any continuum, in either direction, the far boundary stays fixed. The implication is that anything that ever worked for you in the past has a capacity to work for you again. It just needs to be tested and adapted to the present conditions.

2. Growth, or any increase in effectiveness, always occurs at the boundary. A leader's best position in the face of new challenge is at the very edge of his or her Zone of Comfort.

3. As one nears the edge of a sub-boundary and the probability for growth increases, the probability of discomfort, risk, and diminished self-confidence increases proportionally.

CONCLUSION

Regardless of the setting in which it is employed, the Gestalt approach relies heavily on the use of paradox. Several such paradoxes may be very helpful in increasing leadership effectiveness.

Paradox I. The best way to build an effective team is to focus on the individual. The concept of synergy suggests that because the whole (team) is greater than and different from the sum of its component parts (individuals), the stronger each individual member is, the higher the potential for the maximum strength of the team. When the leader focuses on and legitimizes the value of individual differences and common goals, each group member is encouraged to develop the best way to be and to work. Once this differentiation process is established and is well under way, linkages are formed among strong, confident individuals, each of whom is able and more willing to contribute uniquely to the organizational objective.

Paradox II. The best way to change is not to change (Beisser, 1970). The Gestalt approach focuses heavily on what is rather than on what should be. Assisting a leader to be more aware and appreciative of how she is rather than how she should be puts that person in a better position to make a conscious decision to remain in this position or to try something different. In short, once the effective Theory X leader is told, "It's really okay to be how you are," she no longer has to expend effort in defending her position or hiding it. Making it genuinely safe for her to relax and experience her present position more fully is a change! Any modification in her approach that she makes from this position is because she chooses to do so; if successful, the change will become permanent change. Permanent change is the only kind of change that has lasting impact on increasing the effectiveness of the individual and the organization.

Paradox III. No "One Best Way" is the one best way. People are much more different from each other than they are similar, and the same can be said for organizations. The range of uniqueness is infinite and is limited only by an inability to recognize the differences that do exist. No single approach, theory, or set of assumptions is going to be universally applicable to the individual's or the organization's needs—this one included.

If, for example, after reading this article, you reject it, you have, paradoxically, acted in consonance with the approach. That is, you have allowed yourself to try something new, have weighed it carefully, and have then consciously chosen to reject it in favor of an existing position. In this process, you have become more aware of your existing position and how it is of more service to you than the one presented here. You are more aware of how our respective theories and assumptions differ, and at least for now, you are more sure that your position is more useful and correct for you than is mine. At the very minimum, you have gained another alternative that might be useful to you at some later date.

Some direct implications can be shown for the future training and development for the leaders of today's and tomorrow's organizations. Currently, most leadership training and development programs are geared specifically to the expansion of theory, the pursuit of objectives, and the learning of new techniques. What has been missing is the essential first step—assisting individual leaders in becoming more clear and more confident in the assumptions they make about themselves and others and in their ability to provide the necessary leadership to get the organization where it needs to go.

References

Beisser, A.R. (1970). The paradoxical theory of change. In J. Fagan & I.L. Shepherd (Eds.), *Gestalt therapy now.* Palo Alto, CA: Science and Behavior.

Bennis, W.G. (1969). *Organization development: Its nature and origins and prospects.* Reading, MA: Addison-Wesley.

Herman, S.M. (1974). The shadow of organization development. In J.W. Pfeiffer & J.E. Jones (Eds.), *The 1974 annual handbook for group facilitators.* San Francisco, CA: Pfeiffer.

Herman, S.M. (1976). The shouldist manager. In J.W. Pfeiffer & J.E. Jones (Eds.), *The 1976 annual handbook for group facilitators.* San Francisco, CA: Pfeiffer.

Karp, H.B. (1976). A gestalt approach to collaboration in organizations. In J.W. Pfeiffer & J.E. Jones (Eds.), *The 1976 annual handbook for group facilitators.* San Francisco, CA: Pfeiffer.

Karp, H.B. (1995). *Personal power: An unorthodox guide to success.* Lake Worth, FL: Gardner Press.

McGregor, D.M. (1960). *The human side of enterprise.* New York: McGraw-Hill.

Perls, F.S. (1969). *In and out the garbage pail.* Moab, UT: Real People Press.

Polster, E., & Polster, M. (1973). *Gestalt theory integrated.* New York: Brunner/Mazel.

Originally published in The 1996 Annual: Volume 1, Training.

4

An Overview of Ten Management and Organizational Theorists

Marshall Sashkin

What is called for is a complete mental revolution on the part of workers and on the part of managers, such that both take their eyes off the division of profit and together turn toward increasing the size of the profit, until it becomes so large that it is unnecessary to quarrel over how it shall be divided.[1]

The above statement is paraphrased from one of the ten management and organizational theorists who will be discussed in this article. Although the comment may sound idealistic, even humanistic, it is derived from the writing of Frederick Taylor, the father of "scientific management" and a man whom one would never describe as a "humanist" after even a casual inspection of his words and deeds. Most texts cover the details of various management theories reasonably well, explaining the nature of Taylor's "scientific management" and Fayol's "basic functions" of management, defining Weber's elements of bureaucracy, and so on. However, it is possible to really understand what a theory is "all about" only if one has some understanding of the individual who created it. So, although it is not possible to fully describe or explore the creative, complex people who developed the theories and approaches discussed in this brief article, it is possible—and should be interesting—to look at what they said, how

See "Hearings Before Special Committee of the House of Representatives . . ." in reference list.

they behaved (or are reported to have behaved), and the consistency (or lack of it) between each individual's thoughts and actions. The latter, according to Argyris (1976), tells much about the person. This comparison will be made in the context of the historical periods in which these various individuals lived and worked and will focus on the periods of their greatest influence. (Table 1 shows the chronological progression of these influences.)

Historical Management Theory (Pre-1900)

Ancient organizations were considerably more simple than those in which we live and work today. The archetype is the tribe, ruled by a religious leader-authority figure who is obeyed by all. Such a system becomes unwieldy when two conditions occur: (a) the group size increases beyond a dozen or so and (b) the work to be done becomes more complicated than the most primitive of tasks (foraging for food, setting up shelters, etc.). Thus, in a very old text, the Bible, we find a clear description of organizational change. Moses found that he could not cope with being the only leader of the Israelites; the job was too complex, and he simply did not have the time to give instructions to every single person. So he named a group of leaders, each of whom was responsible for ten persons. For every ten "leaders of tens," there was a leader of tens of tens, or hundreds. Thus, an early hierarchy was developed.

Table 1. Periods of Greatest Influence of
Ten Management and Organizational Theorists

Theorist(s)	Period of Greatest Influence
Historical Management	pre-1900
Frederick W. Taylor	1890-1915
Henri Fayol	1890-1920
Max Weber	1885-1920
Elton Mayo	1910-1940
Fritz Roethlisberger and W.J. Dickson	1925-1955
Douglas McGregor	1945-1965
Rensis Likert	1955-1975
Fred Emery and Eric Trist	1965-1980s

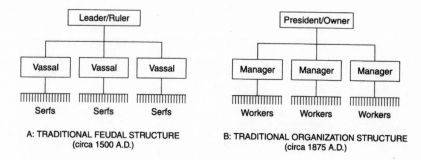

Figure 1. Traditional Structures

Of course, the hierarchical structure that is characteristic of most organizations is even older than the one developed by Moses, but it is important to note that hierarchies taller than Moses' were rare in the ancient world. For example, the Roman armies and others usually contained captains who led anywhere from a few dozen to a few hundred men. The captains reported to a general, who was often the head of the army. Sometimes a very large—or very sophisticated—force might include subcaptains (lieutenants) or "junior" generals who reported to the chief general, but even then the hierarchy would be relatively flat, a characteristic of most organizations throughout history. During the past few centuries, and even in the last century, a typical small factory was organized like a feudal estate. Figure 1 depicts this similarity.

As the world changed, the traditional form of organizational hierarchy began to malfunction because of problems that it was not designed to handle. It could not accommodate the complex interdependencies with which organizations were confronted as technology advanced. Well before 1900, it was clear that most organizations could not operate effectively within this framework. It was around the turn of the century that three men developed modifications of the traditional structure in an effort to aid organizational functioning. This article will present these three men in an artificial order, since they were truly contemporaries and the extent to which they influenced one another is not known.

Frederick W. Taylor: Individually Centered Structure

The author of the statement that is paraphrased at the beginning of this article was a complex and, frequently, contradictory person. He believed that by applying his precepts for the scientific analysis and design of jobs, labor and management cooperatively could create a profit large enough to provide ample

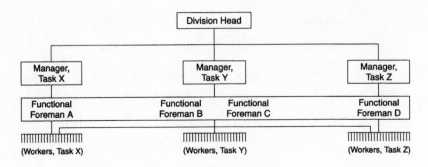

Figure 2. Taylor's Ideal Structures

remuneration for both the workers and the manufacturer. In contrast, Taylor's own description of a worker, in an experiment to increase efficiency, is: "One of the very first requirements for a man who is fit to handle pig-iron . . . is that he shall be so stupid . . . that he more nearly resembles in his mental makeup the ox than any other type" (Hearings, 1912). In instructing this man, Taylor told him, "If you are a high-priced man, you will do exactly as [you are told] . . . from morning till night. When [told] to pick up a pig and walk, you pick it up and you walk . . . . When [told] to sit down and rest, you sit down . . . . And what's more, no back talk" (Taylor, 1911, p. 46). Finally, returning to the issue of the profit so large that there would be no need to argue over its division between labor and management, Upton Sinclair, a popular "expose" writer of the time, noted that Taylor "gave about 61 percent increase in wages, and got 362 percent increase in work" (Copley, 1923, p. 30).

Aside from this view of how to divide increased profits fairly, it is clear that Taylor and his followers went overboard in fractionating jobs by time-and-motion study. Taylor's approach, however, was for many years the defining characteristic of modern industrial work, and many industries still use time-and-motion-study methods to design jobs. It was years before people began to realize the tremendous psychological damage that was done to hundreds of thousands of workers by carrying these methods to an extreme. Ultimately, Taylor's approach led down a dead-end path.

Although Taylor's success was not in dealing with large-scale organizational structures, he did have some interesting, and quite radical, ideas. He would have done away with the principle of chain of command, or one worker/one boss. In his design, shown in Figure 2, each worker was supervised by a number of "functional foremen" who were expert teacher/trainers rather than the traditional overseers. Taylor's idea of the functional foreman failed; it was never fully implemented and was soon forgotten for two reasons: it threatened management supervisory notions of control and it was a far more complex design than was warranted by the nature of jobs at the time (1890–1910).

Years later, a somewhat changed version of Taylor's ideal structure would be known as a "matrix" organization (Davis & Lawrence, 1977). Even so, these organizations differ substantially from Taylor's model because jobs are typically complex and technically demanding rather than fractionated and technically simple

Taylor's statements, then, sounded progressive but were not. He was enough of an influence, however, that Congress investigated him as a possible communist subversive. (This was at the time of the successful Russian revolution, when "red scares" were common in the U.S.) Taylor talked his way out of this, too, and continued to train the next generation of "time-study men."

In France, a contemporary of Taylor also was working on codification of management theory and was aware of Taylor's work. We will examine his achievements next.

Henri Fayol: Organizationally Centered Structure

We describe Fayol as being concerned with the structure of the organization—large-scale structure—as opposed to a focus on task design or small-scale structure. More than this, Fayol was a pragmatist. As head of a French steel-and-coal mining organization for thirty years, he developed a set of fourteen principles that he felt covered most managerial situations. It is not clear just how absolute Fayol meant to be about his principles—whether he intended them to be guidelines or powerful and stable laws. In one essay he wrote, "I became convinced that social phenomena are, like physical phenomena, subject to natural laws independent of our will" (Fayol, 1978). Yet, in his 1916 papers on general and industrial management he wrote, "There is nothing rigid or absolute in management affairs . . . seldom do we . . . apply the same principle twice in identical conditions . . . . Therefore principles are flexible and capable [of] adaptation" (Fayol, 1949, p. 19). As can be seen, later theorists who advocated absolute principles could appeal to Fayol—just as could those who favored more situationally flexible approaches. It was primarily the former type of theorist, however, who followed Fayol's lead in defining law-like principles.

Aside from creating the first set of principles of organization, Fayol added one small note to the traditional theory of organization, a note that was actually the first step toward major change in our view of organizational structure. In a traditional structure (Figure 1B), a worker at any level had only one primary interaction: with his or her supervisor. Fayol called this the "scalar" principle; in the military it is commonly referred to as "chain of command." Fayol, however, modified this principle significantly with still another principle, that of the "gangplank," which is illustrated in Figure 3 with the more recent label "Fayol's Bridge."

Fayol explains it thusly: "Imagine that department F has to be put in contact with department P . . . it is much simpler and quicker to go directly from F to P by making use of a 'gangplank' and that is what is most often done. The scalar principle will be safeguarded if managers E and O have authorized their respective subordinates F and P to deal directly" (Fayol, 1949, p. 35). This may seem ridiculously simple but was revolutionary when Fayol was writing at the beginning of the century.

Fayol was, in a pragmatic way, becoming aware of the increasing need for coordination in organizations, a need brought about by continuing technological development and one that could not be satisfied by traditional organizational structure. Fayol was, however, no radical; in fact, he strongly opposed Taylor's revision of the traditional structure as an unacceptable isolation of the principle of chain of command.

Fayol's principles had a strong and lasting impact on the development of management thought in Europe and in England. His effect on American management was indirect, because his book did not appear in an easily obtainable English language edition until 1949. Nevertheless, his work encouraged others to add more principles until, by the 1930s, some authors had developed hundreds of "principles of management."

Like his gangplank idea, Fayol's principles were generally sensible if sometimes a bit fuzzy. Unfortunately, later authors did not always have his

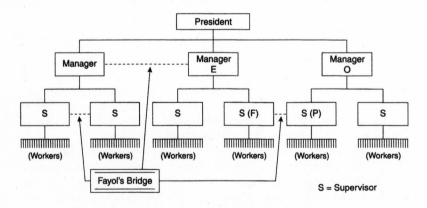

Figure 3. Fayol's Modification of the Traditional Structure

depth of managerial experience, and their principles often were meaning-less lists of trivia. In fact, management theory generally was the product of scholars and academics (such as Max Weber), rather than the result of con-tributions from managers.

Max Weber: Organizationally and Societally Centered Structure

Weber was far more successful than Taylor in his approach to the analysis of organizational arrangements. Most social scientists would agree that Weber was a genius in his field. His name is most closely associated with "bureau-cracy" (although he was also a great religious scholar), but bureaucracy was not his invention.

What Weber (1947) did was first codify (describe) and then slightly mod-ify a system of organization as old as history. A complex, fairly efficient, and very stable bureaucracy has been the basis of the Chinese civilization for over 3000 years. Weber examined and analyzed in detail it and other bureaucratic systems that seemed to have been effective in terms of organizational survival and goal attainment, including the Catholic church and the Prussian army. Weber's anal-ysis of the bureaucratic form, shown in Figure 4, was the first clear, detailed statement of organizational structure.

There were two modifications of the traditional structure in Weber's pre-sentation. The first was the notion of authority based on a rational-legal system, rather than on tradition (e.g., hereditary rule) or force. In Weber's day, many

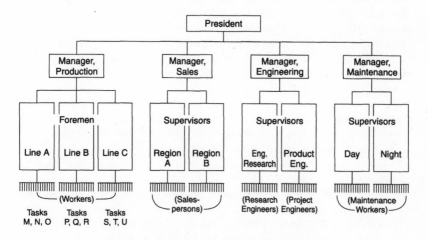

Figure 4. Basic Bureaucratic Structure (Weber)

(if not most) organizations—including business and industrial firms—assumed controls over workers that seem unbelievable today. These included not merely ten-, twelve-, or fourteen-hour working days, but also how the employees' free time might be spent and the assumption of absolute obedience to superiors, however irrational or nonwork-related their orders. The concept of rational-legal authority prescribes clearly defined limits over what may and may not be required of workers. The second thing Weber defined was organizational arrangement as a hierarchy of *offices* rather than of individuals. That is, each "office" carries specified duties along with the legal authority to carry out those duties—no more and no less. The effect of this was twofold: first, the basis of authority—rational and legal—was emphasized, and control over workers was limited to behavior specifically related to the work; second, the activities of the manager—duties, responsibilities, etc.—were clearly defined, thus making it possible to choose people for specific jobs on the basis of their competence and skills.

Although today people often react negatively to the term "bureaucracy," when reading Weber, one is aware that bureaucracy was a great invention. Weber (1946) says, for example, "The decisive reason for the advance of bureaucratic organization has always been its purely technical superiority over any other form of organization" (1946, p. 214). He also writes that bureaucracy "is superior to any other form in precision, in stability, in the stringency of its discipline, and in its reliability . . . [it] is formally capable of application to all kinds of administrative tasks" (1946, p. 214). If this sounds autocratic, one may be reassured by the fact that Weber also said, "The progress of bureaucratization . . . is a parallel phenomenon of democracy" (1946, p. 225). "This results from the characteristic principle of bureaucracy: the abstract regularity of the execution of authority, which is a result of the demand for 'equality before the law' in the personal and functional sense [1946, p. 224] . . . . Bureaucracy . . . strives . . . for a 'right to the office' by the establishment of a regular disciplinary procedure and by removal of the completely arbitrary disposition of the 'chief' over the subordinate [1946, p. 242] . . . . The march of bureaucracy has destroyed structures of domination [such as patriarchialism, feudalism, and charismatic authority] which had no rational character" (1946, p. 244). Thus bureaucracy had two great advantages in Weber's view. First, it was the most efficient and effective form of organization and, second, it was the most humane form of organization.

Weber was more overtly unhappy as a person than Taylor. Plagued with a variety of physical ailments, he was also neurotic and suffered from a number of psychological symptoms. His fascination with rigidly disciplined bureaucratic organizations (e.g., the army and the church) was probably not unrelated to his various psychological problems. Even so, his contributions—which were not limited to defining and delineating bureaucracy—were monumental.

In summary, Weber made organizations rational, just as Taylor made specific tasks rational. Although many organizations had endured and functioned in similar ways for centuries, Weber made a large contribution, observing with acute detail and clarity the organizational form that was so functional for survival and identifying modern modifications to that form that took into account the increasing complexity of organizations in an increasingly technologically sophisticated world.

Elton Mayo: Societally Centered Human Interaction

It is not possible to understand the human-relations movement of the 1930s, 1940s, and 1950s without recognizing that the now-discredited evidence of superiority (in terms of productivity and quality) was never much more than an excuse for what is really a philosophical position. Elton Mayo, a great social philosopher of the 1920s and 1930s, was the major force behind the human relations school. Although Mayo was not one of those who wrote much about the "Hawthorne Studies" (see Carey, 1967; Dickson & Roethlisberger, 1966; Landesberger, 1958; and Shepard, 1971), he was directly involved in that research, and the results seemed to him to offer clear evidence for his philosophy.

Mayo was particularly opposed to the scientific management so forcefully advocated by Taylor. In fact, Mayo's philosophy was partly shaped as a response to Taylor's ideas. Mayo wrote, "as a system, Taylorism effects much in the way of economy of labor; its chief defect is that workmen are not asked to collaborate in effecting such economies" (p. 60). "No social system can be considered satisfactory which deprives the great majority of mankind of every vestige of autonomy. No society is civilized in which the many [work] in the interests of the few. When 'work' signifies intelligent collaboration in the achievement of a social purpose, 'industrial unrest' will cease to be" (1919, p. 63). It is interesting to note that this was written in 1919, before the Hawthorne Studies began and before the term "human relations" was invented. It is also important to recognize that Mayo was not arguing against efficiency or productivity; he is speaking, basically, about how management ought to deal with people in the work environment.

Mayo served as the faculty member, at Harvard, responsible for the industrial psychology experiments at Western Electric's Hawthorne plant near Chicago. It was these studies that led to the term human relations and the subsequent movement. Mayo himself, however, concentrated on larger social issues, as is indicated by the titles of his last books, e.g., *The Human Problems of an Industrial Civilization* (1933). Mayo's student, Fritz Roethlisberger, was more directly involved in the Hawthorne Studies and in creating the human relations movement.

Fritz Roethlisberger and W.J. Dickson: Individually Centered Human Interaction

The Hawthorne Studies (Roethlisberger & Dickson, 1936) have been analyzed and reanalyzed, attacked and defended for over forty years (Carey, 1967; Landesberger, 1958; Shepard, 1971). What was so controversial was not the research findings but their philosophical interpretations. In the guise of scholarly debate and critique, people argued about the worth, importance, and correctness of the human relations approach based on Mayo's values.

A brief review of this historically important research program is worthwhile. In the late 1920s, industrial psychologists were actively applying Taylor's time-study methods as well as analyzing work conditions to determine how human work capacities varied with the physical environment (light, heat, noise, ventilation, etc.). At Western Electric's Hawthorne plant, a special test area was set up. Workers and supervisors were selected to participate in the study, in which work behavior was measured as physical conditions varied. At first everything seemed reasonable, e.g., illumination levels were increased and production increased. However, when the level of light was decreased, production continued to increase, until the workers were producing more than ever under conditions equivalent to bright moonlight. At this point the engineers gave up, and a new research team from Harvard was brought in.

Roethlisberger was on-site head, working with the company's personnel department liaison, W.J. Dickson. What soon became evident was that social relationships in the test area were having a great influence on worker productivity. One view is that the supervisor, who had been chosen because of his excellent reputation, had developed a strongly loyal work group with high morale, and that these workers, who also had been screened, worked hard to satisfy him, even under adverse conditions. Thus, the importance of human relations was demonstrated. A less sanguine view is that the workers responded to the special treatment they were being given by working hard to please the researchers, even when conditions were poor. This explanation, commonly referred to as the Hawthorne effect, was thought to be true during the 1950s and 1960s, when a strong backlash swept toward the human relations movement.

The truth is somewhere in between. Katz and Kahn (1966) observed that the Hawthorne workers had the best supervisor, were given special privileges, and formed a cohesive team. These factors, they argued, go far beyond the effects possible from just special attention, although special attention does have effects.

The importance of the Hawthorne Studies is the demonstration that social factors have strong impacts on work behavior. This is true whether one believes that the social factors were the special attention given the workers or the quality of supervision and group interaction they experienced. Roethlisberger put it this way: "People like to feel important and have their work recognized as important. . . . They like to work in an atmosphere of approval. They like to be praised rather than blamed . . . . They like to feel independent in their relations to their supervisors . . . . They like to be consulted about and participate in actions that will personally affect them. In short, employees, like most people, want to be treated as belonging to and being an integral part of some group" (1950).

Mayo saw that in society the extended family was becoming the nuclear family, with consequent loss of family-group identification for many. He proposed to substitute a new work group for the old family group. Mayo and Roethlisberger conceived an organization along the lines illustrated in Figure 5. Every work unit became self-regulating. The development of positive work relationships (indicated by the work units in Figure 5) was seen as beneficial to workers in that they regained a sense of group identification lost to

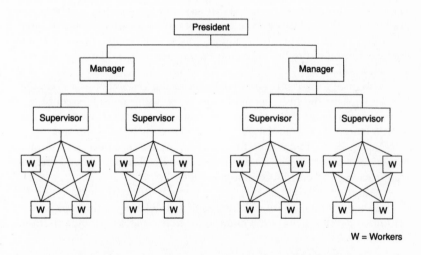

W = Workers

Figure 5. Roethlisberger and Dickson's Human Relations Model

them as their families became smaller (parents and children, not including grandparents, aunts, uncles, etc., as had been true in the last century). Management benefitted because, when treated properly (the human-relations approach), the members of these groups would support high production goals, solve problems, and help one another as needed.

The prescription was simply to allow small groups of workers maximum freedom in controlling their own work. Within the groups, workers would establish their own patterns of coordination. By recognizing and supporting this informal organization, management theoretically could gain the support and cooperation of workers, leading to greater productivity and more efficient job performance.

Over time, these human-relations ideas gained a fair degree of acceptance among managers, although there also was considerable resistance. Many managers feared loss of control or power, which was not an unrealistic concern. The rather laissez-faire, undirected approach prescribed conceivably could generate some anxiety even in a liberal manager.

By the mid-1950s, it was clear that productivity and efficiency were not attainable through the simple solutions generated by the human relations advocates (see Sales, 1966). The Hawthorne Studies actually foretold this, and later parts of the study showed that groups of workers acted to regulate their output, limiting it to no more than a certain average amount per day even though they could have easily produced at far higher levels. This finding was verified in other studies. Still further research showed that very unhappy workers could be highly productive, while very satisfied workers in cohesive work groups could be quite unproductive. The relationships among satisfaction, group morale, and productivity turned out to be much more complicated than Mayo and his colleagues had expected.

Eventually, managers—and not just academic researchers—realized this fact. Perhaps the disillusionment of some accounts for the subsequent backlash, illustrated by articles in the *Harvard Business Review* titled "What Price Human Relations?" (McNair, 1957) and "The Case for Benevolent Autocracy" (McMurray, 1958). In any case, human relations has become a ritual term, a thing that all believe in with no particular action implications (other than generally treating workers with common courtesy).

Although the human-relations approach idealized by Mayo and by Roethlisberger and Dickson ultimately failed, it did provide the basis for the continued development of the behavioral-science theories of organization, which we now will examine.

Douglas McGregor: Individually Centered Behavioral Science

The influence of the human-relations movement provided support for behavioral scientists in business schools. One of the first and best known was Douglas McGregor, a psychologist who served to link a psychological view of human motivation to a theory of management. In doing this he coined the terms "Theory X" and "Theory Y." The former represents traditional assumptions about human motivation, some of which are that people are lazy and work only because they have to and that workers must be controlled and led. Theory Y, in contrast, asserts that workers are responsible and want to be involved more in their work (such that their own needs are met as the organization's are). McGregor said, "The essential task of management is to arrange the organizational conditions and methods of operation so that people can achieve their own goals best by directing their own efforts toward organizational objectives" (1957, p. 26).

McGregor based his approach on the motivation theory of Abraham Maslow (1943). This theory suggests that human needs can be categorized as survival, security, social, esteem, and self-development (or growth). As one type of need is basically fulfilled, the individual progresses toward higher needs (survival is primary, growth is most advanced). This suggests that if management can design work to fulfill the higher needs of workers, the workers' motives can be directed toward organizational, as well as individual, goals. (This assumes, reasonably enough, that for most workers the survival needs are met, and, for the majority, so are the security needs.)

One implication of this approach is that managers must diagnose individual workers' needs and offer opportunities for those needs to be satisfied. If this is so, effective management would seem to be rather impractical. However, although the range of specific individual needs is great, the basic categories of need are few. Furthermore, when workers are involved in defining their own needs, goals, and potential rewards, the task of creating appropriate organizational conditions seems more feasible.

McGregor's great gift was in taking some fairly complex ideas and expressing them in a clear, yet not oversimplified manner. He was able to explain the failure of human relations—and of autocracy—and offer a possible alternative: Theory Y. In 1954, he said, "There are big differences in the kinds of opportunities that can be provided for people to obtain need satisfaction. It is relatively easy to provide means (chiefly in the form of money) for need satisfaction—at least until the supply is exhausted. You cannot, however, provide people with a sense of achievement, or with knowledge, or with prestige. You can provide *opportunities* for them to obtain these satisfactions through efforts directed toward organization goals. What is even more important, the *supply of such opportunities*—unlike the supply of money—*is unlimited"* (1966, pp. 44–45).

McGregor developed a philosophy of how to manage individual workers, based on the best knowledge available about human motivation. Although he presented this philosophy in sugar-coated capsule form—Theory Y—he recognized that it would not be so simple to implement. People's expectations, which were based on past treatment, would have to be radically changed, and such change comes slowly. In 1957 McGregor wrote, "It is no more possible to create an organization today which will be a fully effective application of this theory than it was to build an atomic power plant in 1945" (1966, p. 24).

A major part of McGregor's implementation problem, however, was that his theory was not an *organizational* theory but a theory of how individual managers might better manage. McGregor neglected to consider the organizational framework needed to support such management behavior. We will look next at a theorist who did develop such a framework.

Rensis Likert: Organizationally Centered Behavioral Science

In the work of Likert (1961, 1967), one finds the most complete and sophisticated theory of organization based on behavioral science. It developed out of research conducted during the twenty-five years that Likert was director of the Institute for Social Research at the University of Michigan. Likert's theory is clearly prescriptive; he argues that his approach describes effective organizations and that if it is implemented, the organization will be effective.

Likert can be seen, in one sense, as expanding McGregor's two alternatives to four systems. System 1 is much like an extreme Theory X-organization: rigid, autocratic, and exploitative of workers. System 2 represents benevolent autocracy or paternalism. System 3 is called "consultative" management. Workers are involved to a degree in making decisions, but all real power remains with the managers. System 4 is participative management; all workers are involved in decisions that concern them.

In Likert's words, System 4 has three key elements: "(1) the use by the manager of the principle of supportive relationships, (2) his use of group decision making and group methods of supervision, and (3) his high performance goals for the organization" (1967, p. 47). The principle of supportive relationships states that "the leadership and other processes of the organization must be such as to ensure a maximum probability that in all interactions and in all relationships within the organization, each member, in the light of his background, values, desires, and expectations, will view the experience as supportive and one which builds and maintains his sense of personal worth and importance" (1967, p. 47). These statements mean several things. First, supervision is seen as a group—not a one-to-one, superior-to-subordinate—activity. Second, the group is delegated as much authority as possible; decisions are group decisions, not orders from above. Third, the supervisor or manager is seen as a "link-pin." That is, he or she is the head of one group but a member of another group (at the next level up), as illustrated in Figure 6. Thus, the manager serves as an important communication link between the two levels.

Likert incorporates some of the earlier organizational theories in System 4. He is the only modern behavioral scientist to speak of a "principle" of management. In content, this principle owes much to the human-relations school but also, in a very general way, incorporates Maslow's needs of esteem and growth. The group methods that Likert mentions also derive from Mayo and reflect Maslow's social-need category. Likert's notion of performance goals as well as the basic structure he follows are derived from Weber's theory of bureaucracy. Although the organization shown in Figure 6 may look unusual at first glance, the only modification to the traditional bureaucratic form is that authority is shared at one level below that shown in Figure 4. Instead of the manager making a decision, the decision is made by the manager in collaboration with the manager's subordinates. This is an important change, just as

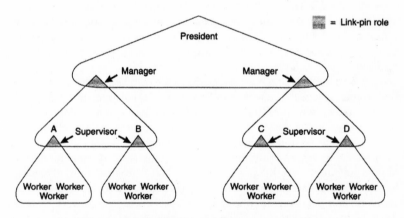

Figure 6. Likert's Overlapping Group/Link-Pin Model[3]

---

3. Managers and supervisors are "link-pins," that is, members of two groups. Their function is to act as coordinative "linkers" (information transmitters) between the two groups.

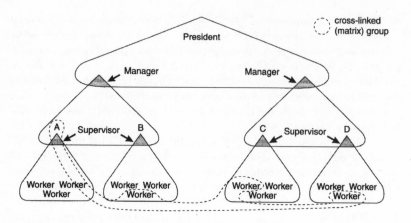

Figure 7. Likert's Combined Behavorial/Matrix Model

Fayol's Bridge was an important change, but like the bridge, it is a modification, not a radical restructuring. Likert even has his own version of Fayol's Bridge; this is shown in Figure 7. Because coordination has continued to become complex since Fayol's time, Likert uses an ad hoc group for this purpose, selecting relevant individuals from each of the units that need to coordinate activities.

Likert should not be underestimated. He has developed what appears (after much study and trial) to be a workable organizational form for implementing the basic human relations approach and for putting Theory Y into practice.

Likert believes that most managers can learn to operate under his theory: "Data . . . show that managers who seek to do so can readily learn better systems of management" (1967, p. 190). He also argues for the utility of sound behavioral science research: "Most organizations today base their standard operating procedures and practices on classical organizational theories. These theories rely on key assumptions; . . . until recently, the shifting sands of practitioner judgment were the major if not the only source of knowledge about how to organize and run an enterprise. Now, research on leadership, management, and organization, undertaken by social scientists, provides a more stable body of knowledge . . . . The art of management can be based on verifiable information derived from rigorous, quantitative research" (1967, p. 1). Likert's position is well stated in the opening lines of his book, *The Human Organization* (1967): "All the activities of any enterprise are initiated and determined by the persons who make up that institution. Plants, offices, computers, automated equipment, and all else that a modern firm uses are unproductive except for human effort and direction . . . . Every aspect of a firm's activities is determined by the competence, motivation, and general effectiveness of its human organization" (p. 1).

This last statement highlights what many consider to be the major flaw in Likert's approach: the conspicuous absence of anything reminiscent of Taylor or Taylorism. Although Taylor could be rejected for a number of reasons, Likert's reason is unusual. He believes that Taylor's basic concept of job technology is irrelevant to organizational effectiveness. At a professional meeting in 1978, Likert was asked why his theory contained no meaningful consideration of the specific characteristics of jobs (design, technology, etc.) or of the motivations of individuals. He replied to the effect that these factors are organizationally irrelevant.

Most current organizational theorists disagree strongly with this view. Some, like Charles Perrow (1972), an organizational sociologist, go so far as to assert the opposite, that technology determines everything and that human variables are essentially irrelevant. Most, however, take a more balanced view, seeing the technical and social aspects of organizations as interdependent.

The best current example of such an approach derives from work at the Tavistock Institute for Human Relations (England), which began in the 1940s and continues today. Many names are associated with this approach; this article will discuss the writings of the two Tavistock members who are most known in the United States.

Fred Emery and Eric Trist: A Comprehensive Behavioral Science Theory

Emery and Trist (1960) are the two names most familiarly attached to the theory called "sociotechnical systems," or, simply, STS (see Pasmore & Sherwood, 1978). This approach was developed in the 1950s and 1960s at the Tavistock Institute. The STS approach has actually involved over a dozen behavioral scientists, including (in alphabetical order) Kenneth Bamforth (Trist & Bamforth, 1951), Wilfred Bion (1961), Wilfred Brown (1960), P.G. Herbst (1974), Elliot Jaques (1951), Eric Miller (1967), A.K. Rice (1958), Einer Thorsrud (Emery & Thorsrud, 1976), and A.T. M. Wilson, among others. The most clear statements of STS as an organized theory have, however, been presented by Emery and Trist, both together and independently.

The STS concept started at the bottom of a coal mine. Trist and a former student, Bamforth (Trist & Bamforth, 1951), were studying the use of new work methods in the mining industry. What they found, however, was that under certain conditions that made the new methods impractical, workers had solved the problem by going all the way back to the small-group team mining that had been abandoned at the time of semimechanization in the 1940s (see Trist, Higgin, Morray, & Pollock, 1963). The team approach not only solved the technical problems, but it fit better with the needs of the miners (e.g., for strong social contacts when faced with a very dangerous task). Trist said, "After going down into the coal mine this time, I came up a different man. I was certain that the things I observed were of major significance" (1980, p. 151). The concept was brilliantly simple: the technological system used in an organization must fit or mesh properly with the social system if the organization is to operate effectively.

In the mid-1950s another British researcher, working independently of the Tavistock group, confirmed this notion. Joan Woodward's (1965) intent was to test some of the basic principles of management by checking to see whether more profitable firms did, in fact, follow the principles more closely than less profitable firms. Her answer was a strong "no." There was no relation at all between effectiveness and adherence to management principles. This seemed odd, because some principles were considered common sense, such as the proper "span of control" or average number of workers to be supervised by a first-line supervisor.

Woodward reexamined her data and found a pattern. All the measures seemed to differ by industry—in fact, by type of technology (which was crudely categorized as production of individual units, mass production, and continuous-process production). Examples of the first would be the manufacture of locomotives, of hand-knit sweaters, or of one-of-a-kind, high-technology items. The second type is the traditional assembly-line operation. The third represents high-technology products that are manufactured in a continuous process, such as oil or chemicals. Each basic technological type did differ, on the average, in number of levels of hierarchy, span of control, ratio of managers to nonmanagers, and a number of other variables. This showed that the principles did not seem to be universal but, rather, were modified depending on an organization's technology.

But what of effectiveness? Woodward then showed that the more effective organizations consistently were characterized at about the average or mean value on each measure. In other words, there seemed to be a best method of organizing to fit each type of technology. Firms that stayed close to this best approach for their technical system were most effective. Firms that had too many or too few levels of hierarchy, too wide or too narrow a span of control, or too small or too large a manager/worker ratio *for their type of technology* were least profitable. The support of Woodward's findings for the STS approach is striking, especially when one realizes that Woodward worked totally independently and was unaware of the Tavistock STS approach. In fact, that approach was most clearly stated at just about the time that Woodward was publishing her findings in 1958, so Trist and Emery could not have been influenced by her work either.

The STS approach does not prescribe one particular organizational form, so there is no one diagram to illustrate it. It is based on the participative involvement of workers in semiautonomous groups and is like Likert's System 4 in this respect. How these groups are set up, their sizes, and the formal structural arrangements in the organization—all these things may vary widely from Likert's modified bureaucratic format.

STS theory does incorporate modern behavioral science as derived from human relations theory and industrial/organizational psychology. Katz and Kahn (1966) comment that the STS approach assumes three basic human work needs: (a) a need for closure, for finishing a whole task; (b) a need for autonomy or control of one's own behavior as a mature adult; and (c) a need for some level of interpersonal contact at work, not as a diversion or tangential to work activity but as a basic part of task activities. It is easy to see how these concepts relate to the human relations approach, to McGregor's Theory Y, and to Likert's group-based approach.

Where STS goes well beyond any of the earlier theoretical approaches is in incorporating technology as a major determinant of how the system should be socially organized. This, of course, directly contradicts Likert's views of organizations while incorporating the key points of his and many earlier theories—as well as parts of some less well-known sociological theories of organization that we have not mentioned, such as Thompson's (1967) and Perrow's (1970). Finally, STS theory incorporates a concern with organizational environments and the effects of the environment on organizations. Likert's and all of the earlier theories totally ignored this dynamic interaction.

Only Paul Lawrence and Jay Lorsch (1969), professors at Harvard, attempted to examine organizations in terms of the demands of their environments. They suggest that more traditional structures (Figure 4) are appropriate when the environment is quite stable in terms of technological complexity and change, market demand, and low internal organizational specialization of tasks and functions. When environments are very unstable (rapid, uncertain changes in the above factors and high internal specialization), more complex devices are needed to coordinate organizational activities. These devices include temporary cross-link teams (as defined by Likert), liaison roles, and even departments whose task is simply to coordinate among other departments.

STS theory, however, deals with this issue through Emery and Trist's (1965) concept of "causal texture" of the environment. They define four types of environment, the first two being subdivisions of the stable environment defined by Lawrence and Lorsch; the second two being unstable. The "type-four" environment is called "turbulent," uncontrollably reactive, almost unpredictable. Trist notes, "We . . . hit on the word 'turbulence' when I was describing how I [once] became airsick" (1980, p. 162).

Unlike the various older approaches, STS theory does not pretend to offer a cure for all organizational ills. In fact, Trist comments that "environmental turbulence has become such a strong dynamic that I'm a pessimistic optimist. I'm scared as hell about what will happen on a large scale during the next few decades. We may well be faced with wholesale unemployment as technological advances continue to replace workers. The 'management of decline' may become a new approach as resources are exhausted and various aspects of our economy wind down. Our focus has been on micro processes, yet we must try to do something at macro levels, at the large-scale system level" (1980, p. 166). Trist's comments seem about as pessimistic as an organizational theorist's can be.

Overview

At this point, it should be clear why this article has labeled each theorist according to the primary social-system level dealt with and the primary orientation taken. From the narrow, structural, individual-behavior focus of traditional theory (Taylor, 1911), there has been steady development in organizational theory. It has passed through a concern with small groups (Mayo, 1919; Roethlisberger & Dickson, 1936), with organizations (Likert, 1961; McGregor, 1957), and finally with all these factors in the context of a broad, social-system approach.

The aim of this article has been to show how organizational theorists have built on one another's ideas and how, even when one individual or group vehemently disagreed with another, the basic ideas of both were usually incorporated into a new approach. By looking at the theorists as people and not just as inanimate sources of ideas, and by examining the social-historical contexts in which they lived, one can see even more clearly how this "thesis-antithesis-synthesis" process has worked. One sees in Likert not merely his new ideas (such as the organizational link-pin concept) but also the reflection of the times he lived in, the days of principles of management and the Hawthorne Studies. In McGregor's work, we can find new ideas about management philosophy and also old ideas about human motivation that were developed in the 1930s and 1940s (and are not unrelated to Mayo's ideas about human needs). In the sociotechnical systems approach, we see the most recent generation of fully developed organizational theory, incorporating much of what came before, accepting and rejecting or correcting earlier elements, and going beyond the prior theories.

Who will become the dominant theorists of the upcoming generation is not clear; even less clear is the possible nature of the theories yet to come. Management and organizational theory has come a long way, from the turn-of-the-century world of Taylor to the world of supersonic aircraft and potential nuclear holocaust. Still, there is no indication that the earlier forms are totally superseded by later developments. Many organizations remain faithful to Weber's bureaucratic model, and there are even a few that still adhere to the traditional structural model. Good arguments can be made that such organizations will continue to decrease in number, but it is unlikely that all will ever disappear, simply because circumstances do exist that make such structural forms not only possible but desirable. In all probability, the world is diverse enough that such circumstances will continue to exist. Nor would it be correct to conclude that the more recently developed structural forms are best in any absolute sense; there is no way of knowing what will succeed them, although it would be reasonable to assume that whatever theories follow will be hierarchical in nature and—to some degree—bureaucratic in orientation.

References

Argyris, C. (1976). *Increasing leadership effectiveness*. New York: John Wiley & Sons.

Bion, W.R. (1961). *Experiences in groups*. New York: Basic Books.

Brown, W. (1960). *Exploration in management*. London: Heinemann.

Carey, A. (1967). The Hawthorne studies: A radical criticism. *American Sociological Review, 32*, 403–416.

Copley, F.B. (1923). *Frederick W. Taylor: Father of scientific management*. New York: Harper & Row.

Davis, S.M., & Lawrence, P.R. (1977). *Matrix*. Reading, MA: Addison-Wesley.

Dickson, W.J., & Roethlisberger, F.J. (1966). *Counseling in an organization: A sequel to the Hawthorne researches*. Boston, MA: Division of Research, Graduate School of Business Administration, Harvard University.

Emery, F.E., & Thorsrud, E. (1976). *Democracy at work*. Leiden, The Netherlands: Martinus Nijhoff.

Emery, F.E., & Trist, E.L. (1960). *Socio-technical systems*. Oxford, England: Pergamon Press.

Emery, F.E., & Trist, E.L. (1965). The causal texture of organizational environments. *Human Relations, 18,* 21–32.

Fayol, H. (1921). *L'incapacité industrielle de l'état: Les* P.T.T. Paris: Dunod.

Fayol, H. (1949). *General and industrial management* (C. Storrs, Trans.). London: Pitman.

Fayol, H. (1978). L'éveil de esprit publique. Quoted in E. Dale, *Management: Theory and practice* (4th ed.). New York: McGraw-Hill.

Hearings Before Special Committee of the House of Representatives to Investigate the Taylor and Other Systems of Shop Management Under Authority of House Resolution 90. pp. 1388–1389. (1912). Washington, DC: U.S. Government Printing Office.

Herbst, P.G. (1974). *Socio-technical design.* London: Tavistock.

Jaques, E. (1951). *The changing culture of a factory.* London: Tavistock.

Katz, D., & Kahn, R. (1966). *The social psychology of organizations.* New York: John Wiley & Sons.

Landesberger, H.J. (1958). *Hawthorne revisited.* Ithaca, NY: Cornell University Press.

Lawrence, P.R., & Lorsch, J.W. (1969). *Organization and environment: Managing differentiation and integration.* Homewood, IL: Richard D. Irwin.

Likert, R. (1961). *New patterns of management.* New York: McGraw-Hill.

Likert, R. (1967). *The human organization.* New York: McGraw-Hill.

Maslow, A.H. (1943). A theory of human motivation. *Psychological Review, 50,* 370–396.

Mayo, E. (1919). *Democracy and freedom: An essay in social logic.* Melbourne, Australia: Macmillan.

Mayo, E. (1933). *The human problems of an industrial civilization.* Cambridge, MA: Harvard University Press.

McGregor, D. (1957, April 9). The human side of enterprise. In *Adventure in thought and action.* Proceedings of the Fifth Anniversary Convocation of the School of Industrial Management. Massachusetts Institute of Technology, Cambridge, MA.

McGregor, D.M. (1957). The human side of enterprise. *The Management Review, 46*(11), 26.

McGregor, D.M. (1966). A philosophy of management. In W.G. Bennis & E.H. Schein (Eds.), with the collaboration of C. McGregor, *Leadership and motivation: Essays of Douglas McGregor.* Cambridge, MA: M.I.T. Press.

McMurray, R.N. (1958). The case for benevolent autocracy. *Harvard Business Review, 36*(1), 82–90.

McNair, M.P. (1957). What price human relations? *Harvard Business Review, 35*(2), 15–39.

Miller, E.J., & Rice, A.K. (1967). *Systems of organization*. London: Tavistock.

Pasmore, W.A., & Sherwood, J.J. (1978). *Sociotechnical systems: A sourcebook*. San Francisco, CA: Pfeiffer.

Perrow, C. (1970). *Organizational analysis: A sociological view*. Monterey, CA: Brooks/Cole.

Perrow, C. (1972). *Complex organizations: A critical essay*. Glenview, IL: Scott, Foresman.

Rice, A.K. (1958). *Productivity and social organization: The Ahmedabad experiment*. London: Tavistock.

Roethlisberger, F.J. (1950). The human equation in employee productivity (Speech before the personnel group of the National Retail Dry Goods Association).

Roethlisberger, F.J., & Dickson, W.J. (1936). *Management and the worker*. Cambridge, MA: Harvard University Press.

Sales, S.M. (1966). Supervisory style and productivity: Review and theory. *Personnel Psychology, 19*, 275–286.

Shepard, J.M. (1971). On Alex Carey's radical criticism of the Hawthorne studies. *Academy of Management Journal, 14*, 23–31.

Taylor, F.W. (1911). *Scientific management*. New York: Harper.

Thompson, J.D. (1967). *Organizations in action*. New York: McGraw-Hill.

Trist, E.L. (1980). Interview: Eric Trist, British interdisciplinarian. *Group & Organization Studies, 5*(2), 144–166.

Trist, E.L., & Bamforth, K.W. (1951). Some social and psychological consequences of the longwall method of coal-getting. *Human Relations, 4*, 3–38.

Trist, E.L., Higgin, G.A., Murray, H., & Pollock, A.B. (1963). *Organizational choice: Capabilities of groups at the coal face under changing technologies: The loss, re-discovery and transformation of a work tradition*. London: Tavistock.

Weber, M. (1946). From Max Weber: *Essays in sociology* (H.H. Gerth & C. Wright Mills, Eds. & Trans.). New York: Oxford University Press.

Weber, M. (1947). *The theory of social and economic organizations* (A.M. Henderson & T. Parsons, Trans., & T. Parsons, Ed.). New York: The Free Press.

Woodward, J. (1965). *Industrial organization: Theory and practice*. London: Oxford University Press.

Suggested Readings

The following are books by the most recent crop of organizational theorists. They provide limits and guidelines for the future development of organizational theory.

Child, J. (Ed.). (1973). *Man and organization: The search for exploration and social relevance.* New York: Halstead-Wiley.

Galbraith, J.R. (1973). *Designing complex organizations.* Reading, MA: Addison-Wesley.

Khandwalla, P.N. (1977). *The design of organizations.* New York: Harcourt Brace Jovanovich.

Mintzberg, H. (1979). *The structuring of organizations.* Englewood Cliffs, NJ: Prentice-Hall.

Pfeffer, J. (1978). *Organization design.* Arlington Heights, IL: AHM Publishing.

Weick, K.E., Jr. (1980). *The social psychology of organizing* (rev. ed.). Reading, MA: Addison-Wesley.

Originally published in The 1981 Annual Handbook for Group Facilitators.

5

McGregor's Theory X-Theory Y Model

Albert J. Robinson

The first acquaintance with "X" and "Y" for many of us was as unknowns in Algebra I. During the decade of the sixties, "X" and "Y" took on some additional meanings for readers in the behavioral sciences and contemporary management thinking.

In 1961, Douglas McGregor published *The Human Side of Enterprise*. This book was a major force in the application of behavioral science to management's attempts to improve productivity in organizations. McGregor was trying to stimulate people to examine the reasons that underlie the way they try to influence human activity, particularly at work. He saw management thinking and activity as based on two very different sets of assumptions about people. These sets of assumptions, called X and Y, have come to be applied to management styles; e.g., an individual is a theory X manager or a theory Y manager.

McGregor looked at the various approaches to managing people in organizations—not only industrial organizations but others as well—and in services, schools, and public agencies and concluded that the styles or approaches to management used by people in positions of authority could be examined and understood in light of those managers' assumptions about people. He suggested that a manager's effectiveness or ineffectiveness lay in the very subtle, frequently unconscious effects of the manager's assumptions on his or her attempts to manage or influence others.

As he looked at the behaviors, structures, systems, and policies set up in some organizations, McGregor found them contrary to information coming out of research at that time, information about human behavior and the behavior of people at work. It appeared that management was based on ways of looking at people that did not agree with what behavioral scientists knew and were learning about people as they went about their work in some, or perhaps most, organizations.

THEORY X

The traditional view of people, widely held, was labeled "X" and seemed to be based on the following set of assumptions:

1. The average human being has an inherent dislike for work and will avoid it if he or she can.

2. Because of this human characteristic of dislike for work, most people must be coerced, controlled, directed, or threatened with punishment to get them to put forth adequate effort toward the achievement of organizational objectives.

3. The average human being prefers to be directed, wishes to avoid responsibility, has relatively little ambition, and wants security above all.

Of course, these assumptions are not set out or stated, but if we examine how organizations are structured and how policies, procedures, and work rules established, we can see them operating. Job responsibilities are closely spelled out, goals are imposed without individual employee involvement or consideration, reward is contingent on working within the system, and punishment falls on those who deviate from the established rules. These factors all influence how people respond, but the underlying assumptions or reasons for them are seldom tested or even recognized as assumptions. The fact is that most people act as if their beliefs about human nature are correct and require no study or checking.

This set of assumptions about people may result in very contrasting styles of management. We may see a "hard" or a "soft" approach to managing, but both approaches will be based on the ideas described above. One theory X manager may drive his employees at their work because he thinks that they are lazy and that this is the only way to get things done. Another may look at her

The Pfeiffer Book of Successful Leadership Development Tools © 2003 John Wiley & Sons, Inc. Published by Pfeiffer.

employees in the same way, but she may think the way to get lazy people to work is to be nice to them, to coax productive activity out of them.

This view of people was characteristic of the first half of the twentieth century, which had seen the effects of Frederick Taylor's scientific-management school of thought. His focus had been on people as an aspect of the productive cycle—much like that of a piece of machinery—and it had allowed for advances in productivity. Yet it was out of this managerial climate—which tended to view people as an interchangeable part of a machine, as a machine element that was set in motion by the application of external forces—that the "human relations" view grew and the behavioral science school developed.

I must hasten to add that the application of understandings of human behavior from the behavioral sciences is not an extension of the human relations focus of the 1940s and 1950s. These two grew up separately. One might construe that the human-relations view of handling people prevalent at that time was manipulative and merely a "soft" theory X approach.

THEORY Y

Another view of people that is not necessarily the opposite extreme of "X" was called "Y" or theory Y. This set of assumptions about the nature of people, which influenced managerial behaviors, is described below.

1. The expenditure of physical and mental effort in work is as natural as play or rest.

2. External control and threat of punishment are not the only means for bringing about effort toward organizational objectives. A person will exercise self-control in the service of objectives to which he or she is committed.

3. Commitment to objectives is dependent on rewards associated with their achievement. The most important rewards are those that satisfy needs for self-respect and personal improvement.

4. The average human being learns, under proper conditions, not only to accept, but to seek responsibility.

5. The capacity to exercise a relatively high degree of imagination, ingenuity, and creativity in the solution of organizational problems is widely, not narrowly, distributed in the population.

6. Under the conditions of modern industrial life, the intellectual potentialities of the average human being are only partially utilized.

It is important to realize that this is not a soft approach to managing human endeavor. Examined closely, it can be seen as a very demanding style: it sets high standards for all and expects people to reach for them. It is not only hard on the employee who may not have had any prior experience with the managerial behaviors resulting from these assumptions, but it also demands a very different way of acting from the supervisor or manager who has grown up under at least some of the theory X influences in our culture. Although we can intellectually understand and agree with some of these ideas, it is far more difficult to put them into practice. Risk taking is necessary on the part of the manager, for he or she must allow employees or subordinates to experiment with activities for which he or she may believe they do not presently have the capability. The learning and growth resulting from this opportunity may handsomely reward the risk.

The focus of a theory Y manager is on the person as a growing, developing, learning being, while a theory X manager views the person as static, fully developed, and capable of little change. A theory X manager sets the parameters of his or her employees' achievements by determining their potential in light of negative assumptions. A theory Y manager allows his or her people to test the limits of their capabilities and uses errors for learning better ways of operating rather than as clubs for forcing submission to the system. He or she structures work so that an employee can have a sense of accomplishment and personal growth. The motivation comes from the work itself and provides a much more powerful incentive than the "externals" of theory X.

A suggestion for your consideration is to make the same assumptions about others that you make about yourself and then act in the appropriate manner. You might be pleasantly surprised.

References

McGregor, D. (1961). *The human side of enterprise.* New York: McGraw-Hill.

McGregor, D. (1967). *The professional manager* (W.G. Bennis and C. McGregor, Eds.). New York: McGraw-Hill.

Originally published in The 1972 Annual Handbook for Group Facilitators.

6

Impact at Ground Zero: Where Theory Meets Practice

Patrick Doyle and C.R. Tindal

The best laid schemes
o' mice and men
gang oft aglee
ROBERT BURNS
("TO A MOUSE")

Ground zero is the point at which managers must convert the organization's philosophy or management "style" into management practices. It is the transition between what a particular management theory or concept says should happen and what the manager actually does. However, as Robert Burns pointed out two centuries ago, things often do not work out as expected. There are numerous examples in the HRD literature of implementations that have "missed the target."

- "Management by objectives works," says Peter Drucker, "if you know the objectives. Ninety percent of the time you don't" (Tarrant, 1976). This may be why management by objectives (MBO) has not always lived up to its advance billing.

- Many organizations have embraced new budgeting techniques such as program budgeting, PPBS (planning-programming-budgeting system), and zero-base budgeting, only to abandon each in disillusionment.

- Many systems of performance appraisal that look so impressive on paper often degenerate into meaningless exercises (McGregor, 1957) involving the completion of forms to satisfy the personnel department.

- Although Peters and Waterman (1982) and others have described various, common-sense approaches to organizational excellence, these approaches seldom are applied successfully.

The answers to these dilemmas are to be found at ground zero: the critical point at which any of these management concepts and approaches actually must be implemented. Although we have an abundance of theories, we appear to lack sufficient understanding of how any particular management approach should be introduced, implemented, measured, and monitored. We need to know more about what happens—and what should happen—at ground zero.

The first part of this article will list some of the problems in attempting to implement theories and describe the symptoms of those problems; the second part of this article will provide prescriptions for turning theory into practice more effectively.

PROBLEMS IN IMPLEMENTING MANAGEMENT THEORY

Everybody Has an Answer

Much of the confusion in the implementation of theory arises from the plethora of theories and concepts being advocated today. Theories change continually and often contradict one another. The following will help to illustrate this.

- There still is some controversy about the reasons for the effects cited in the Hawthorne Studies (Carey, 1967; Dickson & Roethlisberger, 1966; Hersey & Blanchard, 1982; Landesberger, 1958; Rice, 1982; Shepard, 1971), often cited as the beginning of humanistic management practices.

- Although the "Japanese style of management" (Theory Z) has been advocated as the wave of the future (Ouchi, 1981; Pascale & Athos, 1982), we have learned that the Japanese are only practicing management techniques about which Americans have known (Wheelwright, 1981) but which they have failed to practice (Hayes, 1981). In addition, we are told that Japanese management has its own problems and that many of the popular beliefs about Japanese management are either myths or are no longer true because of changes in the nature of the Japanese work force (Kobayashi, 1986).

- Characteristics of America's best-run companies were revealed in a search for excellence (Peters & Waterman, 1982; Peters & Austin, 1985), then some of these same companies experienced organizational problems.

Theories of Management Are Important

Even though their diversity presents problems, the need for management theories has been defended strongly (Granger, 1964). The concept that "practice is static, it does what it knows well," whereas "theory is dynamic" (Urwick, 1952) is important. Theory enables us to build contingency plans for future practices and to consider the influence of change on today's methods. We must appreciate the fact that theory and practice do not exist as independent extremes on the scale of management alternatives. Theory without practice is a luxury that organizations cannot afford. Practice without theory is a one-way ticket to obsolescence. To manage successfully in today's organizations, managers must understand theories of management and must be able to translate them into specific practices. Managers must learn to function effectively at ground zero, where theory meets practice.

Apart from the confusing array of highly touted theories, there are a number of other reasons for the frequent failures at ground zero.

Symbols over Substance

When Ouchi, Pascale, and others wrote about the benefits of the Japanese approach to management, many organizations immediately established quality circles; many announced their commitment to worker involvement in decision-making processes; and a few considered lifetime-employment practices. Most of them, however, adopted only the symbols of Japanese management styles. They did not change their basic attitudes or ways of operating.

In attempting to keep up with the latest management practices, organizations have engaged in a form of show and tell, embracing the terminology and the trappings of a fashionable theory but not (a) understanding the purpose and elements of the theory or (b) training those who were expected to implement the theory well enough to make the substantive changes that were necessary to support the new approach.

"Achiever" Managers and Change for Change's Sake

One of the reasons that many organizations superficially embraced one theory after another without giving sufficient attention and time to any of them is that managers today are expected to implement changes. Furthermore, a large number of managers have ascended the hierarchical ladder because they are achievement driven. Such managers require high reinforcement, accomplished by "doing" and "completing" things. Some of them are characterized by reaction (doing something) without proaction (planning what to do). Because achievers have the tendency to jump in and do things themselves, rather than to invest the time needed to train their subordinates (McClelland, 1976), they may be poor teachers, trainers, or mentors. But they are *noticed* in organizations; they usually are at the center of any activity, working toward its rapid completion. Being noticed is prerequisite to promotion.

In their search for reinforcement, achievers continually look for activities that they can *complete*. Activities such as conceptualizing and planning to meet the organization's needs fifteen years in the future do not have high visibility and, thus, are of limited interest to achievement-driven managers. They are more interested in something with a not-too-distant completion date and with high visibility. Although such behavior is understandable, so is its impact on the organization when achievers are promoted into senior management positions, which call for less doing and more planning.

When promoted, the achiever tends to look for a "new" approach to managing the organization, one that is highly visible or "high profile." Unfortunately, there is little interest in detailed follow-up or in monitoring activities on a daily basis. The achiever tends to be impatient with the lengthy time frames needed to implement most management theories. Thus, an organization that is led by achievers may be introduced to a new management theory or concept every two or three years, primarily to cater to the achievers' needs to be doing things.

The Search for the Simple Solution

In their desire to find solutions that will have predictable success, managers may seek simplistic answers. The search for the simple solution is likely to be based on several questionable beliefs.

- Simple solutions often are associated with rapid implementation and fast results. This psychology is part of management's belief that understanding a change is equivalent to acceptance of the change. The assumption is made that simple solutions are easily understood and, thus, easily accepted. As a result, when planned change is unsuccessful, the excuse often is that those involved failed to understand the purpose and importance of the change (presumably because it was too complicated). In fact, it is more likely that the individuals involved understood the purpose of the change but reached different conclusions about its validity. It also is unlikely that merely because a need and proposed solution is obvious to one person or group, it also will be obvious to others.

■ Another complicating factor is the belief that one can simplify change by presenting it as not being change. When faced with the need to introduce change, managers may attempt to convince employees that they already are operating in the desired manner: For example, a manager may introduce MBO to a subordinate by claiming that "All you do is write out as objectives the things that you are already doing; it's nothing more than a change in terminology."

Such an approach may be quite comforting to the employee in the short run. People often prefer stability and continuity—both of which are insinuated by the manager's comments. But this approach virtually ensures future complications and difficulties. The manager would be ignoring the need for innovative and problem-solving objectives that go beyond the basic job description of the employee and help to ensure the adaptability and survival of the organization. The manager also would be disregarding the fundamental change that should now occur in the basis of evaluating the employee's performance. These are but two of the major implications of MBO that are ignored when a manager attempts to pass it off as nothing more than a change in terminology.

Failure to Follow Through

Much of the difficulty at ground zero is caused by failure to audit the implementation of the theory being adopted. There are a number of reasons why the auditing and follow-up stages may be neglected or ineffective.

■ Unless one is very clear at the outset about the objectives of the new approach and the results that are expected, there may not be much of a basis for measuring change.

■ Even if the process begins with objectives, it still is difficult to translate objectives into measurable work standards that are suitable for auditing purposes.

- If one is able to follow through and measure results, one may not like what one finds. An effective auditing program may confront management with the fact that the planned change has not been successful; and if lack of success is documented rather than merely suspected, it is likely that someone will have to accept responsibility for the failure. Particularly if a change has been directed primarily for the sake of change, auditing the implementation of a theory may be seen as (a) too much trouble and (b) risky. Bad news does not ascend well and tends to become filtered or watered down at each successive level. Avoiding the follow-through phase avoids the strains and repercussions.

Without auditing and follow through, however, it is questionable whether there is any point in introducing any organizational change.

Failure to Focus on Strategy

Organizations tend to deal with isolated, specific changes rather than with an overall strategy of change—a framework within which change will take place. McConkey (1967) states that there must be a foundation of trust within the organization prior to the introduction of MBO. Ironically, MBO is often introduced as a solution to a lack of trust in an organization. Building trust is a slow, laborious undertaking that requires patience and the ability to accept disappointments when progress is not as rapid as anticipated (Argyris, 1971). It requires meticulous consideration of detail in dealing with others. These requirements have a striking contrast to typical characteristics of achiever managers. The search for a quick and simple solution often leads to the adoption of MBO before the organizational climate is prepared for it.

Another problem is that the installation of MBO requires a great deal of time (McConkey, 1972; Odiorne, 1972). From three to four years are necessary to implement the concept successfully. Such long-term results are generally beyond the time focus of the achiever managers to whom the implementation of change is assigned. Typically, such managers would anticipate two or three major changes in responsibility in that period of time. As a result, the implementation of MBO may be passed to several different managers, each of whom is anxious to see the task completed as quickly as possible.

Other Examples

There are many other examples of a misdirected focus on specifics rather than on overall strategy. Many organizations have responded to the publication *In Search of Excellence: Lessons from America's Best-Run Companies* (Peters &

Waterman, 1982) by instituting awards nights and service pins for employees without otherwise changing the ways in which they treat their employees. Similarly, the concept of management by walking around (MBWA) has encouraged some managers to try to avoid spending more than 25 percent of their time in their offices. However, most of them are not sure what to do with the other 75 percent of their time, resulting in a new version of MBWA: management by wandering aimlessly. The specifics may be there, but the overall strategy is missing.

THE SOLUTIONS

The following prescriptions can increase a manager's effectiveness at ground zero—turning theory into practice.

1. Plan Before You Plunge

The change process should begin with the development of a comprehensive plan for implementation. The following questions—along with others, of course—need to be answered in an implementation plan: Who will be responsible for implementing the change? Will the change be introduced throughout the organization simultaneously? When will the change be introduced? What resources will be required to handle the implementation? What follow-up steps will be needed to monitor progress toward implementation?

2. Don't Crusade Alone

It is foolish to introduce a new management system or concept unless there is strong commitment from senior management. Interest in and support for the change need not be unanimous. Under certain circumstances, it may be effective to begin with a pilot project in a department or section that is most enthusiastic about the proposed change. However, to introduce a change when opinions are sharply divided or when key members of the management team are strongly opposed is almost certainly futile.

3. Bring Everyone on Board

Training programs should be developed to familiarize all concerned with the change being introduced and with the specific ways in which they (or their responsibilities) will be affected. In general, managers do not respond favorably to being told to attend a seminar or read a book about an imposed change. Customized training should take into account the distinctive features of the organization, in order to ensure a common understanding of the nature and purpose of the change.

4. Be Sensitive to the Various Impacts of Change Within the Organization and Among Individuals

The introduction of new management theory does not affect all parts of the organization equally. Some individuals are more directly affected than others. Obviously, the nature of the impact on the person's work will influence the degree of reaction and resistance that can be anticipated. Those responsible for implementing change should attempt to assess its probable impact and should develop appropriate strategies to deal with those who are likely to feel threatened (Doyle, 1985). The insights gained from such analysis should be reflected in any implementation plans and training programs.

5. Implement the Entire Change Strategy, Not Just Slogans

Specific management practices take place within a strategy, and both the strategy and the practice must remain within the focus of the manager. For example, a program to generate a positive customer orientation in employees requires that the employees also be treated in a positive, adult manner. In the same vein, superficial compliments or rewards will not enhance productivity if employees are otherwise managed in a dictatorial or competitive environment.

One organization had been attempting to develop excellence and had placed great emphasis on "concern for employees," evidenced by forms of recognition such as service pins and awards. An employee of this organization stated that he found it more productive to work part of the time at home because of the convenience of his microcomputer and research materials there. His manager, however, was unable to cope with this exception to the normal working arrangements. Not surprisingly, the negative effect of the manager's refusal to consider alternatives more than offset the positive effect to the employee (and his colleagues) of the awards and service pins. Although the awards were symbolic, the manager's actions were seen as substantive and as indicative of the organization's real attitude toward employees.

6. Measure, Monitor, Modify, and Maximize

If changes are to be implemented effectively, there must be follow-through. "People respect what you inspect" (Argyris, 1982).

In one organization, a training auditor was appointed to ascertain that the practices of the managers were consistent with the training that had been conducted. The auditor met periodically with the operating managers to determine, through discussion and review of documents, whether the training was having an impact on their activities (at ground zero). Managers who had attended a seminar on reinforcing employees were asked to show any recent letters of appreciation sent to their subordinates. Samples of performance-appraisal documents were examined in the case of managers who had attended a seminar on this topic. As a consequence of this follow-up, managers applied the training suggestions more faithfully than is the norm in organizations that do not conduct such an audit. In addition, the findings of the auditor led to improvements in the training program.

7. Use Time as a Tool

The implementation of almost any theory is measured in years, not months. Do not expect quick results or allow staff members to expect overnight improvements. Such expectations lead only to disillusionment and often result in loss of commitment and the eventual abandonment of the attempt. Time is a tool in implementing any change; as one thing "takes," it makes it easier for others to follow. People must become accustomed to new ideas and new procedures and they must be allowed time to learn ways to implement them most effectively. Feedback on progress and midcourse correction should be built into the change process.

8. Reinforce Desired Behavior and Highlight Progress

Because the successful implementation of change can be a long, slow process, it is important to demonstrate that progress is being made. In the early stages of the implementation of a theory, employees may place more emphasis on the lack of change or the negative aspects of the change (Schein, 1969) than on its positive aspects. Managers must be sensitive to the fact that their actions will be scrutinized closely by employees for evidence of the new strategy. Managerial behavior that is inconsistent with the theory is likely to override the organization's intended message.

A systematic follow-up procedure makes it possible to measure progress. Through the use of reinforcement techniques, individuals can be encouraged to continue their efforts in the desired direction. Moreover, the evidence that progress is being made may help to win over some of the doubters and resisters.

Although specific changes in management approaches can be highly visible in a short period of time, overall strategies are not as visible and take place over a longer period of time. Therefore, reinforcement efforts must highlight the relationship between the two so that the gradual progression of theory into practice (the transition at ground zero) is recognized and appreciated by all employees.

9. Confront and Deal with Dysfunctional Behavior

It is important that dysfunctional behavior not be tolerated or ignored. The difficulty here is that in many organizations low performance levels and other problems have been tolerated for a long time by managers who are eager to avoid conflict. Faced with the task of implementing change, such managers still will be inclined to avoid confrontation if it is at all possible. Although they may be in favor of the change and willing to encourage those who perform in the desired manner, they will try to avoid taking action in connection with the nonperformers.

If managers are allowed to ignore dysfunctional behavior, the organization again is sending out conflicting messages to its employees. In such a situation, the momentum for change may be checked, and the entire effort may be undermined. This problem has been described as "the folly of rewarding A, while hoping for B" (Kerr, 1975).

10. Beware the Half-Way Blues

As Yogi Berra once remarked, "It ain't over 'till it's over." Following the rules outlined here and proceeding well with implementation for a year or so is gratifying; the danger is that it can lead to a false sense of complacency—a feeling that the battle has been won. At this point, an organization is likely to experience the "half-way blues" and a loss of commitment. The newness of the change effort has worn off, and the desire of the achiever managers for instant success has made them restless and anxious to try something new. A well-designed implementation plan and follow-up procedure can help to head off this midpoint slump.

11. Nail Down the Implementation: Integrate the Change into the System

The challenge at this point is to ensure the continuance of the change. Too often, an initiative is introduced with great fanfare, superficially accepted, and yet gradually eroded as time passes (Watson & Glaser, 1965). There may not have been open resistance. The change may not be officially withdrawn. It just does not last!

What is needed is continuing positive reinforcement and efforts to make the new approach a familiar and routine part of the day-to-day activities of the organization. In addition, provision should be made for continuing evaluation of the change and continuing maintenance efforts to prevent erosion and backsliding (Watson & Glaser, 1965).

Summary

The secret to effective utilization of new management theories is to avoid change simply for change's sake and to attempt to implement only those practices that will aid the organization in accomplishing its mission more effectively—those for which there is a need. Dabbling with management theories does more harm than good. If a change is determined to be wise, the substance of the theory must be understood and promoted, not just the trappings. Saying that something will be done does not do it; special attention must be paid to the specific implementation plan. Implementation must be consistent; the process of implementation must be monitored; and follow-up procedures must be installed. Finally, sufficient time must be allowed (without a slackening of effort and with the provision of positive reinforcement) for the change to become part of the procedure of the organization. A long time ago, someone said, "Anything worth doing is worth doing right."

A Checklist for Managers

An organization that is introducing new management practices imposes additional demands on its managers, who must understand not only the new theory but also the strategy used to implement it and the implications for the organization of various changes in behavior. The checklist that follows is designed to stimulate a manager's thinking about how he or she might proceed when called on to take part in the introduction of a new theory or management system.

Reviewing this checklist may help the manager to think of other questions that need to be asked. The challenge is to relate the overall strategy for the proposed change to the actual operating capabilities of the organization.

Characteristic of the Strategy	Implication for Practices
1. Does the strategy assume that a specific type of groundwork has been laid (e.g. that trust exists within the organization)?	Given my present managerial practices, do the employees have reason to believe that the groundwork is in place?

If not: How can I begin to establish that foundation so that the strategy will have an increased probability of success?

What is a reasonable amount of time for this activity?

Characteristic of the Strategy	Implication for Practices
2. Does the strategy assume specific managerial skills (e.g., many strategies require good communication skills)?	Do I have those skills to the degree necessary for successful implementation of the strategy?

If not: Am I able to acquire those skills to the degree required?

How will I acquire the skills?

What is a reasonable amount of time for this activity?

Characteristic of the Strategy	Implication for Practices
3. What assumptions does the strategy make about employees (e.g., maturity level, ability to cope with ambiguity, commitment to organizational goals, level of needs, desire to improve the situation, etc.)?	In the case of my organization, are these assumptions valid?

If not: How serious are the discrepancies?

Will they significantly influence the outcome of the change effort?

Must the discrepancies be handled before implementation or can this be part of the implementation design?

What is a reasonable amount of time for this activity?

Characteristic of the Strategy	Implication for Practices
4. What assumptions does the strategy make about the operational climate of the organization (e.g., does it assume a "Theory X" or "Theory Y" approach)?	Does the operational climate of the organization coincide with that assumed by the theory?

If not: How important is the climate to the success of the theory?

Do changes need to be made prior to implementation or can they be attempted as part of the implementation effort?

If changes are required prior to implementation, what is a reasonable amount of time for this activity?

Characteristic of the Strategy	Implication for Practices
5. What assumptions does the strategy make about the economic environment of the organization (e.g., is the organization currently experiencing reductions in staff, shortage of needed resources, arguments about priorities, or other major problems)?	Is the economic environment of the organization conducive to successful implementation?

If not: Can the economic problem be overcome during implementation?

How long would implementation be delayed if we were to wait until a more conducive economic environment exists?

What can be done to change the situation? How long will this take?

Characteristic of the Strategy	Implication for Practices
6. What assumptions does the strategy make about the commitment of top management (e.g., is the support of top management critical or just desirable? Can this approach be forced from the bottom up?	Is the level of top-management commitment sufficient to ensure the success of the approach?

If not: How necessary is the support?

Would communication with top management increase the level of support or would it be better to proceed and then demonstrate positive results to top management?

Should time and effort be spent in trying to convince top management of the value of the strategy or would this effort be in vain?

Characteristic of the Strategy	Implication for Practices
7. What level of resource commitment does the strategy assume (e.g., time demands for both managers and employees, financial and staff resources for training, etc.)?	Does the organization have sufficient resources to allocate what is needed to the change effort?

If not: Are there less costly ways in which to implement the change?

Are various levels of implementation feasible, given the present allocation of resources?

Can the theory be implemented (i.e., can management practices be changed as desired) with less commitment of resources?

References

Argyris, C. (1971). *Management and organizational development.* New York: McGraw-Hill.

Argyris, C. (1982). *Reasoning, learning and action.* San Francisco, CA: Jossey-Bass.

Carey, A. (1967). The Hawthorne studies: A radical criticism. *American Sociological Review, 32,* 403–416.

Dickson, W.J., & Roethlisberger, F.J. (1966). *Counseling in an organization: A sequel to the Hawthorne researches.* Boston, MA: Harvard University, Division of Research, Graduate School of Business Administration.

Doyle, P. (1985). Considerations for managers in implementing change. In L.D. Goodstein & J.W. Pfeiffer (Eds.), *The 1985 annual: Developing human resources.* San Diego, CA: Pfeiffer & Company.

Granger, C.M. (1964, May-June). The hierarchy of objectives. *Harvard Business Review,* pp. 63–74.

Hayes, R.H. (1981, July-August). Why Japanese factories work. *Harvard Business Review,* pp. 57–66.

Hersey, P., & Blanchard, K.H. (1982). *Management of organizational behavior: Utilizing human resources* (4th ed.). Englewood Cliffs, NJ: Prentice-Hall.

Humble, J.W. (1973). *How to manage by objectives.* New York: AMACOM.

Kerr, S. (1975). On the folly of rewarding A, while hoping for B. *Academy of Management Journal, 18,* 769–783.

Kobayashi, M.K. (1986). *Japanese management: Myth and reality* (video package and booklet). San Diego, CA: Pfeiffer & Company.

Landesberger, H.J. (1958). *Hawthorne revisited.* Ithaca, NY: Cornell University Press.

McClelland, D.C. (1976). *The achieving society.* New York: Irvington.

McConkey, D.D. (1967). *How to manage by results.* New York: American Management Association.

McConkey, D.D. (1972, Winter). How to succeed and fail with MBO. *Business Quarterly,* pp. 58–62.

McGregor, D. (1957, May-June). An uneasy look at performance appraisal. *Harvard Business Review.* Reprinted in *The performance appraisal series,* No. 21143, (1972), pp. 5–10.

Odiorne, G.S. (1972). *Management by objectives: A system of managerial leadership.* New York: Pitman.

Ouchi, W. (1981). *Theory Z: How American business can meet the Japanese challenge.* Reading, MA: Addison-Wesley.

Pascale, R.T., & Athos, A.G. (1982). *The art of Japanese management: Applications for American executives*. New York: Warner Books.

Peters, T., & Austin, A. (1985). *A passion for excellence: The leadership difference*. New York: Random House.

Peters, T.J., & Waterman, R.H., Jr. (1982). *In search of excellence: Lessons from America's best-run companies*. New York: Warner Books.

Rice, B. (1982, February). The Hawthorne defect: Persistence of a flawed theory. *Psychology Today*, pp. 70–74.

Schein, E. (1969). *The mechanisms of change*. In W. Bennis, K. Benne, & R. Chin (Eds.), *The planning of change* (2nd ed.), (pp. 98–107). New York: Holt, Rinehart and Winston.

Shepard, J.M. (1971). On Alex Carey's radical criticism of the Hawthorne studies. *Academy of Management Journal, 14*, 23–31.

Tarrant, J.J. (1976). *Drucker: The man who invented the corporate society*. London, England: Barrie & Jenkins.

Urwick, L.F. (1952). *Notes on the theory of organization*. New York: American Management Association.

Watson, G., & Glaser, E.M. (1965, November). What have we learned about planning for change. *Management Review, 54*(11), 34–46.

Wheelwright, S.C. (1981, July-August). Japan: Where operations really are strategic. *Harvard Business Review*, pp. 67–74.

Originally published in The 1987 Annual: Developing Human Resources.

7

A Model for the Executive Management of Transformational Change

Richard Beckhard

The focus of this article is the management of a transformational-change effort in a significant system or a
complex organization. The management of this type
of change is distinctly different in a number of ways
from the management of change in many other are-
nas that concern HRD practitioners daily. A transformational change is orchestrated by the organization's
executive managers, who must have access to a model
that enables them to diagnose and manage the
change process. In addition, employing such a model
effectively is dependent on the managers' understanding of a number of important issues: the nature
of transformation, the implications of transformational change, the organizational conditions and behavioral changes that are necessary for transformation
to succeed, and the challenges and dilemmas that are
likely to be encountered. This article presents a model
for transformational change that HRD practitioners
may suggest to managers facing this difficult task, and
it provides useful information that practitioners can
pass along to managers to help them develop the understanding of the process that is so critical to success.

THE NATURE OF TRANSFORMATION

The definition of transformation in Webster's is "A change in the shape, structure, nature of something." This definition coordinates well with the needs and practices of organizations involved in transformational change. There is no question that there is an increasing need for a complex organization in today's world to change its shape to accommodate changing demands; an organization faces a heavy responsibility in attempting to determine the shape, in terms of both size and complexity, that will allow it to function effectively in the dynamic world in which it operates. Merely altering the configuration or writing new job descriptions is an inadequate and possibly even inappropriate response, given the difficulty of the task.

Transformation in an organization can also address *structure*, or the basic parts of the organization that are responsible for its character or its *nature*. Structure includes values, beliefs, reward systems, ownership, patterns, and so on. Sometimes environmental factors change and necessitate significant reappraisals of the organization's nature: consumer interests and demands, work force, technology, telecommunication, and competition.

However, an in-depth assessment of shape, structure, character or nature, and environment—difficult and essential as that task may be—is insufficient of itself. Undertaking transformational change also necessitates reexamining the organization's mission and creating a vision or desired future state as well as the strategies by which the organization can move toward that vision. The strategic issues involved in formulating an organization's mission and vision are quite different from those involved in "running the store" or increasing profits in the short term, and HRD practitioners need to ensure that executive managers who attempt transformation are aware of these differences.

The types of organizational changes that can be called transformational are as follows:

1. *A change in what drives the organization.* For example, a change from being production driven or technology driven to being market driven is transformational.

2. *A fundamental change in the relationships between or among organizational parts.* Examples include redefining staff roles and moving from central management to decentralized management or from executive management to strategic management.

3. *A major change in the ways of doing work.* Such transformational changes include moving from low-technology to high-technology manufacturing sys-

tems, implementing computers and telecommunications, and redesigning the customer interface (for example, by providing salespeople with lap computers so that they can interact directly with both customers and suppliers).

4. *A basic cultural change in norms, values, or reward systems.* An example of a cultural change is moving from standardized incentive rewards to individualized ones.

ORGANIZATIONAL PREREQUISITES

The following ten conditions or elements, which are discussed in order of priority, must exist before transformational change can be achieved in an organization.

Prerequisite 1: Committed Top Leaders

One or more of the organization's top leaders, including the chief executive officer (CEO), must be committed champions of the change. In assisting executive managers with transformational change, the HRD practitioner cannot overemphasize the importance of top-level commitment and the visibility of that commitment. Those at lower organizational levels who will be responsible for implementing various aspects of the change cannot be expected to commit to the effort until they see for themselves that the organizational leadership is similarly committed. Although it is possible to achieve some degree of change without top-level commitment, that change is likely to be ephemeral at best.

Prerequisite 2: Written Description of the Changed Organization

It is essential to have a statement, written in behavioral terms, of how the changed organization will function. This statement should include a description of the basic organizational character, policies, values, and priorities that will exist as a result of the transformational change. The HRD practitioner should stress that this statement is not a list of short-term objectives and should monitor the writing process carefully to ensure that the statement is sufficiently detailed and focused on behavior.

Prerequisite 3: Conditions That Preclude Maintenance of the Status Quo

Another critical prerequisite is the existence of a set of external conditions that makes the choice of maintaining the status quo either unlikely or impossible. The HRD practitioner should explain to the executive managers that the transformation will not occur unless people are feeling so much pain in the present situation that they are motivated to change it; in the absence of such pain, resistance will take over and make the change difficult or even impossible.

Prerequisite 4: Likelihood of a Critical Mass of Support

The organizational situation should be studied carefully to determine the potential that a critical mass of support for the change will develop. The HRD practitioner can assist in this task through the use of such means as surveys and interviews. The key players involved in the change, both inside the hierarchical system and in the immediate environment, must be identified and their commitment to the change solicited and obtained.

Prerequisite 5: A Medium- to Long-Term Perspective

Transformational changes take years, not months; it is important that the executive managers understand and accept this time perspective. The HRD practitioner might want to cite examples from his or her own experience of the fact that "quick-fix" changes tend to be just that—first-aid treatments that do not have a base for perpetuation. However, it should also be stressed that it is sometimes necessary in the turbulent transitional environment to make quick, dramatic changes in the organization's character. When this is the case, a trap is to mistake such an event for the completion of the entire change effort; instead, it represents only the beginning of the change-management process. Executive managers may need help in discerning the difference between the individual changes that take place during transformation and the completion of the transformation itself. They also may need help in developing a clear strategy for managing the tension between the need for stability—the need to "run the store"—and the need for change.

Prerequisite 6: Awareness of Resistance and the Need to Honor It

Those managing a transformational change need to be helped to understand and accept resistance to that change. It is essential to devise strategies for working with rather than against resistance. Many executive managers assume that resistance is a representation of "the enemy," whereas the reality is that no change can occur without it. Resistance is the process of internalizing, taking on and letting go, and moving into the new state. This process is totally normal, not neurotic. The tension between the status quo and change is an inherent part of transformation. The appropriate response is to set up ways to manage the resistance productively and to ensure that its effects further the organization's progress in its journey from here to there.

Prerequisite 7: Awareness of the Need for Education

The executive managers must develop awareness of the need to educate the people and groups involved in or affected by the change. This education may go well beyond simply fostering understanding of the change itself; it may include needs assessment and subsequent training in the skills and knowledge that are shown to be essential to functioning successfully in the changed environment. Education is also one of the best tools for reducing resistance and obtaining commitment to a change. The HRD practitioner can play a vital role in developing awareness of the need, pinpointing the kinds of education required, and providing such education through various training programs.

Prerequisite 8: The Conviction That the Change Must Be Tried

This conviction on the part of executive management should include willingness to sustain an experimental attitude throughout the change effort and to stick with the effort. Inherent in this willingness is the assumption that occasional failures will be experienced and will be accepted as a normal part of the learning process that accompanies change. Intolerance of such failures will convince those implementing the change that executive management is not, in fact, committed to the change process and that the old ways of doing things are safer. It is essential that management reward rather than punish the risk taking required in abandoning the old and trying the new. The HRD practitioner can assist in assessing people's orientations toward risk, fostering risk-taking behaviors, and developing an appropriate reward system.

Prerequisite 9: Willingness to Use Resources

Executive management must be willing to "put its money where its mouth is" and use all kinds of resources—technical, consultative, and expert—in support of the change effort. Those responsible for implementing the change will be thwarted in their efforts if they cannot have access to the resources they need. The HRD practitioner can provide useful assistance in specifying the resources that are needed, in serving as a resource, in identifying other internal and external resources, and in encouraging people to generate creative ways of using resources.

Prerequisite 10: Commitment to Maintaining the Flow of Information

From the outset of a transformational-change effort, information must flow freely between and among the different parts of the organization. All employees must receive explicit information about the vision, values, priorities, and rewards that will govern the new state or condition. This often means issuing such information before all of the details are complete. In addition, information about the progress of the effort and about what has worked and what has not worked is extremely valuable. When information is not shared appropriately, mistakes can be repeated and valuable time and other resources can be wasted. Inadequate information also can lead to morale problems. The HRD practitioner can help by stressing the importance of communication; by suggesting appropriate ways to communicate; and by recommending, setting up, and/or conducting training in communication if necessary.

A MODEL OF TRANSFORMATIONAL CHANGE

The process of transforming inputs (needs and raw materials) into outputs (goods and services) is the "work" of an organization. When an organization needs to transform itself, it is, in fact, transforming its work. In any such change, there are three states that must be dealt with: (1) the *present state,* which is things as they are; (2) the *future state,* which is what the changed condition will be; and (3) the *transitional state,* which is the one that exists when evolving from the present to the future—the state during which the actual changing takes place.

The author's model addresses the critical relationships among these three states as well as the ten prerequisites previously discussed. It consists of the following steps:

1. *Designing the future state.* The future state can be defined as the vision for the organization or the strategic objectives of the change. It includes not only the end state but also an intermediate state, which, for example, might be a year or two from the time during which the future state is being planned. The model assumes that for either the end state or the intermediate state,

a scenario is needed—a written description of the envisioned behavior of the operation at some point in time. Generally the existing situation is seen as a problem and the future state as the solution to that problem.

2. *Diagnosing the present state.* This diagnosis is performed in the context of the future state. The model suggests that during this step the entire gamut of issues embedded in the defined change problem must be identified, analyzed, and prioritized in terms of any probable domino effects. This means determining whether the individual parts of the change process should or must be completed in a particular order.

3. *Extrapolating what is required to go from the present state to the transitional state.* This step consists of identifying in detail what is required to get from here to there: the activities that must be completed, the resources that must be allocated, the relationships that must be in place, the management structures that are necessary for the transition, and the rewards that must exist. These requirements should be listed in sequence and some time frame established for meeting them.

4. *Analyzing the work that occurs during the traditional state.* This step consists of formulating a complete picture of how the organization will function during the transitional state.

5. *Defining the system that is affecting the problem.* This step does not necessarily mean that everyone affected by the problem must be identified. What is essential is to identify a "critical mass" of people inside and directly outside the organization who must be committed to the change in order for it to succeed. The smallest number of people or groups is the optimum.

6. *Analyzing each of the members of the critical mass with regard to readiness and capability.* *Readiness* refers to an individual's attitude toward the change, and *capability* refers to an individual's capacity to do whatever the change requires of him or her. This step is important in that organizational transformation always necessitates the need for changes in the behavior of those who hold key roles in the organization. For example, the types of decision making that are appropriate for a functionally controlled organization are inappropriate for a matrix organization or an organization driven by business areas.

When managing a transformational change, the CEO must behave in ways that indicate commitment to the new state; demonstrating such commitment may be a new and unfamiliar form of behavior. In addition, the goals, priorities, and even activities of the human resource manager may require major modification as a result of transformational change; he or she may need to switch from controlling to facilitating, from providing services only to leading the change, and/or from simply implementing policies to actively initiating new mechanisms like improved reward systems. Finally, a transformation can involve agonizing changes in the power structure, expectations about performance, and the control wielded by heads of major staffs in their own functional areas. The staff heads may have to develop new relationships among themselves and with the business leaders; new rewards must be negotiated; and many questions must be answered. The staff heads, who are accustomed to functioning as "experts" in their particular functions, may need to become supporters, facilitators, and leaders in long-range thinking—a major change requiring behavioral modification. It is a good idea to know at the outset whether the members of the critical mass will be willing and able to respond appropriately to the change; then, if it is determined that certain members are unwilling or unable, that situation can be planned for and dealt with.

7. *Identifying the power relationships and resources necessary to ensure the perpetuation of the change.* It is not enough to carefully analyze what is required to get from here to there; it is equally important to analyze and provide what is necessary to make the change stick.

8. *Setting up an organization (or structure or system) to manage the transformation.* The company's executive managers are responsible for managing the organization that is set up, not necessarily for managing the change work itself. In the absence of such a setup, the transformational effort may deteriorate into a series of undocumented experiments from which people fail to learn.

EXAMPLES OF THE MODEL AT WORK

Case 1: A Cultural Change Initiated Within the Organization

The large, multinational chemical company that is the subject of Case 1 had facilities in over eighty countries and produced a variety of products from pharmaceuticals to heavy chemicals. It operated in many markets, and its competitors were all over the world. Its ownership relationships varied from a wholly owned territory to joint ventures to a partnership.

The company was organized in approximately ten areas of business, each of which had its own board of directors and its own CEO, but all of which were wholly owned by the parent company. The enterprise governance was achieved through a board of directors, half of whom were designated as executive directors who provided the company's active leadership and half of whom were designated as nonexecutive (external) directors who fulfilled the more traditional board functions. The organization had historically operated through executive management in which the executive directors were the CEOs of the individual businesses as well as the heads of the territories and the functions, such as finance and personnel.

This organization was a leading part of the economy of its home country. It was traditional, highly people oriented, somewhat paternalistic, and a comfortable place to work. Relations with the trade unions were excellent; the company was one of the first to start joint consultations many years ago.

Eventually it became apparent to several members of both the main board and the heads of the businesses that the technically controlled, decentralized divisions, which were primarily local in nature, were not appropriate for addressing the market of the future. Technical innovation had slipped; markets had been eroded in various ways; some of the products were too mature for growth.

Some of the members of the executive board decided to rethink the organizational culture with the following aims:

1. To focus on moving toward a world-wide business;

2. To place the authority for running the businesses with the heads of those businesses rather than with the central directors;

3. To reduce the central directorate to a small number of enterprise directors and to limit their influence; and

4. To revitalize research and development and relate it more to the businesses, replacing the highly centralized research effort with a smaller central effort.

For a number of years the efforts of those who were proponents of this vision were either contained or circumvented by the majority, who resisted such a massive change. The resistance followed classic patterns. For example, commissions and study groups were set up to study organizational changes and changes in board functioning. Through various tactics such as postponing, returning reports for further clarification, and stalling based on excuses like "bad timing," the change efforts were effectively squashed.

A few proponents of the change effort saw themselves as having to provide the executive leadership for the change and having to develop a strategy for doing so. Two or three of them who were on the main board solicited support from other board members; they worked even harder to obtain commitment from the heads of the businesses, who would soon be board members. Over a six-year period the board membership moved from a minority of three people who supported the change to a "critical mass" of individuals who were firmly committed to the change and concerned only about how to implement it.

As some of the leaders of this effort moved into top positions, they began to strengthen the division leadership and to exert their influence in various meetings of the leaders of the businesses around the world. They engaged in goal setting and envisioning for the enterprise and changed the methodology by which the business heads reported to control groups from the center. They began to institute the actual changes that were necessary:

1. They reduced the number of board members to seven and granted group control to all members.

2. They redefined the role of the business head to that of CEO with control over all of his or her resources.

3. They changed to a strategy-management mode in which each of the business heads met with the entire executive board once a year to define strategic objectives and once a year to establish a budget. No other contact with the board was required of the business heads, although each had a contact on the board who provided ongoing support.

4. They revised the budget process.

5. They significantly reduced overhead by combining various subheadquarters of related businesses, thereby eliminating well over twenty thousand overhead positions. With the new, smaller board, they were able to reduce the support staff. The smaller staff allowed them to move their headquarters to a building half the size, thus providing one more visual symbol of the change in the organizational culture.

Despite all of these changes, the leaders of the change effort consciously supported and maintained those values and ways of work that had been productive in the past, such as joint consultation with the unions. They set up specific change-management systems that were administered by committees, subgroups of board members, and special study groups and closely monitored the resulting efforts.

In this case the driving force for transformational change came from within the organization and was led by the top leadership. For the last several years the transformation has been led by one particular member of that leadership, who was designated as the "project manager" of the entire change effort. He used his position power to effect the critical mass that was necessary to make the change.

Case 2: A Change Induced by Competitor Activity

For many years the large, consumer-goods enterprise that is the subject of Case 2 had virtual monopoly on its products. It sold world-wide, was a household name, and had virtually no competition. It was driven primarily by technology, the making of its products, and the quality of those products. Although there were stores all over the world, manufacturing and distribution were highly centralized; most of the products were made in one giant plant. The majority of the company's employees worked at this home plant, with relatively few workers located at other plants. The function of research and development was very active, constantly upgrading product quality and in recent years moving into related products.

The organization was humanistic, caring, and paternalistic. Employees were never fired; a job at the company was a career for life that paid very well, included excellent benefits, and afforded a nice place to work.

The organization's market share had been relatively stable for a long time and even growing in concert with the growth in the world economies. However, it suddenly began to erode as a result of the emergence of a Japanese competitor that managed to produce a product that was not only competitively priced but also of comparable or better quality. This situation had never existed before. For a time the company failed to acknowledge the problem until the numbers began to be serious, at which time management decided to "regroup, become leaner, and work differently." As is often the case, the first thing the management planned to do was to eliminate people. Programs were instituted to reduce 20 percent of the work force, and these programs were implemented in various ways—generally in a humanitarian manner.

At this point the manufacturing entity, which was the largest facet of the organization in terms of people, initiated a change effort that was very creatively managed. Although the starting point was the requirement of reducing numbers of employees, this requirement was translated into a productivity-improvement program that was implemented under the leadership of a transition-management team composed of high potential managers. The team members solicited improvement suggestions from the entire organization, received several hundred, and culled these to approximately fifteen. Then they set up fifteen study groups, each of which was charged with designing a new state for one of the fifteen suggestions. When the study-group reports and recommendations had been submitted and approved by the hierarchy, transition teams were established to manage the process of implementing the recommendations. Finally the new states began to emerge.

This change process enabled the manufacturing entity to effect not only the required reduction in numbers of employees, but also an improvement in operation. With many fewer people, ideas that had been considered impossible, such as combinations of major functions, were now implemented successfully. For example, five levels of management were cut; this development sent a message to the work force that the required reductions were not to take place only at the lower levels of the hierarchy.

Other parts of the enterprise made cuts, but not as radically. However, top management became aware that all of the work-force reductions, although necessary, were not attacking the basic problem: the organization had been designed for another time in history rather than for the competitive world in which it now lived. The business was not driving the organization; instead, the organization was driving the business.

It became apparent that the company needed to reorganize fundamentally. After consultation and planning, the company set up the organization in approximately fifteen lines of business, each representing a separate product line and each with a general manager. Clusters of these general managers reported to three group vice presidents. The manufacturing, technical, sales, and other staffs were matrixed. Part of each functional staff was now dedicated to the new businesses, but significant parts were kept functional in order to achieve the synergy necessary for certain processes to occur.

As it is easy to imagine, these changes produced a whole new set of issues. It became necessary to develop a number of change-management organizations to cope with the various matrices and to move the company toward some of the major changes that were essential to the total transformation. Ultimately, the transition state led to several thousand new jobs, important shifts in management, and a test of top management's commitment.

To achieve the critical mass, it was necessary to accomplish the following:

1. Make changes among the key leaders in the organization;

2. Provide new, highly committed leadership that would coordinate all manufacturing efforts; and

3. Make changes in the leadership of the various parts of the manufacturing process, the sales process, the advertising process, and so on.

It took a year to train a group of people to function as the general managers. A task force was set up to provide the training, most of which occurred on the job.

This case presents a situation in which the commitment for change was high at the top; but the methods for achieving the change were confused at first, and not enough effort was expended to infuse the total organizational environment with commitment. Each of the organizational parts was working on its specific concerns, and no one analyzed the domino effect. Subsequently the organization centralized the management of the change effort and instituted information linkages among the parts. Today the change tends to be managed in a more system-wide way than it was previously. The critical dimensions of this transformational effort were starting with a vision that was at first unclear or at least insufficiently communicated, focusing too much on cost reduction and not enough on developing a new state, trying to function without adequate transition-management structures, and consciously intervening in the matrix-management issues until they became acute.

THE CHALLENGES OF TRANSFORMATIONAL CHANGE

As discussed in this paper, a number of challenges must be met any time a transformational change is attempted:

1. Ensuring the commitment of the CEO and key leaders;

2. Ensuring that adequate resources are allocated to support the change and to maintain it once it has been achieved;

3. Reaching an appropriate balance between managing the change and managing the stability of the organization;

4. Ensuring appropriate use of special roles, temporary systems, study groups, consultants, and transition teams;

5. Continually evaluating both the total effort and its individual parts in terms of planning improvement;

6. Establishing and maintaining continuity of leadership during the change process;

7. Appropriately allocating rewards (and punishments) consistent with the priority of the change effort;

8. Ensuring adequate information flow among various parts of the organization; and

9. Constantly monitoring the system to ensure that people know what is happening during the change, understand their roles in the process, and comprehend the total effort rather than only isolated elements of it.

This impressive list could be quite intimidating to any executive managers faced with planning and implementing an organizational transformation. Consequently, the HRD practitioner's role in helping managers meet these challenges can be extremely useful and challenging in its own way.

Originally published in The 1985 Annual: Developing Human Resources.

Visionary's Disease and the CEO

George M. Smart, Jr.

Abstract: As consultants, we all know the value of vision. Vision as a leadership concept is not new. Almost every consultative model has a vision component, and tools to help an organization create and sustain a vision continue to crowd the shelves of bookstores. Indeed, without vision, achieving that elusive synergy we consultants promote to our clients is difficult.

The article describes what happens when an organization's problem isn't a lack of vision but too much of it, when a CEO bulges with vision, or the vision changes monthly, weekly, or even daily—driving the organization crazy. The author calls this "visionary's disease." The article presents a detailed case study of Visionary's Disease and offers several steps you can take to combat the condition.

A CASE HISTORY

A number of years ago, I was brought into a high-profile, high-tech company to assess its poor morale and lack of project management ability. I was able to isolate most of the presenting problems as symptoms of being overwhelmed and doing too much rework. The wheel was not only being reinvented daily, but everything was always behind schedule and over budget. When I met the CEO, the problem became clear. It was my first exposure to Visionary's Disease, and he had a serious case.

Like many techno-CEOs, he was young, brilliant, and completely unorganized. His ability to integrate the marketplace and the technology the company was developing was stunning, and his kooky but persuasive style with investors kept the money rolling in, although at the time there were no profits; all the money was going to R&D. Don (not his real name) had been very focused during the company's first few years when he and two others were all there were. They developed the software in their spare bedrooms and, like so many other entrepreneurs, evolved into a company of twenty-five.

Don's exposure to Visionary's Disease began with the travel made possible by a major cash infusion from a Fortune 500 company. He could attend virtually any conference he wanted. Because of his knowledge, he was asked to present as well. He networked with men and women who shaped the industry. Each time, he would return home with a new grand idea, and within forty-eight hours he would call a special management meeting to "discuss" the idea. In truth, the meeting was always the forum for an announcement. Managers soon began to understand the nature of such "discussions."

By the end of each meeting, everyone could see that each new initiative would require heroic amounts of extra effort. Only in the most passive way ("I know we're all busy, but . . .") would Don acknowledge that everyone was already working above capacity. The obvious next step—an honest discussion of what the company would stop doing or do less of—could not happen in this company, and it rarely does in others. In fact, most CEOs treat the very idea of prioritizing work projects as organizational heresy. And Don was no exception. He would note that those who suggested such a discussion "lacked vision."

Don's newest vision always involved a substantial redirection of resources: marketing and PR communications, new product development, programming schedules, and production. And each time, no one could object. Don's ideas were brilliant and well-advised—for a much larger company with many more resources. Managers would return to their departments to dismantle what had been underway. Then an endless series of meetings and e-mails would bring the company to a screeching halt as frustration levels soared, planning ceased to exist, and everyone scrambled to redirect customers, suppliers, and one another. After a short time, Don would leave for another trip. This happened almost *monthly*.

The fallout of this behavior was incredible. No serious thought or planning went into anything, because managers knew it would be undone forty-eight hours after Don's next trip. After Don had a cell phone and laptop computer, he actually tried to conduct these meetings *from the plane.* Solid professionals hired for their competence at project management threw up their hands and gave up trying to follow through. The culture of tentativeness created by Visionary's Disease undermined accountability and added hundreds of additional hours to an already overtaxed staff schedule.

No one wanted to confront Don. He treated their practical concerns about stability, capacity, and leadership as signs of disloyalty, laziness, or the most deadly sin of all—technical ignorance. His reaction to feedback was a Jack Nicholson-style stare, coupled with a lecture about "getting left behind," staying on the "bleeding edge," drilling down into the market, and altering the course of the industry. Don placed much emphasis on the *millions* of dollars to be lost if the company failed to follow the latest, greatest vision.

Within six months of Don's beginning to travel so often, the company had greater than 25 percent turnover, the investors were nervous, and sales dropped because the salespeople were never sure what to sell or to what market. Project management stalled and employees took on glazed, catatonic looks.

I'd like to report a fitting moral conclusion to this story, perhaps saying that Don went out of business because of his failure to sustain a vision, or that investors forced him to have a leadership epiphany. Unfortunately, Visionary's Disease is not usually fatal in high-tech industries. After all the money ran out, Don simply went out and found more. The promise of his software was so alluring that it really didn't matter whether people were managed well or not. Companies who have deep-pocketed investors can and do get away with this behavior. Now, with the Internet pouring millions (sometimes billions) into firms, Visionary's Disease is on the rise.

A TOUGH CONDITION

Visionary's Disease is extremely resistant to conventional treatments. CEOs in particular are prone to it because their unique position gives them access to money and a low level of accountability. Authority, capital, and autonomy allow them to use denial as a powerful protective shield against criticism. CEOs rarely see their behavior as symptomatic of anything negative. In fact, they herald their ability to "turn on a dime" as a great strength that mere mortals (their employees) can only dream of attaining. As it was with Don, the collusion of cash and genius, along with feelings of creative liberation, often marks the beginning of the infection.

Contracting Visionary's Disease is easier than ever. CEOs once only caught it on the road, but now the Internet brings many of the benefits of travel to the desktop. The Internet and its attendant phantasms of instant wealth via e-commerce start-ups is a breeding ground for new infections. The Internet itself (and its significant contribution to the state of the stock market) is little more than a coalition of glimmering visions that the marketplace has rapidly transmuted into cyber-cash. The insight of a generation ago—not "plastics," but that power and wealth in the future will reside with the symbol makers and manipulators—has become true. Visionary's Disease allows the aspiring business leader to exploit post-modern beliefs in the predominance of symbols over things, of promise over people. The product is no longer as important as the idea of the product.

WHAT YOU CAN DO

You can help your CEO when he or she begins to show symptoms of infection. Figure 1 provides a list of effective suggestions for how to temper the effects of Visionary's Disease in your organization or your client's organization. Further exploration of these suggestions follows:

1. *Use crises as teachable moments to give CEOs feedback on the capacity of their organizations.* When things are going poorly, the CEOs resistance to feedback can be lowered enough that he or she will be more willing to engage in a frank discussion of organizational capacity.

2. *Reduce the number of times the vision can change in a fiscal year.* Establish a quarterly strategy conference in which the CEO and others can share any new ideas they've learned during the last quarter. These scheduled exchanges of information reduce the stress that frequent, sudden changes in direction can cause.

3. *Require a second management meeting before the vision changes.* Establish at least a two-week "cooling off period" between the initial presentation of the proposed change and any decision to start working on it. Have the CEO agree that nothing changes until he or she calls this second meeting to sanction any new vision formally. It is amazing how frequently the second meeting never is called.

4. *Honor the reality of organizational capacity.* A common corporate fantasy is that the organization has unlimited capacity and that the employees can

---

□ Use crises as teachable moments to give CEOs feedback on the capacity of their organizations.

□ Reduce the number of times the vision can change in a fiscal year.

□ Require a second management meeting before the vision changes.

□ Honor the reality of organizational capacity.

□ Honor the reality of employee productivity.

□ Surface the assumptions a new vision implies.

□ Keep Operations in the loop.

Figure 1. Suggestions for Tempering the Effect of Visionary's Disease

do everything, but we all know this isn't true. Help the CEO to decide what to stop doing before adding new projects.

5. *Honor the reality of employee productivity.* Working longer hours is not the answer to all project management problems. Nearly every CEO I have coached is proud of working sixty-hour weeks. They wear the long hours as a badge of honor. But any sane plan has to start with reality. Help the CEO to see that if he or she really wants to work "smarter," the *really* unimportant tasks will fall away if the hours are cut back.

6. *Surface the assumptions a new vision implies.* For example, determine whether the vision requires that new specialists must be hired and decide on a realistic timeframe. Will the change mean that the CEO has to stay home more to cheerlead and/or direct the project? Surfacing assumptions immediately puts boundaries on a vision (keep reminding the CEO this is a *good* thing) and begins the essential process of crystallizing the plans.

7. *Keep Operations in the loop.* In many companies, Operations is the last area to know about a change, yet it is often the most directly affected. Including this function earlier in vision development is a wonderful reality check. Given half a chance, the Operations people can show the CEO grander and substantially more implementable ideas.

While seldom fatal financially, Visionary's Disease can have a devastating impact on organizational stability, squelch human potential, and just generally drive everyone crazy. By surfacing assumptions, setting quantitative limits on change, and establishing checks and balances that incorporate employee input at all stages of the change process, consultants can help the overzealous CEO recover from Visionary's Disease. And let's not forget the adage, "physician, heal thyself." Take the time to look at your own behavior and your own business practice. As with most diseases, the cure starts at home.

Originally published in The 2001 Annual, Volume 2, Consulting.

Part 2
Experiential
Learning Activities

Experiential learning activities are exercises in which people learn by doing something as opposed to just listening to a lecture or watching a demonstration. Since to date no substitutes have been found for practicing the skill you're trying to learn, or for witnessing, directly, the truth of a lesson someone is trying to impart, experiential activities have special power as a training method.[1]

The activities in this section were chosen from thirty years of the Pfeiffer *Annuals* as the best experiential exercises pertaining to leadership development. They are designed as complete packages. Each includes full instructions for the facilitator and participants, as well as all necessary handouts. Each includes suggested variations the facilitator might find useful to fine-tune the activity for a particular group or situation (you are welcome to create your own variations, as well). Each recommends specific questions to be asked and discussed in order to ensure that learning took place.

---

1. That special power is a double-edged sword. Experiential learning exercises also have special dangers. This is not the place for a discussion of caveats, but trainers who lack experience in the use of such activities are strongly urged to read the Introduction to the *Reference Guide to Handbooks and Annuals* (1999 Edition). It presents the theory behind the experiential-learning cycle and explains the need to complete each phase of the cycle to allow effective learning to occur.

The recommended group size and time required for every activity are listed, as are the learning goals each one was designed to meet. (*Note:* You are better positioned than any exercise's creator to determine whether it will suit the needs of your group.)

The activities adopt several different formats and processes. Some are problem-solving exercises, some are role plays, and some draw their material from the participants' real-life experiences as leaders and as followers.

We have organized the twenty activities into three categories: *Style and Approach, Organizations and Systems,* and *Skill Building.* The divisions are somewhat arbitrary, but the categories should help speed your search for the right exercise for the learning need you have in mind.

Style and Approach These are activities that explore, teach, and demonstrate the traits and interpersonal behaviors that effective leaders exhibit. What can a leader do to persuade followers to perform to the best of their abilities? What persuades people to choose or to follow a particular leader in the first place? Why have *you* come to regard certain people as leaders worth following?

Organizations and Systems Management consultant Geary Rummler (CQ "GEARY") famously said that if you put a good performer up against a bad system, the system will win every time. The maxim is true, and every aspiring leader needs to know it. The first four activities in this section demonstrate the effects of organizational factors that can frustrate and demoralize job performers despite the skills or efforts of leaders at any level in the corporate hierarchy. The last two, aimed at higher-level managers, deal with strategic planning—a core task for those who intend to lead organizations instead of just individual work groups.

Skill Building Here we risk opening a can of semantic worms because these activities would fit as easily into a classic management-training curriculum as into a leadership-development initiative. A manager can lack credibility with subordinates and continue to function, however poorly. A leader cannot. But where does credibility come from in a business or government organization? In part, it comes from effectiveness at classic management tasks such as delegating, delivering performance feedback, choosing priorities, and running productive meetings. The activities in this section teach skills that lay the groundwork for credibility as both a manager and a leader. We offer them, with no apologies, for consideration in your leadership-development programs.

Here is the lineup of experiential learning activities:

Style and Approach

- Choose Me: Developing Power Within a Group: Participants experience for themselves what works and what doesn't when trying to gain a leadership role in a group of peers.

- Successful Leadership Traits: Reaching Consensus: Groups analyze traits of famous leaders, past and present. Which traits are most needed today? Which ones can be taught (or learned)?

- Motivation: A Feedback Activity: Exercise built on an introduction to Maslow's Hierarchy of Needs and Frederick Herzberg's distinctions between motivational and "hygiene" factors.

- Management Skills: Assessing Personal Performance: A questionnaire and group discussions identify a broad range of leadership and management skills that individual

- Leadership History: Searching the Past for Insight: Participants recall and discuss their reactions to leaders they have followed (or rejected) in the course of their own lives.

- Management Perspectives: Identifying Styles: Role play illustrating four different leadership styles brought to bear on a complex workplace problem.

Organizations and Systems

- MACE: Demonstrating Factors that Affect Performance: Activity demonstrating the relative influence of motivation, ability, working conditions, and clarity of management expectations on followers' performance of a task.

- Organizational Structures: A Simulation: Exercise showing the effect of bureaucratic vs. "organic" organizational structures on people attempting to solve a problem.

- There's Never Time to Do It Right: A Relay Task: Demonstration of what happens when followers are led to believe that speed or quantity count more heavily than quality in performing a task.

- The Flip-It Company: Exploring the Impact of Work Quotas: A slightly misleading title for a good exercise showing the effects of *any* system of rewards and punishments based on factors the performers cannot control.

- The Robotics Decision: Solving Strategic Problems: Case study for higher-level leaders that presents a method to surface and test both the obvious and hidden assumptions inherent in a strategic decision.

- Reviewing Objectives and Strategies: A Planning Task for Managers: An intact management team devises actual goals and strategies for the coming year.

Skill Building

- Feedback Awareness: Skill Building for Supervisors: Supervisors practice giving performance feedback that is clear, constructive, and specific.

- Delegation: Using Time and Resources Effectively: Managers discuss principles of effective delegation, then make plans to delegate actual tasks to specific subordinates.

- Constructive Discipline: Following Organizational Guidelines: A case study introduced by a brief but solid lecture on the legal and ethical issues of disciplining a subordinate.

- Vice President's In-Basket: A Management Activity: In-basket exercise focused on setting priorities and identifying tasks that can and cannot be delegated.

- Under Pressure: Managing Time Effectively: Another good in-basket exercise centered on time management, priority setting, and delegation.

- Interviewing: Gathering Pertinent Information: Straightforward practice at determining the skills necessary for a job and then role playing interviews with candidates.

- Meeting Management: Coping with Dysfunctional Behaviors: Case studies identify and suggest coping strategies for snipers, saboteurs, and other types who undermine meetings—with cautions against leaping to conclusions about who's a saboteur.

Style and Approach

1

Choose Me:
Developing Power Within a Group

Larry Porter

Goals

- To explore issues related to power and influence within a group.

- To offer each participant an opportunity to influence the other members of his or her group.

- To allow the participants to give and receive feedback about their personal approaches to developing power and influence within a group.

Group Size

Three to five subgroups of five to seven members each.

Time Required

Approximately two hours and fifteen minutes.

Materials

Blank paper and a pencil for each participant.

Physical Setting

A room with plenty of space for each subgroup so that its members may make oral presentations to one another and engage in discussions without disturbing the other subgroups. A chair and a writing surface should be provided for each participant.

Process

1. The participants are assembled into subgroups of five to seven members each.

2. The goals of the activity are explained.

3. The facilitator states that each subgroup is to select a leader and clarifies the sequence of events whereby each subgroup is to make its selection: Each member is to prepare a self-nominating presentation, making the best case that he or she can for being selected as the subgroup's leader. The members are to take turns making their presentations to the subgroup. Using all information available to them, the subgroup members are to engage in their selection process. Then, under the guidance of the newly selected leader, the members are to prepare a report on their selection process. Subsequently, each subgroup is to share its report with the total group.

4. Each participant is given blank paper and a pencil for the purpose of making notes, if desired, while preparing his or her presentation. The participants are instructed to spend five minutes on their preparations and to restrict their presentations to a maximum of three minutes each.

5. The facilitator asks the members of each subgroup to begin the presentation process. The participants are encouraged to listen carefully to each presentation and to take notes about each member's qualifications if they wish. (Three minutes per presentation.)

6. Each subgroup is instructed to use the data presented by the members to select its leader. The facilitator emphasizes that volunteering, choosing rotating leaders, opting to share leadership responsibilities, and deciding not to choose a leader are unacceptable approaches.

7. After the choices have been made, the members of each subgroup are asked to provide one another with feedback: One member at a time receives feedback from every other member regarding the effectiveness of

the approach that he or she used to develop power and influence during steps 5 and 6. (Twenty minutes.)

8. Each leader is instructed to lead his or her subgroup in preparing an oral report on the subgroup's selection process and deciding who is to present this report. (Thirty minutes.)

9. The facilitator reassembles the total group and asks the subgroups to take turns reporting. (Twenty minutes.)

10. The facilitator leads a discussion about the activity, asking the following questions:

   - How did you feel about having to present yourself as a leader to your subgroup? On what basis did you make your choice of characteristics to present to the subgroup?

   - What do the things you chose to say about yourself and the way you chose to say them have to do with your concept of power and influence?

   - How would you describe your subgroup's concept of power and influence as illustrated in the subgroup's process of choosing a leader?

   - From your individual decisions and your subgroup's operation, what can you generalize about power and influence in a group?

   - What are some specific ways to gain power in a group? How can power be lost or forfeited?

   - What can you do in the future to exert your power and influence more effectively in your home life or in your organization?

Variation

   - This activity may be altered to be used for the purpose of giving and receiving feedback related to leadership abilities or assertiveness.

Originally published in A Handbook of Structured Experiences for Human Relations Training, Volume X *(1985).*

2

Successful Leadership Traits: Reaching Consensus

Robert Alan Black

Goals

- To examine the traits, behaviors, and skills of highly successful leaders.

- To discuss learnable traits, behaviors, and skills associated with leadership.

- To identify skills and attributes required for reaching consensus.

Group Size

Any size in subgroups of five.

Time Required

Fifty to sixty minutes.

Materials

- A copy of the Successful Leadership Traits Listing for each participant.

- A Successful Leadership Traits Collage of current leaders' photos on one sheet as a handout, prepared by the facilitator prior to the session.

- A feature photo from a magazine or newspaper of each of the leaders to be discussed, prepared in advance by the facilitator. The photos may be posted on the wall.

- A copy of the Successful Leadership Traits Sample List of Successful Leaders for the facilitator.

- Paper and pencils for participants.

- Two flip charts and felt-tipped markers.

Physical Setting

A room arranged with tables that will accommodate five people.

Process

1. Lead a short discussion about traits, skills, and behaviors of highly successful leaders. Post the participants' ideas about them on the flip chart. (Five minutes.)

2. Give everyone copies of the Successful Leadership Traits Listing and compare it with the list generated by the participants. (Five minutes.)

3. Distribute the prepared Successful Leadership Traits Collage with photos of ten to twelve well-known contemporary leaders on it. Also distribute paper and pencils.

4. Explain to the group that they are to answer the first two questions that you write on the flip chart individually. Write the following on a flip chart.

   - Which individual traits stand out for you in the leaders shown on the handout?

   - Which traits do all the leaders have in common?

   (Five minutes.)

5. When everyone has finished, form subgroups of five at tables and ask them to reach consensus on the next two questions after you post them on the flip chart:

   - Which of the leadership traits you listed earlier can be taught?

   - Which traits are most needed in today's workplaces?

   (Ten minutes.)

6. When the time is up, ask for two volunteer scribes to record the traits that *can be taught* and the traits that *are most needed* on two separate flip charts at the front of the room. Have the scribes capture the responses from the groups one at a time. Facilitate the capturing of the answers while they record. (Ten minutes.)

7. Bring closure with the following discussion questions:

   - What are the most common traits listed?

   - What are the most significant ones in today's workplaces?

   - How easy was it to reach consensus on the most desirable traits required in today's workplace?

   - Which ones can be taught easily?

   - Given what you believe are the most necessary, how easy will it be for leaders to learn those particular behaviors and traits?

   - What behaviors hindered your group reaching consensus?

   - What behaviors/skills helped you reach consensus?

   - How can you use what you have learned through this activity to work in groups in the future?

   - To reach consensus in the future?

   - To select leaders in your organizations?

   (Twenty minutes.)

Variations

- Warm up the group with a list of leaders from the past representing different nationalities, races, cultures, professions (governmental, military, business, educational). (See the sample listing.)

- Include leaders from an occupation or profession that is familiar to group members.

Originally published in The 2002 Annual: Volume 2, Consulting.

Successful Leadership Traits Listing

Adventurous

Boundless energy

Committed

Creative

Curious

Dedicated

Encouraging

Focused

Goal-oriented

Headstrong

Intelligent

Jewels (finds them in people)

Kaleidoscopic, willing to try anything

Loyal

Measures the odds of risk

Negotiates when necessary

Organized for success

Passionate about their cause

People-focused

Praises others

Quick to act when necessary

Reduces wasted effort

Secure in his/her thinking

Supportive

Task-focused

Tough

Unwilling to give up

Valiant

Willing to work hard

X-ray vision of problems

Zealous

SUCCESSFUL LEADERSHIP TRAITS SAMPLE LIST OF SUCCESSFUL LEADERS

Adolf Hitler

Alexander the Great

Anita Roderick (The Body Shop)

Attila the Hun

Ben and Jerry

Betty Friedan

Bill Gates

Billie Jean King

Caesar Chavez

Chang Kai-shek

Colin Powell

Confucius

Dwight D. Eisenhower

Eleanor Roosevelt

Fidel Castro

General Norman Schwartzkoff

Gloria Steinem

Harry S. Truman

Henry Ford

Henry Kissinger

Joseph Stalin

Julius Caesar

Karl Marx

Malcolm Baldrige

Margaret Sanger

Margaret Thatcher

Martin Luther

Martin Luther King, Jr.

Mohandas Gandhi

Mother Teresa

Napoleon Bonaparte

Nelson Mandela

Pearl Buck

Rosa Parks

Teddy Roosevelt

The Dalai Lama

Walt Disney

William Safire

William Shakespeare

Winston Churchill

3

Motivation: A Feedback Activity

Donald F. Michalak

Goals

- To learn the concepts in Maslow's Need Hierarchy.
- To get feedback on one's use of motivational techniques in terms of Maslow's Need Hierarchy.

Group Size

Up to thirty participants.

Time Required

At least one-half hour, depending on the length of the lecturette and final discussion.

Materials

- One copy of the Motivation Feedback Opinionnaire, Parts I & II, for each participant.
- A pencil for each participant.
- One copy of the Motivation Theory Sheet for the facilitator.

Physical Setting

A room large enough to hold all participants.

Process

1. Each participant completes the Motivation Feedback Opinionnaire, Part I.

2. The facilitator presents a brief lecturette on motivation, based on the Motivation Theory Sheet. The congruence of Maslow's Need Hierarchy and Herzberg's concepts should be pointed out.

3. Each participant completes the Motivation Feedback Opinionnaire, Part II, scoring his or her own answers to Part I.

4. The facilitator leads the group in a discussion of the job relevance of this activity. If the group is large, the participants should form into subgroups of five or six for this discussion. Reports can be solicited from each of these processing subgroups.

Originally published in The 1973 Annual Hamdbook for Group Facilitators.

MOTIVATION FEEDBACK OPINIONNAIRE
PART I

Directions: For each of the statements below, refer to the following scale and decide which number corresponds to your level of agreement with the statement; then write the number in the blank to the left of the statement. Complete every item. You have about 10 minutes to do so.

Strongly Agree	Agree	Slightly Agree	Don't Know	Slightly Disagree	Disagree	Strongly Disagree
+3	+2	+1	0	-1	-2	-3

_____ 1. Special wage increases should be given to employees who do their jobs very well.

_____ 2. Better job descriptions would be helpful so that employees will know exactly what is expected of them.

_____ 3. Employees need to be reminded that their jobs are dependent on the company's ability to compete effectively.

_____ 4. Supervisors should give a good deal of attention to the physical working conditions of their employees

_____ 5. Supervisors ought to work hard to develop a friendly working atmosphere among their people.

_____ 6. Individual recognition for above-standard performance means a lot to employees.

_____ 7. Indifferent supervision can often bruise feelings.

_____ 8. Employees want to feel that their real skills and capacities are put to use on their jobs.

_____ 9. The company retirement benefits and stock programs are important factors in keeping employees on their jobs.

_____ 10. Almost every job can be made more stimulating and challenging.

_____ 11. Many employees want to give their best in everything they do.

_____ 12. Management could show more interest in the employees by sponsoring social events after hours.

Strongly Agree	Agree	Slightly Agree	Don't Know	Slightly Disagree	Disagree	Strongly Disagree
+3	+2	+1	0	-1	-2	-3

_____ 13. Pride in one's work is actually an important reward.

_____ 14. Employees want to be able to think of themselves as "the best" at their own jobs.

_____ 15. The quality of the relationships in the informal work group is quite important.

_____ 16. Individual incentive bonuses would improve the performance of employees.

_____ 17. Visibility with upper management is important to employees.

_____ 18. Employees generally like to schedule their own work and to make job-related decisions with a minimum of supervision.

_____ 19. Job security is important to employees.

_____ 20. Having good equipment to work with is important to employees.

MOTIVATION FEEDBACK OPINIONNAIRE
PART II

Scoring

1. Transfer the numbers you circled in Part I to the appropriate places in the chart below:

Statement No.	Score	Statement No.	Score
10	_____	2	_____
11	_____	3	_____
13	_____	9	_____
18	_____	19	_____
Total (Self-Actualization Needs)	_____	Total (Safety Needs)	_____

Statement No.	Score	Statement No.	
6	_____	1	_____
8	_____	4	_____
14	_____	16	_____
17	_____	20	_____
Total (Esteem Needs)	_____	Total (Basic Needs)	_____

Statement No.	Score
5	_____
7	_____
12	_____
15	_____
Total (Belonging Needs)	_____

2. Record your total scores in the chart below by marking an "X" in each row next to the number of your total score for that area of needs motivation.

	−12	−10	−8	−6	−4	−2	0	+2	+4	+6	+8	+10	+12
Self-Actualization													
Esteem													
Belonging													
Safety													
Basic													

Low   High
Use   Use

Once you have completed this chart, you can see the relative strengths of your use of each of these areas of needs motivation.

There is, of course, no "right" answer. What is right for you is what matches the actual needs of employees and that, of course, is specific to each situation and each individual. In general, however, the "experts" tell us that employees are best motivated by efforts in the areas of Belonging and Esteem.

MOTIVATION THEORY SHEET

Maslow's Need Hierarchy

Abraham Maslow theorized that needs are the primary influences on an individual's behavior. When a particular need emerges, it determines the individual's behavior in terms of motivations, priorities, and action taken. Thus, motivated behavior is the result of the tension—either pleasant or unpleasant—experienced when a need presents itself. The goal of the behavior is the reduction of this tension or discomfort, and the behavior, itself, will be appropriate for facilitating the satisfaction of the need. Only unsatisfied needs are prime sources of motivation.

Understanding behaviors and their goals involves gaining insight into presently unsatisfied needs. Maslow developed a method for gaining insight by providing categories of needs in a hierarchical structure. He placed all human needs, from primitive or immature (in terms of the behaviors they foster) to civilized or mature needs, into five need systems. He believed that there is a natural process whereby individuals fulfill needs in ascending order from most immature to most mature. This progression through the need hierarchy is seen as the climbing of a ladder whereby the individual must have experienced secure footing on the first rung in order to experience the need to step up to the next higher rung. The awareness of the need to climb further up the ladder is a function of having fulfilled the need of managing the preceding rung, and only satisfactory fulfillment of this need will allow the individual to deal with the new need or rung. Inability to fulfill a lower-order need or difficulty in fulfilling a lower-order need may result in an individual's locking in on immature behavior patterns or may produce a tendency to return to immature behaviors under stress any time an individual feels a lower-order need not fulfilled to his or her satisfaction. The individual may also revert to behaviors that fulfilled lower-order needs when the satisfaction of higher needs is temporarily blocked. That is not to say that any need is ever completely satisfied; rather, Maslow indicates that there must be at least partial fulfillment before an individual can become aware of the tensions manifested by a higher-order need and have the freedom to pursue its fulfillment.

The Maslow Need Hierarchy is comprised of five levels: Basic, Safety, Belongingness, Ego-Status, and Self-Actualization (Figure 1). The Basic level represents needs that reflect physiological and survival goals. At this level are such factors as shelter, clothing, food, sex, and other necessities. In cultures where these basic needs are almost automatically met there is not likely to be any need tension concerning the fulfillment of Basic needs. However, individuals may adapt this basic level upward to include such needs as avoidance of physical discomfort, pleasant working environment, or more money for providing creature comforts.

The second level of the hierarchy consists of Safety needs. When the individual has at least partially fulfilled the Basic needs, he or she will experience the tensions relating to needs of security, orderliness, protective rules, and general risk avoidance. These needs are often satisfied by an adequate salary, insurance policies, a good alarm system for his or her business, etc.

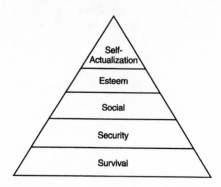

Figure 1. The Maslow Need Hierarchy

When Safety needs have been met, the individual will become less preoccupied with self and will endeavor to form interpersonal relationships. The relative success of this need for Belongingness will result in his or her feeling accepted and appreciated by others. Thus the third-level needs concern family, friendship, and group membership.

When an individual feels secure in his or her relationships with others, he or she will probably seek to gain special status within the group. The need tension will be associated with ambition and a desire to excel. These Ego-Status needs will motivate the individual to seek out opportunities to display his or her competence in an effort to gain social and professional rewards.

Because Ego-Status fulfillment is greatly dependent on the ability of others to respond appropriately to the individual's efforts to perform in a superior way, these needs are the most difficult to fulfill satisfactorily. However, if the individual has gained satisfaction on level four, he or she may be able to move up to level five—Self-Actualization. At this level, the individual is concerned with personal growth and may fulfill this need by challenging himself or herself to become more creative, demanding greater achievement of himself or herself, and, in general, directing himself or herself to measure up to his or her own criteria of personal success. Self-Actualizing behaviors must include risk taking, seeking autonomy, and developing freedom to act.

Job Enrichment

The motivation-hygiene theory, underlying what is known as job enrichment, grew out of research on job attitudes conducted by Frederick Herzberg. In establishing his theory, Herzberg draws heavily upon the hierarchy of needs developed by Abraham Maslow. Herzberg stresses that the factors that truly motivate work are "growth" factors, or those that give the worker a sense of personal accomplishment through the challenge of the job itself. In other words, motivation is *intrinsic* in the content of the job, the internal dynamics that the worker experiences in completing his or her task.

Herzberg also maintains that the context, or environmental factors (hygiene), that surround the job cause dissatisfaction when they are in unhealthy conditions. These *extrinsic* dissatisfiers may be classed as "deficit" needs in that their importance is felt only in their absence. For example, good working conditions rarely motivate workers. However, bad working conditions are frequently cited by workers as sources of dissatisfaction.

The chart that follows (Figure 2) outlines the differences between motivation factors and hygiene factors. A simple example of motivation and hygiene factors present in the work environment might be the case of the telephone installer who is given the list of places to cover during the day and asked to order them in the way he or she believes will be most efficient, rather

Motivation Factors (Job Content) Satisfiers	Hygiene Factors (Job Environment) Dissatisfiers
Work Itself	Company Policy & Administration
Achievement	Supervision
Recognition	Working Conditions
Responsibility	Interpersonal Relations
Growth and Advancement	Salary

Working Figure 2. Motivation Factors and Hygiene Factors

than having been given an itinerary preplanned by the manager who doesn't "know the territory" first hand in the way the installer does.

The responsibility of planning his or her route demonstrates not only a challenging task for the telephone installer, but also a proper level of supervision in the workplace.

Rererences

Maslow, A.H. (1970). *Motivation and personality* (2nd ed.). New York: Harper and Row. [Orig. ed., 1954.]

Herzberg, F., Mausner, B., & Snyderman, B.B. (1959). *The motivation to work* (2nd ed.). New York: John Wiley & Sons.

4

Management Skills: Assessing Personal Performance

Carol J. Levin

Goals

- To increase the participants' awareness of the wide range of behaviors that are encompassed by management.

- To enable the participants to assess their own needs for changes in their management-related behaviors.

Group Size

Any number of trios.

Time Required

One hour and twenty-five minutes.

Materials

- A copy of the Management Skills Inventory for each participant.

- A pencil for each participant.

- A clipboard or other portable writing surface for each participant.

Physical Setting

A room with movable chairs for the participants.

Process

1. The facilitator distributes a copy of the Management Skills Inventory and a pencil to each participant and asks them to complete this instrument. (Twenty minutes.)

2. The participants are assembled into trios. The members of each trio are instructed to help one another to develop ways to improve in areas of deficiency as well as ways to gauge and monitor improvement. (Thirty minutes.)

3. The total group is reassembled to discuss the experience. The following questions are helpful:

   - What did this instrument tell you about your management skills? How do you feel about the way you assessed yourself?

   - Were you previously aware that you used the types of behavior dealt with in the instrument?

   - Did the items in the instrument differ from the behaviors that you feel are necessary for managers? If so, how? Are there any that you do not feel are necessary? Are there any necessary ones that were not included in the instrument?

   - Did you uncover any areas of activity that you have neglected? Any biases that may require examination?

   - With regard to any of the behaviors dealt with in the instrument, do you conduct yourself in a particular way because of established norms within your organization? Would you change your behavior if these norms did not exist? Why or why not?

   - What types of activities are you prepared to begin to work on?

Variations

- Staff members may be asked to predict one another's responses to particular items and subsequently to compare their predictions with actual responses.

- The participants may be asked to develop a set of organizational learning skills from the responses and the discussions.

- The entire group may be reassembled several times over a long period to complete the instrument and to study improvement.

Originally published in A Handbook of Structured Experiences for Human Relations Training, Volume IX *(1983)*.

Management Skills Inventory[1]

Instructions: This form is designed to stimulate your thinking about your skills and relationships with others as a manager. It is intended to help you to set your own goals for development. The steps for using it are as follows:

1. Read through the list of activities and assess your performance for each one. Mark an X for each item in the appropriate blank. Some activities that you think are important may not be listed. Blank lines are provided in each category so that such an item may be added.

2. Go back over the entire list, choose the three or four items on which you would most like to improve at this time, and mark each of these items with an asterisk.

3. List the three or four activities in the space provided under "Action Plan." Then make preliminary notes about specific actions that you might take to improve your performance in each of these areas. Later you will be asked to share these notes with others who will help you to develop a final plan.

Communicating Skills

	Present Performance Sufficient	Need to Do More	Need to Do Less
1. Making clear statements	_____	_____	_____
2. Being brief and concise	_____	_____	_____
3. Being forceful	_____	_____	_____
4. Drawing others out	_____	_____	_____
5. Listening alertly	_____	_____	_____
6. Checking out assumptions	_____	_____	_____
7. Writing clearly and effectively	_____	_____	_____
8. _____	_____	_____	_____

Adapted from "Goals for Personal Development Inventory," in J.W. Pfeiffer and J.E. Jones (Eds.), *The 1976 Annual Handbook for Group Facilitators,* p. 59.

	Present Performance Sufficient	Need to Do More	Need to Do Less
Problem-Solving/Decision-Making Skills			
9. Defining problem or goal	_____	_____	_____
10. Establishing criteria for solutions	_____	_____	_____
11. Asking for and researching alternative ideas and opinions	_____	_____	_____
12. Giving ideas and opinions	_____	_____	_____
13. Evaluating ideas critically before choosing one	_____	_____	_____
14. Evaluating results of the solution of decision	_____	_____	_____
15. _____	_____	_____	_____
Planning Skills			
16. Establishing a clear goal or mission statement	_____	_____	_____
17. Determining specific objectives	_____	_____	_____
18. Involving others in the planning process	_____	_____	_____
19. Foreseeing barriers	_____	_____	_____
20. Developing contingency plans	_____	_____	_____
21. Integrating budget into the planning process	_____	_____	_____
22. Evaluating results on a regular basis	_____	_____	_____
23. _____	_____	_____	_____
Staffing Skills			
24. Developing clear job descriptions	_____	_____	_____
25. Recruiting appropriate candidates	_____	_____	_____
26. Interviewing fairly and effectively	_____	_____	_____

	Present Performance Sufficient	Need to Do More	Need to Do Less
27. Negotiating salary and/or benefits fairly and effectively	_____	_____	_____
28. Evaluating performance on a regular basis	_____	_____	_____
29. Firing when appropriate	_____	_____	_____
30. Providing ongoing supervision (coaching and feedback on a frequent basis)	_____	_____	_____
31. _____	_____	_____	_____

Organizing Skills

32. Clarifying work flow	_____	_____	_____
33. Establishing departments or units as needed	_____	_____	_____
34. Developing coordination between units	_____	_____	_____
35. Holding effective meetings as necessary	_____	_____	_____
36. Delegating tasks to others	_____	_____	_____
37. Developing systems to improve or simplify task accomplishment	_____	_____	_____
38. _____	_____	_____	_____

Group-Dynamics Skills

39. Initiating ideas	_____	_____	_____
40. Clarifying and elaborating on discussion	_____	_____	_____
41. Summarizing others' ideas	_____	_____	_____
42. Gatekeeping (ensuring that people are heard)	_____	_____	_____

	Present Performance Sufficient	Need to Do More	Need to Do Less
43. Compromising or mediating	_____	_____	_____
44. Standard testing	_____	_____	_____
45. Consensus seeking	_____	_____	_____
46. Noting tension and interest levels in a group	_____	_____	_____
47. Encouraging	_____	_____	_____
48. Noting when the group avoids a topic	_____	_____	_____
49. Sensing individuals' feelings	_____	_____	_____
50. Recognizing and understanding the stages of group development	_____	_____	_____
51. Controlling dysfunctional behavior	_____	_____	_____
52. _____	_____	_____	_____

Morale-Building Skills

53. Showing interest in individuals	_____	_____	_____
54. Expressing praise or appreciation	_____	_____	_____
55. Consulting with employees before making decisions that affect them	_____	_____	_____
56. Providing opportunities for growth and development	_____	_____	_____
57. Promoting from within the organization	_____	_____	_____
58. Treating people fairly and equitably	_____	_____	_____
59. Helping people to reach agreement; harmonizing	_____	_____	_____
60. Upholding rights of individuals in the face of group pressure	_____	_____	_____
61. _____	_____	_____	_____

	Present Performance Sufficient	Need to Do More	Need to Do Less
General/Personal Skills			
62. Telling personal feelings to others	_____	_____	_____
63. Facing and accepting conflict and anger	_____	_____	_____
64. Facing and accepting closeness and affection	_____	_____	_____
65. Understanding personal motivation (self-insight)	_____	_____	_____
66. Soliciting feedback on personal behavior	_____	_____	_____
67. Accepting help willingly	_____	_____	_____
68. Criticizing oneself constructively	_____	_____	_____
69. Managing stress and tension	_____	_____	_____
70. Managing time effectively (setting priorities)	_____	_____	_____
71. Taking good care of oneself (nutrition, rest, etc.)	_____	_____	_____
72. Taking time for relaxation and recreation	_____	_____	_____
73. _____	_____	_____	_____

Action Plan

Activity	Actions to Take to Improve Performance
1. _____	_____
2. _____	_____
3. _____	_____
4. _____	_____

5

Leadership History: Searching the Past for Insight

Frank A. Prince

Goals

- To increase participants' awareness of their leadership styles.

- To compare and contrast individual leadership experiences within a group.

- To allow participants to share their past learnings in a creative forum.

Group Size

Ten to twenty participants.

Time Required

Sixty to ninety minutes, depending on the number of participants sharing their leadership histories.

Materials

- A copy of the Leadership History Survey for each participant.

- Pens and paper for each participant.

- Flip-chart paper for each participant.
- A variety of colored markers for each participant.
- Masking tape.

Physical Setting

A room with chairs and a surface on which participants can spread out and work on their drawings.

Process

1. Give all participants paper and pencils to take notes.

2. Announce the goals of the activity, briefly explaining that the leadership styles we currently exhibit come from experiences we have had with leaders in our past. Say that they will have an opportunity to reflect on those people who have influenced their leadership styles.

3. Give everyone a copy of the Leadership History Survey. Read the first question and have participants individually write their answers. Continue through the questions, reading them out loud to give participants time to reflect and write their answers. (Five to ten minutes.)

4. Once the participants have all completed the Survey, tell them that they will now create a poster of their "Leadership History." Give everyone a sheet of flip chart paper and colored markers, and ask participants to create a drawing of their own leadership history, based on their answers to the Survey.

5. Tell them there is one very important rule for creating their leadership history posters. They must not use any words, but only pictures. (Fifteen to twenty minutes.)

6. Once all participants have completed their drawings, have them hang their posters on one of the walls of the room with masking tape.

7. Ask each participant, one at a time, to share his or her leadership history poster with the rest of the group, describing the events depicted. (Two minutes per person.)

8. Once all participants have described their posters, debrief the activity by having the group compare and contrast the different experiences that were shared and their learnings. (Ten minutes.)

9. Conclude with a discussion about the impact we have on others and their leadership styles. Encourage participants to think about the influence they have in their reporting relationships. Address the following questions:

- What common leadership experiences did you notice?

- What were some of the most significant events in people's leadership histories?

- In what ways might we actively impact leadership within an organization?

(Ten minutes.)

Variation

- Instead of participants drawing their Leadership Histories, they can use magazines and cut out pictures that represent the events of their past, then tape or glue them to a poster.

Originally published in The 2001 Annual: Volume 2, Consulting.

LEADERSHIP HISTORY SURVEY

Instructions: Answer each of the following questions in as much depth as possible. Wait for the facilitator to read each question rather than reading ahead.

1. Where were you born? What type of neighborhood was it (city, suburb, or country)?

2. How large was your family? Any brothers or sisters? Were you youngest, oldest, or in the middle?

3. What games did you enjoy playing as a child? Did you usually lead, follow, or do a little of both?

4. List your best friends as you grew up. What did you especially like about each of them?

5. Name an adult (a parent or other adult) you were close to as you grew up. What leadership qualities did this person exhibit?

6. Name a teacher who had a strong influence on you as you grew up. What did this person do that influenced you?

7. What was your first "real" job? What leadership learnings did you obtain from that job?

8. List all the jobs you have had in your career.

9. Who was your best boss? In what ways was this person a good leader?

10. Who was your worst boss? In what ways was this person a poor leader?

11. Identify mentors (formal or informal) who have influenced you. What changes have you made as a result of their influence?

12. What one significant piece of leadership advice would you give to others?

6

Management Perspectives: Identifying Styles

Patrick Doyle

Goals

- To help the participants to identify various managerial styles.

- To illustrate the ways in which these managerial styles can affect an organization.

- To acquaint the participants with the advantages and disadvantages of these styles.

Group Size

Three to six subgroups of four participants each.

Time Required

Two hours and fifteen minutes.

Materials

- A copy of the Management Perspectives Situation Sheet for each participant.

- A set of Management Perspectives Role Sheets for each subgroup (a different sheet for each member).

- Four name tags for each subgroup. Prior to conducting the activity, the facilitator labels each subgroup's tags as follows:
  - Manager A
  - Manager B
  - Manager C
  - Manager D
- A copy of the Management Perspectives Theory Sheet for each participant.
- A copy of the Management Perspectives Discussion Sheet for each participant.
- Blank paper and a pencil for each participant.
- A clipboard or other portable writing surface for each participant.

Physical Setting

A room large enough to afford each subgroup an opportunity to work without disturbing the other subgroups.

Process

1. The facilitator announces that the participants are to be involved in a role play and then assembles them into subgroups of four members each.

2. Each participant is given a copy of the Management Perspectives Situation Sheet and is asked to read this handout. (Five minutes.)

3. The facilitator distributes copies of the role sheets and the corresponding name tags to each subgroup, ensuring that each of the four members is assigned a different role. The participants are instructed to read their handouts and to wear their name tags throughout the entire activity. In addition, the facilitator cautions the participants not to reveal the contents of their role sheets to their fellow subgroup members. (Ten minutes.)

4. Each participant is given blank paper, a pencil, and a clipboard or other portable writing surface and is instructed to spend fifteen minutes devising and recording a solution to be presented at the upcoming managers' meeting. The facilitator emphasizes the importance of maintaining assigned roles during this step and the meeting that follows.

5. At the end of the fifteen-minute period, the subgroups are told to begin their meetings.

6. After thirty minutes the facilitator stops the subgroup meetings, distributes copies of the Management Perspectives Theory Sheet, and asks the participants to read this sheet. (Ten minutes.)

7. Each participant is given a copy of the Management Perspectives Discussion Sheet. The facilitator states that each subgroup is to discuss answers to the questions on the sheet and that the subgroup should select a reporter to record answers, summarize them, and report the summarized answers later to the total group. (Thirty minutes.)

8. The total group is reconvened, and the reporters are asked to share the summarized results of the subgroup discussions. (Twenty minutes.)

9. The facilitator leads a concluding discussion concerning how the participants might apply what they have learned in their individual environments.

Variations

- Additional participants may be asked to serve as observers. In this case the facilitator should devise an observer sheet to guide the participants who fulfill this role.

- A role and corresponding role sheet may be created for a member of top management within each subgroup. The facilitator should note that this option may necessitate changes to the situation sheet.

- The facilitator may devise additional roles and role sheets that are based on other management models or theories.

- If the group is homogeneous, the situation sheet and the role sheets may be altered to reflect a situation that the participants deal with regularly.

Originally published in The 1985 Annual: Developing Human Resources.

MANAGEMENT PERSPECTIVES SITUATION SHEET

You are a branch manager of a large local bank. A year ago another manager's branch was selected to be redesigned as "the bank of the future." New, state-of-the-art word-processing equipment, automatic tellers, and computer terminals were installed. These changes meant that one employee working with a single piece of equipment could provide immediate responses to inquiries that were previously processed through the joint efforts of several employees over a period of days.

At the same time, two new staff members joined the branch. One was hired as an office supervisor because of an understanding of the word-processing and microcomputer equipment, and the other was named as supervisor of the tellers because of an understanding of the main computer. The rest of the staff was trained in the use of the new equipment. This training seemed to proceed as planned, and the employees developed a level of understanding and competence that was determined to be acceptable.

Top management announced these changes throughout the organization and had high hopes that the branch would evolve into a model of increased productivity and efficient operation. However, this has not been the case.

Before the changes took place, the branch employees and their manager functioned productively as a close-knit, content group. But soon after the changes were instituted, it became known that the employees were beginning to complain. They were disappointed in the new equipment, which malfunctioned frequently, and in their new work environment, which they described as cold and impersonal. Another situation that distressed them involved the removal of the time clock. When the clock was first removed and the employees were no longer required to "punch in" and "punch out," they saw this development as a sign that the organization had more trust in them; but subsequently they discovered that the newly installed computer equipment was verifying their comings and goings. Discontent over these concerns and others grew, and, despite a healthy economy, the branch began to experience a drop in performance. Things progressively worsened until finally, a week ago, the branch manager became frustrated enough to quit.

Now the branch is without leadership, and top management has asked you and three other branch managers to meet to *determine the source of the problems within the redesigned branch and to arrive at a solution to these problems.* Each manager has been instructed to work independently to develop a solution and to bring this proposal to the meeting, which is to take place shortly.

MANAGEMENT PERSPECTIVES ROLE SHEET A

Manager A

You feel that the present problems in the redesigned branch are obviously attributable to the people who work there. If the branch employees have not yet adapted to the new equipment and procedures, they probably are incapable of functioning in "the bank of the future." It is also possible that the two new supervisors are not the equipment experts that they were assumed to be and are, therefore, to blame for inadequately training the employees.

If you had had your way from the beginning, you would have chosen only one type of employee for the redesigned branch: the type who strictly follows and does not deviate from instructions. In the actual process used to institute the changes at the branch, too much emphasis was placed on helping existing employees to understand the new procedures. Actually, all they needed to know was what buttons should be pushed and at what time.

One issue about which you are particularly sensitive is the new equipment at the redesigned branch. You believe this equipment to be the best available. In fact, you were a member of the task force that investigated different kinds of equipment and ultimately suggested that the present models be purchased. Although you know it is true that the equipment malfunctions occasionally, you attribute such breakdowns to the incompetence of the people who use it. You even have support for your position in this matter: A recent report on the "down time" of the equipment was submitted by the supplier, and it implies that the branch employees are to blame rather than the machinery itself. Therefore, during the upcoming meeting, you plan to make it clear that the new equipment cannot possibly be the source of the present problems.

You are certain that the solution you come up with will be the best alternative, and you plan to support it at all costs.

MANAGEMENT PERSPECTIVES ROLE SHEET B

Manager B

You are convinced that the source of the problems at the redesigned branch is the lack of emphasis on human relations. Throughout the year since the changes were instituted, the branch employees have been complaining. As you suspected from the outset, the employees were not consulted about the type of equipment or procedures that should be used, just as they were excluded from the decision-making process that led to the creation of "the bank of the future."

Furthermore, the employees state that the new equipment continually breaks down and makes it impossible for them to work efficiently. Although you recently read a report implying that the malfunctions were caused by human error, you dismissed the contents; because the report was submitted by the supplier of the equipment, its conclusions can scarcely be regarded as legitimate.

It seems to you that top management, in redesigning the branch, was operating under the philosophy that the equipment should control the flow of work, a viewpoint that you consider unacceptable. Instead, the primary emphasis should be on the employees, without whom the equipment is useless. As you have always said, when the organization fulfills its responsibility to meet the employees' needs, everything else falls into place and organizational goals are met automatically. After all, the branch employees were happy before the redesigning process, and productivity then was considerably higher than it is now. Under the new system, they have to cope not only with a reduction in the amount of teamwork that previously had promoted morale and satisfaction, but also with new supervisors who were hired because of their computer skills instead of their management skills. During the upcoming meeting, you plan to point out top management's error in judgment.

You are certain that the solution you come up with will be the best alternative, and you plan to support it at all costs.

MANAGEMENT PERSPECTIVES ROLE SHEET C

Manager C

In your opinion the problems in the redesigned branch are attributable to one source: a failure to provide the employees with opportunities to fulfill their individual needs and their natural desire to do competent work. You formed this opinion on the basis of what you have learned about employees in general as well as those at the troubled branch. The branch employees, like your own subordinates, are mature adults who want to do their best for the bank; they enjoy their work and supervise themselves well in completing it. Indeed, their performance record and their level of job contentment before the redesigning prove that this is the case.

In its plans to redesign the branch, the bank's top management has overlooked these facts and has chosen to treat the employees like lazy children. New supervisors were brought in to monitor their work, and new equipment was programmed to keep track of their comings and goings. The employees were expected to meet new organizational goals for increased productivity while their needs for autonomy, self-direction, and a sense of fulfillment were ignored. Under the circumstances, a drop in productivity was inevitable. You feel strongly that the present organizational attitude toward employees is counterproductive, and you plan to make your feelings known during the upcoming meeting.

You are certain that the solution you come up with will be the best alternative, and you plan to support it at all costs.

MANAGEMENT PERSPECTIVES ROLE SHEET D

Manager D

As far as you are concerned, the source of the problems at the redesigned branch is a failure to analyze and respond to all of the factors involved before the changes were implemented. The situation at the branch was and is complex. Top management had no choice but to respond to technical advances that would allow the bank to remain competitive, but too much was attempted too fast and without adequate preparation. In addition, the needs of the branch employees should have been met to a greater degree, and the social climate within the branch should have been considered.

However, you feel that it is time to face the situation and rectify it. It is highly impractical to consider such solutions as firing all of the branch employees, abandoning concerns about productivity and competitiveness, or attempting to effect overnight changes in the way in which the organization and top management operate. The solution must incorporate social and technological goals within the context of internal and external environmental pressures. Your objective during the meeting is to convince your fellow members to see the whole picture as it really is rather than as their special interests may compel them to see it.

You are certain that the solution you come up with will be the best alternative, and you plan to support it at all costs.

MANAGEMENT PERSPECTIVES THEORY SHEET[1]

Over the years a number of approaches to management have been developed and promulgated in an attempt to provide effective leadership within organizations. The role-play situation in which you have just been involved has characterized four of these approaches, which are described below.

The Scientific Approach (Manager A)

Frederick Taylor is known as the father of the scientific approach to management. In the early 1900s he analyzed the loading of pig iron onto railroad cars at Bethlehem Steel and determined that he could devise techniques for increasing the workers' productivity.

After observing the workers carefully, Taylor selected a few who he felt could tolerate the new pace he would set, and from this group he ultimately chose one individual for his project. This worker was instructed to do exactly as he was told and only as he was told. By closely adhering to Taylor's methods, the worker was able to increase his average loading per day from 12.5 to 47.5 tons.

Although this initial effort was deemed successful, Taylor's work, reputation, and the entire approach of scientific management eventually suffered because of his negative opinion of workers. He defined the worker in the Bethlehem Steel situation as "mentally sluggish," and he described the ideal pig-iron worker as closer to an ox in his mental abilities than any other form of life. Taylor made these statements in a fairly public manner and subsequently was condemned by many, not because of his devotion to increasing productivity through applying the results of time-and-motion studies, but because of his lack of sensitivity to the human element.

Today we tend to associate Taylor's approach with the attitude that success must be achieved at any cost. This high concern with the mechanics of task, when combined with a low concern for people, is now thought to be quite psychologically damaging to workers. Nevertheless, it characterized industrial work for a number of years and is still prevalent in many areas of our society.

---

1. Adapted from M. Sashkin, "An Overview of Ten Management and Organizational Theorists," in J.E. Jones and J.W. Pfeiffer (Eds.), *The 1981 Annual Handbook for Group Facilitators.*

The Human-Relations Approach (Manager B)

Elton Mayo, a social philosopher of the 1920s and 1930s, held views that were in direct opposition to those of Frederick Taylor. While Mayo was a faculty member at Harvard, he was responsible for experiments that took place at Western Electric's Hawthorne plant. These experiments formed the basis of the human-relations approach to management.

Mayo believed that productivity could be increased by involving workers in the decision-making process. After analyzing the results of the Hawthorne experiments, Mayo concluded that they supported his belief, although many have debated this conclusion in the years since.

Whereas the scientific approach came to be maligned because its originator held unacceptable views of the workers, the human-relations approach ultimately came to be maligned because it excluded a concern for profit in favor of the contentment of workers. Although Mayo himself recognized the legitimacy of the profit motive and sought to incorporate this motive with that of worker involvement in decision making, those who adopted his approach eventually became convinced that if a company's workers were happy, the company itself would automatically prosper. Managers who espoused this notion saw their responsibility as catering to the needs of their workers almost to the exclusion of their companies' needs. This approach developed a considerable following during the 1930s, 1940s, and early 1950s, but by the mid-1950s it became obvious that increased productivity could not be achieved solely by assuring the happiness of workers.

Behavioral-Science Approach (Manager C)

One of the important outcomes of the human-relations approach was that it prepared the way for the behavioral-science approach. Douglas McGregor, one of the earliest and most influential proponents of this approach to management, began to expound his ideas in the late 1950s. McGregor based his view of management on different managerial attitudes toward worker motivation. He designated as "Theory X" a managerial style based on the assumption that workers are basically lazy, do not wish to accept responsibility, must be closely controlled, and do not wish to be involved in the solution of organizational problems. The opposite style, which McGregor called "Theory Y," is governed by the assumption that workers actively seek and willingly accept responsibility, are naturally goal oriented and self-controlled at work, and are willing and able to help in solving organizational problems.

McGregor's answer to the excesses of the scientific and the human-relations approaches was Theory Y: Management must, of course, meet organizational goals, but it should also design work in such a way that it provides workers with opportunities to meet their own needs as well. This approach takes full advantage of workers' natural motivation to the mutual benefit of the workers and their organization. Because worker needs fall generally into the categories of social, esteem, and self-development, ample opportunities can be offered to fulfill them. For example, it is perfectly conceivable that a worker's job can be designed to afford him or her an opportunity to gain prestige, a sense of achievement, or knowledge.

When managers tried to apply this theory, however, they encountered a problem. A certain kind of organizational structure and environment is required to support Theory Y behavior on the part of a manager. An organization that adheres predominantly to Theory X, for instance, is no place in which to try this approach.

Sociotechnical-Systems Approach (Manager D)

The sociotechnical-systems approach, set forth by Fred Emery, Eric Trist, and others during the 1950s, 1960s, and 1970s, combines elements from the three approaches previously discussed in an attempt to address the complexity of variables that exists within contemporary organizations. This approach recognizes the concerns of an organization that must adapt to technical advances, but still must attend to its internal social environment as well as the larger environment within which it functions. The responsibility of each organization, if it is to survive, is to analyze its own situation with regard to social, technical, and environmental factors and then to choose a structure and a method of operating that work within the context of these factors. Therefore, not all organizations can or should be alike.

This concept recognizes that just as no organization operates within a vacuum, so does no manager. In order to know how to behave, a manager must weigh human needs, technological concerns, and both internal and external environmental pressures. Although the sociotechnical-systems approach does offer managers and their organizations a way to respond to changing conditions, it is not a panacea and does not pretend to be one. Even Trist has expressed a fear that the technological advances of the next few decades will outdistance the ability of the sociotechnical-systems approach to deal with them.

MANAGEMENT PERSPECTIVES DISCUSSION SHEET

1. What positive reactions did you have while playing your assigned role? What were your negative reactions?

2. Which comments from other subgroup members had the greatest impact on you? What meaning did you attribute to these comments?

3. What do you consider to be the advantages of the managerial approach that you represented during the role play?

4. What do you consider to be the disadvantages?

5. How closely does your assigned role-sheet style resemble your own managerial approach?

6. Which approach is most characteristic of your own organization? How does this approach affect your organization?

7. How acceptable would your assigned role-sheet style be in your own organizational environment? What elements of the style would be acceptable or unacceptable?

Organizations and Systems

7

MACE: Demonstrating Factors that Affect Performance

Stephen Dakin and Russell Robb

Goal

- To demonstrate that individual performance within a group is influenced by four major factors: motivation, ability, conditions, and expectations (MACE).

Group Size

Ten to fifteen pairs.

Time Required

One to one and one-half hours.

Materials

- Blank paper and a pencil for each participant.
- A one-dollar bill.
- A five-dollar bill.
- A chalkboard and chalk or a newsprint flip chart and a felt-tipped marker.

Physical Setting

A room with a chair and a writing surface for each participant.

Process

1. The facilitator introduces the activity and begins the first phase:

   "To illustrate the main factors that influence performance, we are going to conduct some experiments. During the first of these experiments, do exactly as I say, but do not ask any questions or compare notes with other people."

   Each participant is given blank paper and a pencil.

2. To show the effects of unclear *expectations* on performance, the facilitator gives the following instructions:

   "I want you to perform a simple clerical task. Listen to the instructions, but do not start until I tell you to do so. Write the letters of the alphabet. For each letter that has a fully enclosed component, place a dot inside that component. For each letter that does not have a fully enclosed component, draw a circle around the entire letter. For example, 'a' and 'e' have fully enclosed components, and you should place a dot inside each of these components."

   The facilitator demonstrates by writing the letters on a chalkboard or a newsprint flip chart:

   "On the other hand, 'f' and 'z' do not have fully enclosed components and should, therefore, be circled."

   As before, the facilitator demonstrates:

   "Your objective in completing this task is to dot and circle as many letters as you can in the allotted time of thirty seconds. When I say 'go,' start working and continue until I tell you to stop. Ready, 'go.' "

3. At the end of the allotted time, the participants are told to stop working. Each participant is asked to exchange papers with the person seated next to him or her. Then the facilitator gives directions for scoring:

"Now score your partner's work. Give one point for each *lower-case* letter that is correctly dotted or circled."

It is explained that those who used uppercase letters are disqualified and that this requirement should have been evident from the examples given. The facilitator asks each participant to state his or her partner's score. As these results are announced, they are recorded on a chalkboard or a newsprint flip chart.

4. The facilitator leads a discussion to explore various ways in which the instructions were and might have been interpreted. It is emphasized that performance can be influenced dramatically by failure to agree on expectations. The discussion should include the following questions:

■ How did you feel about the instructions that you were given?

■ How did these feelings affect your performance?

(Ten minutes.)

5. To show the effects of *ability* on performance, the facilitator begins the second experiment:

"Let's consider the experiment we just completed to be a practice session. We'll try the same task again. Does everyone now know what is expected?"

After answering any questions that the participants have, the facilitator starts the experiment in the manner indicated in step 2.

6. After the participants have worked for thirty seconds, the facilitator stops the experiment, asks the participants to trade and score their papers as they did previously, and records the results next to those of the first experiment.

7. The facilitator leads a discussion of the results, emphasizing the following points:

■ Performance is affected by ability; some people are better than others at specific tasks.

■ There is a range of ability in many groups in both work and nonwork settings.

■ The following questions should be included in this discussion:

■ How was this experience different from the first one?

■ How do you explain the effect of ability on performance?

(Ten minutes.)

8. To show the effects of *motivation* on performance, the facilitator conducts the third experiment:

> "Now let's repeat the same task, but change the goal. This time your objective is to exceed your last score. In addition, the person who exceeds his or her previous score by the greatest number of points will win one dollar."

A one-dollar bill is displayed prominently, and the facilitator starts the experiment in the same manner as before.

9. Step 6 is repeated.

10. After awarding the one-dollar prize to the winner, the facilitator leads a discussion. It is emphasized that performance is improved by motivation and that there are many different ways to motivate, such as those used in step 8. Questions to be included in this discussion are as follows:

- How did this experience differ from the previous one?

- What can you conclude about the effect of motivation on performance?

(Ten minutes.)

11. To show the effects of changed conditions on performance, the facilitator begins the last experiment:

> "Let's try the task once more. This time the person who can most improve his or her performance over the last trial will win five dollars. However, you must complete the task this time with your nonpreferred hand."

A five-dollar bill is displayed, and the facilitator starts the experiment.

12. Step 6 is repeated.

13. If there is a winner, the facilitator awards the five-dollar prize. Then the following points are emphasized in discussion:

- Performance depends on the conditions under which a task is performed. With many tasks, the conditions may have a more dramatic effect on people than motivation, ability, or expectations.

- Factors that may affect performance negatively include rules or regulations as well as the anticipation of failure, which leads to lowered motivation.

The discussion questions should include the following:

- How did this last experience differ from the previous three?
- How do you explain the impact of conditions on performance?

14. In conclusion, the facilitator elicits answers to the following questions:

- How can you relate what you have learned about performance to your back-home work group?
- What can be done to maximize the positive effects of expectations, ability, motivation, and conditions on performance?
- What can be done to minimize the negative effects?

Variations

- The facilitator may prefer to conduct all four experiments before leading a discussion on the determinants of performance.
- The participants may be asked to work in teams rather than individually.

Originally published in The 1984 Annual: Developing Human Resources.

8

Organizational Structures: A Simulation

Rudi E. Weber

Goals

- To assist the participants in their efforts to understand the relationships between organizational structure, problem-solving performance, and organizational climate.

- To provide participants with an opportunity to experience and explore these relationships in a simulated environment.

- To encourage participants to examine the structures that prevail in their own work environments.

Group Size

At least two groups of eight members each. (The activity can be conducted with seven in a group, but it is preferable to have eight.)

Time Required

Approximately two hours to two hours and fifteen minutes.

Materials

- One set of index cards for each group, one card per member. [If there are more than seven members in the group other than the observer(s), repeat the information on one or more of the cards.] The information displayed on each card is as follows:

- **Card 1:**

  (a) The problem you have to solve is to figure out the total cost of Project X.

  (b) Is Maslow's theory applicable here?

  (c) Try to reach consensus

  (d) $e = mc^2$

- **Card 2:**

  (a) $S = m$

  (b) The fixed cost is 50 (Project X)

  (c) $TC = F + n \times V$

  (d) a = Number of units produced in Project B

- **Card 3:**

  (a) Deadline for Project B is tomorrow

  (b) F = Fixed cost

  (c) Total cost of Project A = PA

  (d) b = 184

- **Card 4:**

  (a) Use the PC

  (b) We have tried that before!

  (c) The correct oil is SAE 40

  (d) $NaCL + H_2O$?

- **Card 5:**

  (a) n = Number of parts

  (b) $PA = a + bx - 12$

  (c) The company has a good EEO policy

  (d) The variable cost per part is 0.2 (Project X)

- **Card 6:**
  - (a) The machine uses roller bearings
  - (b) $E = 12$
  - (c) The total cost of Project $X = TC$
  - (d) M
- **Card 7:**
  - (a) $X = M^{-2} \log y$
  - (b) You need to produce 1000 parts for Project X (i.e., $n = 1000$)
  - (c) $V = $ Variable cost per part
  - (d) $E + M = L$

- Copies of the Organizational Structures Mechanistic Task Sheet for half of the groups (one copy per member) and one for each observer.

- Copies of the Organizational Structures Organic Task Sheet for the other half of the groups (one copy per member) and one for each observer.

- One copy of the Organizational Structures Background Sheet for each of the participants.

- An Organizational Structures Observer Sheet for each observer.

- Blank paper and a pencil for each participant.

- A clipboard or other portable writing surface for each participant.

- A newsprint flip chart and felt-tipped markers.

Physical Setting

A room that is large enough so that all groups can work without distracting one another or several smaller rooms. A chair should be provided for each participant.

Process

1. Participants are formed into groups of eight members each. One person in each group is selected to serve as the leader, and one person in each group is selected to serve as the observer. Any additional participants also can be assigned to groups as observers. (Five minutes.)

2. To half of the groups, the facilitator gives copies of the Organizational Structures Mechanistic Task Sheet (one copy for each member, including observers). To the other half of the groups, the facilitator gives copies of the Organizational Structures Organic Task Sheet (one copy for each member, including observers). Each observer also receives a copy of the Organizational Structures Observer Sheet. The facilitator tells the participants to read their task sheets and to arrange themselves as directed. (Five minutes.)

3. After the group members have occupied their respective positions, the facilitator allots a set of seven cards to each group, distributing the cards randomly among the group members. The members are instructed not to exchange cards or to discuss their content. [Note to facilitator: Some of the information on the cards is relevant (R) and some is irrelevant (I), as follows: Card 1: a-R, b-I, c-I, d-I; Card 2: a-I, b-R, c-R, d-I; Card 3: a-I, b-R, c-I, d-I; Card 4: a-I, b-I, c-I, d-I; Card 5: a-R, b-I, c-I, d-R; Card 6: a-I, b-I, c-R, d-I; Card 7: a-I, b-R, c-R, d-I. The pieces of information distributed across the six "relevant" cards together allow the correct solution to be determined.] (Five minutes.)

4. The facilitator introduces the activity by announcing that the groups will be in competition with one another in an attempt to solve the problem that is contained in the set of cards. The winner will be the group that produces the correct solution first. Each group is to work according to its task instructions. No further clues are provided. (Five minutes.)

5. The groups work separately on the problem. The facilitator checks any proposed solutions and records on a newsprint flip chart the time taken by each group to produce the correct answer. If a group arrives at the correct solution before time is called, its members are instructed to discuss among themselves the reasons that they finished the task satisfactorily. The simulation is terminated after forty-five minutes. (Forty-five minutes.)

6. The total group is reassembled (with the members of each work group seated together). The facilitator posts the solution to the problem on a newsprint flip chart. The solution is shown below.

- Total Cost of Project X = TC   (extracted from cards 1 and 6)
- TC = F + n x V   (extracted from card 2)
- F = Fixed Cost = 50   (extracted from cards 2 and 3)
- n = Number of Parts = 1000   (extracted from cards 5 and 7)
- V = Variable Cost per Part = 0.2   (extracted from cards 7 and 5)

Therefore:

Total Cost of Project X = 50 + 1000 x 0.2 = 250

(Five minutes.)

7. The facilitator leads the following discussion:

   - Which members felt satisfaction with the experience? What was it about the roles or tasks that contributed to that? How did that affect the organizational climate?

   - Which members felt dissatisfied? What was it about the roles or tasks that contributed to that? How did that affect the organizational climate?

   - How did members learn (a) what the problem was, (b) who had relevant and useful information, and (c) who was most capable of solving this type of (algebraic) problem? Did this latter recognition affect the leadership role? If so, how?

   - Did member(s) who held the card that contained the problem statement recognize the key to potential success? If not, why not? [Typically, the person either did not expect it or was awaiting instructions from the leader.]

   (Fifteen minutes.)

8. The facilitator distributes a copy of the Organizational Structures Background Sheet to each participant. The facilitator explains the information on the sheet. An important part of the debriefing at this point is to reassure the participants, particularly those who played the role of leaders, that their performance was not a function of their ability but, rather, of the structures they had to work under. (Ten minutes.)

9. Observers are asked to report their findings, particularly in relation to differences they observed in the behaviors of the various groups. (Ten minutes.)

10. The facilitator leads a discussion of the recorded outcomes of the simulation. Participants are asked to discuss the following items and their responses are recorded on a newsprint flip chart:

    - Reasons that the organic structure(s) performed more successfully.

    - Under what conditions the different types of structures are effective or ineffective.

    (Ten minutes.)

11. The facilitator then informs the participants that the simulation has been used with numerous participants in organizational training programs. The performance of groups working in an organic structure on uncertain problem situations was vastly superior to that of groups working within the constraints of a mechanistic structure. This superiority is evident in terms of both the rate of success and the time taken to arrive at the correct solution. The results also suggest that oral communication is more effective than written irrespective of the type of structure utilized, but that changing a mechanistic structure to an organic one while maintaining only written communication is more conducive to success than trying to achieve the same end by allowing members of the mechanistic structure to communicate orally. In other words, a suitable structure appears to be more critical to success than the communication mode under conditions of uncertainty. These findings are compatible with those obtained in classical studies of communication networks (for example, Leavitt, 1951; Shaw & Rothschild, 1956). However, they go beyond these contributions inasmuch as they also account for the concept of uncertainty. (Five minutes.)

12. The participants are asked to form small discussion groups of four to five members each. Utilizing the experience as a "trigger," participants are encouraged to offer examples from their own work environments that demonstrate dynamics similar to those observed in the simulation and to develop possible solutions or recommendations for improvement. (Fifteen minutes.)

Variations

- In addition to the groups, individual participants can be given complete sets of cards and allowed to complete the task in competition with the groups. Such participants will sit outside the groups. Individuals will process the experience along with the group members. In the processing discussion, it can be pointed out that, typically, individuals working on their own are even more successful than the organic/oral communication group in terms of the average time taken to solve the problem—probably because they have all the information they need and do not have to rely on others for information exchange—but they tend to have a lower success rate, probably because incorrect assumptions cannot be checked by others.

- Compromise structures (for instance, a basically mechanistic structure within which members are allowed to talk with one another or an essentially organic structure in which members have to communicate in writing) also can be utilized. This approach is most useful with a large number of participants.

- Steps 10, 11, and 12 can be replaced with a total-group discussion of back-home applications.

References

Leavitt, H.J. (1951). Some effects of certain communication patterns on group performance. *Journal of Abnormal and Social Psychology, 46,* pp. 38–50.

Shaw, M.E., & Rothschild, G.H. (1956). Some effects of prolonged experience in communication nets. *Journal of Applied Psychology, 40,* pp. 281–286.

Originally published in The 1999 Annual: Volume 2, Consulting.

ORGANIZATIONAL STRUCTURES
MECHANISTIC TASK SHEET

Instructions: Quickly pick a leader for your group. Arrange yourselves in the configuration shown below:

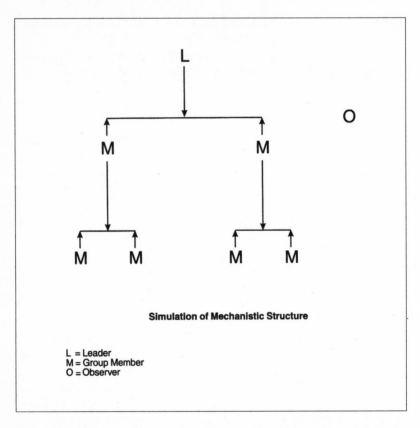

Simulation of Mechanistic Structure

L = Leader
M = Group Member
O = Observer

During this activity, your group is to function in a strictly hierarchical and bureaucratic fashion. That is, you are allowed to communicate only through the formal channels shown on your organizational chart and only in writing. You are not allowed to talk. You are not allowed to bypass anyone in the system.

Let the facilitator know when you have found the solution to the problem.

Organizational Structures
Organic Task Sheet

Instructions: Quickly pick a leader for your group. Arrange yourselves in the configuration shown below:

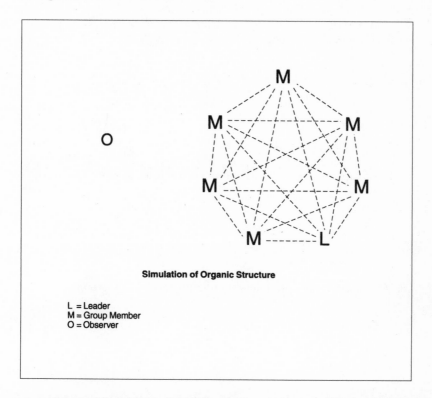

Simulation of Organic Structure

L = Leader
M = Group Member
O = Observer

During this activity, you are allowed to communicate within your group in any way you like, that is, with anyone and in any form (oral or written) that you wish to use. (The dashed lines above show possible patterns of communication.)

Let the facilitator know when you have found the solution to the problem.

ORGANIZATIONAL STRUCTURES
OBSERVER SHEET

During this activity, you are encouraged to move about and observe the various groups in order to allow yourself to become aware of major characteristics of and differences in the groups' working patterns.

Make notes about the primary characteristics of the various groups' working patterns in the following space:

Try to answer the following questions:

1. What happened to the leaders in the mechanistic group(s)?

2. What happened to communication in the mechanistic group(s)?

3. What happened to the participants situated at the lower levels of the mechanistic group(s)?

4. Did the leader of the mechanistic group(s) ask for all of the information to be transmitted to him/her and then proceed to solve the problem singlehandedly or did he/she delegate?

5. Did the members of the organic group(s) engage in a multidirectional exchange of information? Did the members share their perceptions, test their ideas, and either verify or correct their assumptions and solutions?

6. What happened to the role of leader in the organic group(s)?

ORGANIZATIONAL STRUCTURES
BACKGROUND SHEET

In order to ensure success, organizations need to be structured to be prepared for environmental contingencies. Burns and Stalker (1961) suggest that mechanistic structures work best under stable environmental conditions and that organic structures are needed in times of rapid change (for the characteristics of both types of structure, see Table 1). More generally, Kanter (1983) shows that organizations operating in our changing environment need to maintain "structural flexibility."

Students of organizational behavior frequently find it difficult to understand these principles at a theoretical level. Other people are overwhelmed by the complexity of real-world organizational processes and their relationship to change. The purpose of the activity is to reduce this complexity to a simple, concrete experience—to a context and task situation that participants are familiar with and can relate to in a meaningful way.

Table 1. Characteristics of Organic and Mechanistic Structures

Organic	Focus	Mechanistic (Bureaucratic)
Decentralized	HIERARCHY OF AUTHORITY	Centralized
Few	RULES AND PROCEDURES	Many
Ambiguous	DIVISION OF LABOR	Precise
Wide	SPAN OF CONTROL	Narrow
Informal and Personal	COORDINATION	Formal and Impersonal

The Effect of Structure on Problem Identification and Problem Solving

The type of problem in this simulation frequently is observed in situations that arise in uncertain (that is, rapidly changing) organizational environments:

1. It is unique (it has never occurred before in its present form), undefined, and unexpected. Hence, the organization may not possess—or may not even be aware of—what expertise, experience, resources, structure, or procedures are needed to deal with the problem.

2. It may be recognized as a problem (or impact the organization) at any level—frequently at lower levels—or in any functional area. That is, top management—or management in general—might be unaware of its presence or may fail to interpret it as a problem.

3. Although some members of the organization may have certain skills, bits of information, or experiences that are useful in the definition or solution of the problem, others may have no resources that could be employed in the problem-solving effort. Additionally, the types of personal resources required may be unknown to both employees and management.

The implications of such a problem situation are that:

1. Organizational members other than management may need to initiate appropriate action if the problem is to be solved; and

2. Members need to be able to communicate freely (without being hampered by undue structural barriers) to allow them to recognize that there is a problem; define it; discover who has the resources needed to solve it; and combine their skills, knowledge, and experience in an effort to generate a solution.

It clearly can be seen that an organic structure will facilitate this process while a mechanistic structure will interfere with it.

References

Burns, T., & Stalker, G.M. (1961). *The management of innovation.* London: Tavistock.

Kanter, R.M. (1983). *The change masters.* New York: Simon & Schuster.

9

There's Never Time to Do It Right: A Relay Task

Russell J. Denz

Goals

- To help participants understand the dilemma of quality versus quantity in terms of productivity.

- To help participants explore the consequences of focusing primarily on quality or quantity in teamwork.

Group Size

Four or more subgroups of four or five members each.

Time Required

Approximately one hour.

Materials

- A copy of the Relay Task A-Team Leader's Instruction Sheet for each leader of the A Teams.

- A copy of the Relay Task B-Team Leader's Instruction Sheet for each leader of the B Teams.

- One copy of the Relay Task Problem Sheet for each team.

- A sheet of blank paper for each participant.

- A pencil with an eraser for each participant.
- A clipboard or other portable writing surface for each participant.
- A newsprint flip chart and a felt-tipped marker.
- Masking tape for posting newsprint.

Physical Setting

A room that is large enough for the subgroups to work without disturbing one another.

Process

1. Without revealing the goals of the activity, the facilitator divides the group into teams of four or five members each. (The ideal number is five members. If some teams have only four members, one of the four will also serve as leader of the team.)

2. The facilitator designates one person from each team as the leader. If the team has five members, the leader plays no other role.

3. Copies of the A-team leader's instruction sheet are distributed to half the leaders, and copies of the B-team leader's instruction sheet are distributed to the other half. The facilitator does not reveal that the leaders have received two types of instruction sheets.

4. Leaders are instructed to read their sheets without allowing anyone else to see them. If clarification is needed, the leaders are instructed to walk over to the facilitator and ask their questions privately. Each participant is given a pencil and a sheet of blank paper. (Five minutes.)

5. When every leader has indicated that he or she is ready to proceed, each team is given a copy of the problem sheet.

6. The leaders are asked to explain the task and give instructions to their team members, and the participants are instructed to wait until the facilitator tells them to begin.

7. When all teams have indicated that they are ready to proceed, the facilitator instructs them to begin and records the time on newsprint. As each team arrives at the correct answer, the leader announces, "Our team has finished," and the facilitator records the time on newsprint. (Ten minutes.)

8. When every team has either found the correct answer or conceded defeat, the results of the experiment are tabulated on newsprint. The goals of the activity are explained, the facilitator reveals the differences in the

leaders' instructions, and each team is identified as an A team or B team. (Ten minutes.)

9. The facilitator leads a discussion on the following questions:

- If your leader pressured you to finish the task, how did you react? How did the pressure affect your morale? How was your productivity affected?

- If your leader encouraged you to take time, work carefully, and obtain the correct answer, how did you react? How did you feel when you realized that other teams would finish the problem before your team did?

- If your leader encouraged you to concede defeat, how did you react?

- What results did the two methods produce? What differences are evident from the tabulations?

- What might you have done differently if you had known what the goals of the activity were?

- In what ways can members of work teams cooperate in order to enhance both quality and quantity?

(Twenty minutes.)

Variations

- Three-member teams can be used. In this case, one member would be the leader, another member would do the work outlined for the "first person" and "third person," and the third member would do the work outlined for the "second person" and "fourth person."

- A problem that does not involve mathematics could be substituted for the given problem.

- The following question can be added to the discussion questions in step 9: How does your organization view the value of quantity when contrasted with quality? The participants can then be asked to give examples to illustrate their views.

- The following additional questions can be discussed: What are your views on focusing on quality? On quantity? What kinds of situations call for giving priority to quality? To quantity?

Originally published in The 1987 Annual: Developing Human Resources.

RELAY TASK A-TEAM LEADER'S INSTRUCTION SHEET

Do not allow anyone else to read these instructions. Take time to read this sheet thoroughly. If you need clarification on any point, walk over to the facilitator and ask your questions in private.

Your team will be given the following problem but will not be given the answer.

First person, add: 14
                           62
                           28
                         114
                         56
                        921
                         17
                         49

Total =   _____

Second person, multiply the above total by 256. Product = _____

Third person, subtract 384 from the above product. Difference = _____

Fourth person, divide the above difference by 16. Final Answer = 20,152

Important Note to Leader: If your team has only four members, including yourself, you must participate as a problem solver. However, you must not assign yourself the role of the "fourth person," because as the leader of the team you are given the solution to the fourth person's task.

Before your team members begin work on the problem, give them the following instructions:

1. You will be competing with all the other teams.

2. You will be given a problem to work on together. The most important thing is to obtain the correct answer.

3. Do not worry about how long it is taking you, because if you do not have the correct answer you will have to do the problem over again.

4. The problem is in four parts. You can decide among yourselves how to assign these parts.

5. You may ask me for suggestions, and you may ask one another for help in solving your part of the problem. If you have a calculator, you may use it. This is a team effort and the most important thing is to get a correct answer. If our team also finishes first, that is even better; but be sure to work carefully and take all the time you need.

After you have read this sheet and have clarified any questions, raise your hand to indicate to the facilitator that you are ready to proceed. When all team leaders are ready, your team will be given a copy of the problem.

You will then give the above instructions to your team and again raise your hand to indicate that your team is ready to proceed. The facilitator will tell your team when to begin.

If your team members have difficulty with the problem, feel free to discuss the task with them. You may not supply the answers, but you may offer suggestions about how to solve the problem. If your team obtains the wrong answer, you may help them discover which part of the problem was worked incorrectly.

When your team arrives at the correct answer, call out loudly enough for everyone to hear, "Our team has finished."

Remember, the correct answer is 20,152.

Relay Task B-Team Leader's Instruction Sheet

Do not allow anyone else to read these instructions. Take time to read this sheet thoroughly. If you need clarification on any point, walk over to the facilitator and ask your questions in private.

Your team will be given a problem to solve. You may not give the team any help or suggestions. The only instructions you may give your team are the following:

1. You will be given a simple math problem. It is divided into four parts. The person I hand it to will work the first part and hand it to someone else. That person will work the second part and hand it to another person. That person will work the third part and hand it to the last person to finish.

2. This is a very simple task and should be finished quickly. We are competing against the other teams to see who can finish first. So the important part is to work as quickly as you can.

3. You may not receive help from me or from one another. I cannot answer any questions. The object is to work quickly and quietly and get through the problem.

Important Note to Leader: If your team has only four members, including yourself, you will play the role of the "first person" in solving the problem.

After you have read this sheet and have clarified any questions, raise your hand to indicate to the facilitator that you are ready to proceed. When all team leaders are ready, your team will be given a copy of the problem.

You will then give the above instructions to your team and again raise your hand to indicate that your team is ready to proceed. The facilitator will tell your team when to begin.

While your team is working, occasionally make comments like "Now Chris, hurry up; we want to win, you know"; "Don't spend that much time on it; after all, this is just plain old arithmetic"; or "One team has already finished. Let's try to come in second at least." Also refuse to answer any questions. The object is to put the team under pressure to finish quickly.

The correct final answer is 20,152. If the fourth person does not arrive at that answer, just hand the problem back to the first person and tell the team members they will have to check their work and find out where the error is. Then add, "But do it quickly."

When your team arrives at the correct answer, call out loudly enough for everyone to hear, "Our team has finished." If most of the other teams finish first, encourage your team to concede defeat.

Remember, the correct answer is 20,152.

RELAY TASK PROBLEM SHEET

The following problem has four parts, and four people should work on it. General instructions are given here, but you should also follow your leader's instructions.

First person, add: 14
                      62
                      28
                     114
                      56
                     921
                      17
                      49

Total =   _____

Second person, multiply the above total by 256. Product = _____

Third person, subtract 384 from the above product. Difference = _____

Fourth person, divide the above difference by 16. Final Answer = _____

10

The Flip-It Company:
Exploring the Impact of Work Quotas

James L. Costigan

Goals

- To illustrate what happens when work quotas are assigned without consideration of the variables that affect results.

- To offer the participants an opportunity to experience typical worker reactions to work quotas.

- To give the participants a chance to generate and share ways to motivate employees and achieve organizational goals other than using work quotas.

Group Size

At least twenty participants.

Time Required

Approximately one hour and ten minutes.

Materials

- Ten pads of paper and ten pencils.

- Eleven coins (one for each of the ten production workers and one for the facilitator to use in demonstrating the procedure).
- A newsprint reproduction of Figure 1, prepared in advance.
- Masking tape for posting the newsprint reproduction of Figure 1.
- A felt-tipped marker.
- A calculator.

Physical Setting

A room large enough to allow the production workers to complete the flipping procedure and hold meetings while the observers watch. An elevated stage is helpful but not essential.

	Round 1			Round 2			Round 3			Round 4		
Worker	Salary	HP	%	Salary	HP	%	Salary	HP	%	Salary	HP	%
1												
2												
3												
4												
5												
6												
7												
8												
9												
10												
Total												
Average												

Legend: HP = "Heads" produced

Figure 1. Suggested Configuration for Recording Information on Newsprint

Process

1. The facilitator asks for ten volunteers to be production workers for the Flip-It Company. All other participants are to observe the activity and participate in the concluding discussion. The facilitator adds that he or she will function as a manager of the company until the discussion period. (Five minutes.)

2. The ten production workers are instructed to form a row in an area where they will be easily visible to the observers. Each worker is given a coin, a pad of paper, and a pencil. Then the facilitator leads an orientation session by explaining that the Flip-It Company produces "heads" (rather than "tails") in flipping coins. The facilitator gives verbal instructions and demonstrates by flipping a coin in the air with his or her right hand, catching it in that same hand, and then putting it on the back of his or her left hand. The facilitator states that each worker is to record the results of each flip, either "heads" or "tails," on the pad of paper provided. (Five minutes.)

3. The facilitator asks the workers to practice the procedure for a couple of minutes. When all of them have mastered the procedure, the facilitator announces that the beginning pay for the job is $20,000 per year. Each production worker is instructed to complete Round 1 by flipping the coin ten times and recording the results after each flip. The facilitator posts the newsprint reproduction of Figure 1, records the names of the production workers, and lists their beginning salaries under "Round 1" in the "Salary" column. When all workers have completed the ten flips, the facilitator asks for individual results and records those results under "Round 1" in the "HP" column. In addition, the facilitator calculates the percentage of heads for each worker and records that percentage under "Round 1" in the "%" column. Average heads produced and an average percentage for the worker group are also calculated and recorded. *Note:* The boxes for Total Salary and Average Salary are not applicable. (Ten minutes.)

4. The facilitator (acting as manager) calls for a meeting of the Flip-It Company workers. During this meeting the facilitator announces that the Flip-It Company has hired the Variance Corporation (VARCO) to help streamline the work process and ensure worker motivation. After extensive study VARCO has informed Flip-It that the average worker should produce 50 percent "heads" per year. The facilitator then announces the company average for the year thus far (recorded under "Round 1" in the box for Average %) and subsequently either praises or blames the production workers,

depending on whether they met or failed to meet this percentage. The facilitator delivers the praise or blame in an impassioned way, pointing with pride to the workers who met or exceeded 50 percent and stating that those who did not meet the 50-percent level did not try hard and were unwilling to pull their own weight. (Five minutes.)

5. The facilitator then announces that the company management has implemented a new incentive plan. All those who met the level of 50 percent "heads" in Round 1 will continue to be paid $20,000; those who exceeded the standard will receive $1,000 per year for each 10-percent increase over 50 percent; and those who failed to meet the standard will have their pay reduced $1,000 per year for each 10 percent under 50 percent. The facilitator records the new salaries under "Round 2," reminding the workers that this pay reflects their performance during Round 1. (Five minutes.)

6. Round 2 (another ten flips per worker) is initiated and the results recorded as in Round 1. A meeting is held with the same format as the first meeting. Salaries are adjusted as indicated in Step 5 and are recorded under "Round 3." Then the facilitator announces a bonus plan for Round 3: Those who exceed the work quota by 30 percent will earn an all-expense-paid trip to Disneyland, and those who exceed the quota by 40 percent will earn a trip to Hawaii with all expenses paid. (Ten minutes.)

7. Round 3 (another ten flips per worker) is held and the results recorded as in the previous two rounds. The facilitator presents bonus trips to the appropriate workers and then announces that the Flip-It Company has found it necessary to reduce its number of worker personnel: Any worker who did not produce 50 percent or more "heads" in Round 3 is fired. (Ten minutes.)

8. The facilitator announces the end of the role play, drops the role of manager, and asks the following questions:

   ■ What did you experience as you worked under this system of work quotas? What worker behaviors did the observers notice? What systems or situations like this one have you experienced before?

   ■ What are the similarities in people's reactions to this quota system? What are the differences? What can you generalize about reactions to working under a system of work quotas?

   ■ What does the work-quota system take into account in terms of expected results? What does it not account for?

- What are the results for the organization in operating under the work-quota system?

- What are some ways to motivate employees to achieve organizational goals without using work quotas?

- What ideas can you apply in your own job or organization as a result of this activity?

(Fifteen to twenty minutes.)

Variation

- To reduce the time required, the facilitator may omit a round.

Originally published in The 1996 Annual: Volume 2, Consulting

11

The Robotics Decision: Solving Strategic Problems[1]

Charles H. Smith

Goals

- To introduce the participants to the Strategic Assumption Surfacing and Testing (SAST) process as a tool for solving complex strategic problems.

- To offer the participants an opportunity to use the SAST process in solving a sample problem.

Group Size

Four subgroups of three to seven members each.

Time Required

Approximately three and one-half hours.

---

1. This activity is based on the Strategic Assumption Surfacing and Testing (SAST) process developed by R.O. Mason and I.I. Mitroff and described in *Challenging Strategic Planning Assumptions* by R.O. Mason and I.I. Mitroff, 1981, New York: Wiley Inter-Science, copyright © 1981 by John Wiley & Sons. The SAST process is incorporated into this design by permission of the publisher and R.O. Mason.

Materials

- A copy of The Robotics Decision Theory Sheet for each participant.
- A copy of The Robotics Decision Case History Sheet for each participant.
- A copy of The Robotics Decision Assumption Rating Work Sheet for each participant.
- Several sheets of blank paper and a pencil for each participant.
- A clipboard or other portable writing surface for each participant.
- A newsprint flip chart and several felt-tipped markers for each subgroup.
- A newsprint flip chart and a felt-tipped marker for the facilitator's use.
- Masking tape for posting newsprint.

Physical Setting

A room large enough so that the individual subgroups can work without disturbing one another. Movable chairs should be provided.

Process

1. The facilitator introduces the goals of the activity, distributes copies of the theory sheet, and instructs the participants to read this sheet. (Ten minutes.)

2. The facilitator leads a discussion on the content of the theory sheet, emphasizing the importance of stakeholders and their assumptions and eliciting and answering questions as necessary. (Fifteen minutes.)

3. Each participant is given a copy of the case history sheet and is asked to read this handout. After all participants have read the handout, each is asked to decide individually whether he or she is for or against the robotics proposal. The facilitator offers these guidelines for deciding on a pro or con position:

   - If you find that you want to focus primarily on issues like profit, competition, and trends within the industry that could affect Elmire Glass and Plastics, choose the pro position.

- If you find that you want to focus primarily on issues like the social consequences of the robotics proposal and the potentially adverse reactions from the employees of Elmire Glass and Plastics, choose the con position.

The facilitator stipulates that no participant is allowed to remain undecided; designates one side of the room as the "pro" area and the other as the "con" area; and asks each participant to go to the area that represents his or her choice, emphasizing that each participant must be willing to complete the next several steps of the activity in support of the pro or con position chosen. After the participants have made their choices, the facilitator asks the members of the pro group to assemble into two subgroups of approximately equal size; the members of the con group are instructed to do the same. Each of the four resulting subgroups is given a newsprint flip chart and several felt-tipped markers; each participant is given blank paper, a pencil, and a clipboard or other portable writing surface. (Fifteen minutes.)

4. The members of each subgroup are instructed to spend thirty minutes completing step 3 on their theory sheets by listing the stakeholders in the robotics decision facing Elmire Glass and Plastics as well as one assumption about each stakeholder. The facilitator asks each subgroup to select one member to record on newsprint the stakeholders and assumptions that the subgroup ultimately identifies. (Thirty minutes.)

5. The facilitator distributes copies of the assumption rating work sheet, and the members of each subgroup are asked to spend fifteen minutes completing step 4 on their theory sheets by rating the assumptions generated during the previous step. Each recorder is instructed to complete a newsprint version of the sheet after the subgroup has discussed and debated the issue and determined final ratings. (Fifteen minutes.)

6. The facilitator instructs the members of each subgroup to spend ten minutes first reviewing step 5 on their theory sheets and then preparing a short presentation (three to four minutes maximum) on the identified stakeholders, assumptions, and ratings of assumptions. The participants are told that the purpose of the presentation is to express the results of the subgroup work as forcefully as possible, in the form of arguments for the pro or con position that was chosen. They are also told that the newsprint generated during steps 4 and 5 should be posted during the presentation. (Ten minutes.)

Variations

- With an ongoing group, the facilitator may substitute a real organizational problem for the Elmire Glass and Plastics case.

- The activity may be continued by having the total group extract the most important elements from each of the subgroup plans and use them to devise a final action plan to solve the robotics problem.

- A different approach may be used to create the subgroups in step 3 by having the different subgroups represent the richer stakeholder roles, such as unions, employees, stockholders, and the local community.

- If the major focus is on surfacing assumptions, the activity may be stopped after step 5.

Originally published in The 1989 Annual: Developing Human Resources.

THE ROBOTICS DECISION THEORY SHEET[2]

Those who attempt to solve strategic problems in an organization find it extremely challenging to try to consider all the issues and constituents involved. People often make the mistake of trying to simplify such situations and avoiding the more complex aspects. The Strategic Assumption Surfacing and Testing (SAST) process (Mason & Mitroff, 1981) offers a systematic way to analyze a strategic problem, particularly one involving ambiguous information, uncertainty, many stakeholders with competing interests, and/or a number of constraints. The following summary describes the basic steps of the process.

Step 1: Understand the Objectives of the SAST Process

Pfeiffer, Goodstein, and Nolan (1992) define "stakeholders" in this way:

> A stakeholder in the Applied Strategic Planning process is any person or group that believes it will be affected in some significant way by the outcome of that process, [such as] owners, employees, customers/clients, community, government, media, board of directors, vendors/suppliers, stockholders, competitors, social advocates. (p. 109)

It is important to study any strategic problem from the vantage points of all stakeholders and to surface not only the current assumptions of these stakeholders but also how they and their assumptions affect the problem. Either as a result of conscious consideration or by accident, any plan that addresses a strategic problem incorporates many assumptions about stakeholders and how they will react to an organization and its actions. For example, a plan for a health service organization might incorporate a conscious assumption that the number of possible clients in a given geographic area will grow at 5 percent yearly. On the other hand, an organization that is dependent on a supply of electronic components might assume, without conscious consideration, that the presence of many suppliers and large supplies at low prices will continue.

---

2. This theory sheet explains the Strategic Assumption Surfacing and Testing (SAST) process developed by R.O. Mason and I.I. Mitroff and described in *Challenging Strategic Planning Assumptions* by R.O. Mason and I.I. Mitroff, 1981, New York: Wiley Inter-Science, copyright © 1981 by John Wiley & Sons. Adapted by permission of the publisher and R.O. Mason.

Step 2: Form Subgroups

The optimal number of subgroups needed to complete the SAST process is three or four; two is the minimum, and seven or eight the maximum. Ideally, each subgroup would have three to seven members.

It is crucial to create subgroups that are very different in their perspectives on issues, and there are a variety of ways to form these subgroups. If SAST is being used to evaluate a pro or con position or clearly differing alternatives, opposing subgroups that support the positions may be formed. An alternative method is to engage in an activity that surfaces the differing orientations of participants, such as the Nominal Group Technique (Delbecq & Van de Ven, 1971). With this technique each participant writes the ten major issues that he or she perceives as critical to the problem under discussion. Individuals then share their lists and vote on the importance of the issues; those with the most similar voting profiles are placed in subgroups with one another. Still another alternative is to complete a value-clarification instrument such as the Decision Style Inventory (Rowe, Mason, & Dickel, 1986, p. 234) or a problem-solving style instrument such as a shortened version of the Myers-Briggs Type Indicator (see McKenney & Keen, 1974); subgroups are then formed on the basis of similar styles.

Step 3: Each Subgroup Generates a List of Stakeholders and Their Assumptions

The usual method used to generate a list of stakeholders is to think of the organization in its environment and identify all the key parties that affect or are affected by the problem being addressed. The stakeholders chosen should be ones that are important in relation to the position or perspective that the subgroup represents. The following questions are useful to consider when identifying stakeholders:

1. Who has an interest in the problem and its resolution?

2. Who can affect the adoption, implementation, and execution of any plan to resolve the problem?

3. Because of demographics or other factors, who ought to care or might care about the problem?

Then the subgroup members identify one or more crucial assumptions about each stakeholder's interests and behavior with regard to the subgroup's position on the problem. For example, if a government agency is identified as an important stakeholder, the impact that this agency is expected to have on the organization should be identified in the form of an assumption. The assumption might be that the government will pressure the organization to meet environmental guidelines sooner than financially possible.

In generating assumptions the members of the subgroup consider these questions:

1. What effect will our position/perspective have on the stakeholder?
2. How can we assume the stakeholder will react if a course of action reflecting our position/perspective is adopted?

Step 4: Each Subgroup Rates Assumptions

The assumptions generated during the previous step are rated with respect to importance and certainty. The most important of the assumptions are those having the greatest bearing (either supporting or resisting the subgroup's position) on the problem. The most certain of the assumptions are either those that are self-evident or those for which there is a good deal of evidence supporting their validity.

After discussion and debate among the members, each subgroup completes an assumption rating graph representing the results of this step (see Figure 1). Each assumption is assigned a letter and plotted on the graph to depict its certainty and importance.

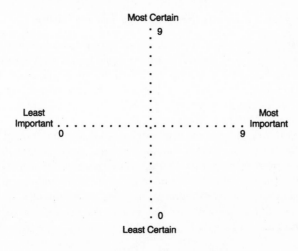

Figure 1. Assumption Rating Graph

Step 5: Subgroups Present Information

Each subgroup presents the total group with its list of key stakeholders and assumptions as well as the importance and certainty of these assumptions as indicated by the completed rating graph. One possible format for the presentation is as follows:

1. A clear statement of the subgroup's position and its four most important assumptions;

2. A list of the key stakeholders and an explanation of why they are important in relation to the subgroup's position; and

3. Display of a newsprint reproduction of the assumption rating graph with the four most important assumptions highlighted and an explanation of why these assumptions are critical to the subgroup's position.

As each subgroup presents, the remaining participants listen carefully and make notes about the assumptions that they believe are most damaging or threatening to those of their own subgroups. At this point the only listener comments permitted are requests for clarification.

After all presentations have been made, the individual subgroups reconvene so that the members can share their notes about damaging and threatening assumptions. Then a summary list of these assumptions is prepared.

Step 6: Subgroups Debate with One Another and Generate Solutions

The final step consists of debate among subgroups based on the summary lists of unresolved issues created during the previous step. After the debate new "synthesis" subgroups are created, each of which is composed of individuals representing the conflicting positions. Each of the new subgroups is given the challenge of competing with the others to generate the best integrative plan for solving the problem.

The winning plan should not be considered to be an optimal solution. Instead, after the winner has been announced, the participants should review all the plans presented, extract the important perspectives and recommendations from each, and create an integrated plan to which the total group is willing to commit. If final resolution of the issues is incomplete or impossible, the group can identify all unresolved issues and plan possible ways to move toward resolution.

References

Delbecq, A.L., & Van de Ven, A.H. (1971). A group process model for problem identification and program planning. *Journal of Applied Behavioral Science*, 7, 466–492.

Mason, R.O., & Mitroff, I.I. (1981). *Challenging strategic planning assumptions.* New York: Wiley Inter-Science.

McKenney, J., & Keen, P. (1974, May-June). How managers' minds work. *Harvard Business Review*, pp. 79–90.

Nolan, T.M., Goodstein, L.D., & Pfeiffer, J.W. (1986). *Applied strategic planning: The consultant's kit.* San Francisco, CA: Pfeiffer.

Rowe, A., Mason, R.O., & Dickel, K.E. (1986). *Strategic management: A methodological approach.* Reading, MA: Addison-Wesley.

THE ROBOTICS DECISION
CASE HISTORY SHEET

Elmire Glass and Plastics, Inc., is one of the nation's leaders in the production of glass and plastic for industrial use. The company has just received a proposal from United Robotics for the automation of its main production facility in Elmire. The change would entail full conversion from human operation to robotic production lines in the Plastic Components Division plant. This plant is the company's principal facility for the production of plastic components, which are used primarily in electronic equipment.

Elmire Glass and Plastics has been an innovator in the plastic components industry, and its components division has consistently yielded a 30-percent pretax return on investment. Although the demand for the company's component products appears to be strong, many of its competitors have recently switched to robotic production operations. This shift toward robotics is a source of concern to the company. Some industry analysts believe that robotics will transform the industry and will be a critical success factor in the future. Other analysts warn that robotics is a temporary solution, that it diverts attention from productivity and morale problems, and that the high capital investment required is not warranted because robotic tooling is not flexible enough to adjust to changing plastic product needs.

United Robotics claims that the pessimism of some industry analysts is totally unwarranted and that its products contain built-in design features that will ensure adaptability. The management at United argues that although the risk of obsolescence might naturally be high over a long period—say twenty years—the robotic equipment will have paid for itself five times during that period in terms of labor savings. Financial analysts at Elmire concur with this claim, estimating that the incremental rate of return from the equipment can reasonably be expected to range from 25 percent to 40 percent (pretax). This estimate is based on an expected capital investment of $50,000,000 and the generation of yearly savings between $12,500,000 and $20,000,000. The savings computations are based on current labor costs that will be eliminated by the changeover and do not include the cost savings due to increased efficiency. Although efficiency-related savings could be substantial, the components division at Elmire Glass and Plastics is noted to be a highly efficient operation with low defect rates and minimal employee absenteeism and turnover.

In addition to financial considerations, there are numerous other factors involved in the investment decision. This morning local representatives of the union (to which all of the company's manufacturing workers belong) met with top management. They voiced concern, resentment, and their strong opinion that even considering the robotic transition was inconsistent with Elmire's history and reputation as a family organization. They noted that although the transition might bring a substantial return in the short term, it would have an overwhelmingly negative effect on the entire company in the long term. The union leaders pointed out that other Elmire Glass and Plastics divisions, located both in Elmire and in other locations, would not stand for the changeover. They noted that the interdependent divisions that make up the company rely on many unionized skilled artisans and technicians and that these workers would be mobilized to strike if the robotic operation were implemented. The union leaders said that the integrity of the entire company was being threatened. Interestingly, middle managers and the secretarial staff were recently overheard in the cafeteria voicing the same concern and questioning the ethics involved in the changeover.

Other pressures are being placed on the company from the local community. The town of Elmire, with a population of 50,000 and located in an already-impoverished anthracite-mining area, has been hurt recently by other plant closings. The prospect of five hundred more layoffs as well as the possibilities of strikes by other workers and layoffs from future robotic implementations are bringing many strong reactions. Several members of the town council and the Chamber of Commerce have phoned Elmire Glass and Plastics to express their concern, as have several congressional representatives and a number of local businesspeople. For the past two days, picketers from Citizens Against Corporate Irresponsibility (CACI) have been in town, organizing demonstrations in front of the components division offices and carrying signs with slogans like "Another Step Toward Greed," "Your Choice: Robots or Food for Elmire's Children," and "Robots or Responsible Management?" Although the CACI is viewed as a moderate group and advocates nonviolent protest, a number of more threatening protesters, believed to be part of an organized radical group that has used sabotage in other manufacturing plants, jeered at managers and office employees who were entering and leaving the facility.

Three-year union contract negotiations come up for the components division in one year, just about the time the robotic operation could begin if a contract were signed now. At this point the top managers are divided regarding the best way to proceed. All agree that Elmire Glass and Plastics has survived through its years because of dedicated employees and that it has maintained a commitment to caring for its employees like family members. Layoffs have occurred in the past during difficult economic periods, but none of the magnitude of the one that would ensue with the robotic transition. The industry competition has never been so intense, and there is a fear that missing the opportunity to go with robotics and gain further competitive advantage would be disastrous and an injustice to Elmire's stockholders. A gradual transition to robotics would yield significantly lower returns in at least the next five years; also, replacements of retiring workers by automation would have its own unique set of problems, possibly acting like salt in a wound.

The need for a solution to this dilemma is critical.

THE ROBOTICS DECISION
ASSUMPTION RATING WORK SHEET

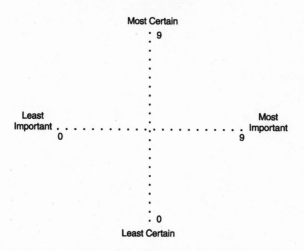

Figure 1. Assumption Rating Graph

12

Reviewing Objectives and Strategies: A Planning Task for Managers

Cyril R. Mill

Goals

- To review and evaluate an organization's accomplishments of the past year.
- To clarify and reaffirm the organizational mission.
- To prepare objectives and action steps for major organizational efforts in the next year.

Group Size

Eight to twelve people who comprise the top management of an organization or organizational unit, including the chief executive officer.

Time Required

Approximately three hours.

Materials

- At least six copies of the Reviewing Objectives and Strategies Sheet for each participant.
- Blank paper and a pencil for each participant.

- Newsprint and felt-tipped markers.
- Masking tape.

Physical Setting

One large room furnished with a work table, chairs, and easel for newsprint. Smaller rooms, furnished similarly, for individual or small-group work are helpful but not necessary.

Process

1. The facilitator reviews the goals of the activity (which have been listed previously on newsprint) and indicates that these goals will serve as the agenda for the session and that the majority of the time will be spent on the third goal.

2. Explaining that planning must be based on some data, the facilitator invites the participants to review the organization's accomplishments for the past year. The facilitator leads the group in brainstorming answers to the question "What have we accomplished during the past year?" The facilitator may ask prodding questions during this step and/or may post a list to encourage the participants to think in terms of such things as size, growth, profit, new organizational structures, new policies, new personnel, new technical resources, new linkages to outside groups, impact on the market or community, events (e.g, conferences), awards, and new learnings. All answers are listed on newsprint, and the list then is reviewed to eliminate redundancies and nonpertinent items. (Fifteen minutes.)

3. Immediately following the brainstorming phase, the facilitator distributes blank paper and pencils to the participants and asks for a rating of degree of individual satisfaction with the past year. Each member is directed to prepare a rating based on the following scale:

   I feel satisfied (or dissatisfied) with what we have done, to the following extent:

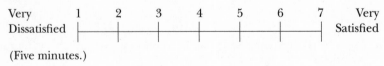

   Very Dissatisfied 1 2 3 4 5 6 7 Very Satisfied

   (Five minutes.)

4. The ratings are collected, and the results are posted on newsprint on a single scale so that everyone can see the overall ratings. The facilitator solicits comments on the ratings. (Ten minutes.)

5. The brainstorming procedure is repeated for the question "What have been our organizational failures or shortcomings during the past year?" (Participants may be reluctant to speak openly about failures because these often are perceived as personal—rather than as organizational—weaknesses. If this proves to be the case, before beginning the brainstorming activity, the facilitator can initiate a standard of confidentiality and discuss the issue of openness in confronting weaknesses.) (Ten minutes.)

6. The list of organizational weaknesses is reviewed and narrowed down by the participants. (Ten minutes.)

7. The facilitator introduces the goal of clarifying and reaffirming the organizational mission by commenting on the following points:

   - A management team should be clear about and in agreement on the organization's mission.

   - All activities of an organization should help to achieve its mission.

   - A mission statement may be a phrase, a few sentences, or even a lengthy document.

8. The facilitator announces that the group's task at this point is to state the organization's mission in a few sentences with which all agree. The facilitator serves as process and catalytic consultant during the group's discussion, which concludes with the writing of a mission statement on newsprint. Guidelines for the discussion may include:

   - State a goal rather than *operations*. A mission is more related to purpose than it is to activities.

   - A statement can be too broad or too narrow, thus limiting its usefulness. Avoid high-sounding generalities as well as specifics.

   - The statement should distinguish this organization from others.

   - Throughout the discussion, be alert to problems of interpretation or emphasis and work to clarify and rationalize these differences.

   (Thirty minutes.)

9. The facilitator explains that the third goal, to prepare objectives and action steps for the next year, will be accomplished in two phases. In the first phase, which will take about thirty minutes, the participants will work

individually on familiar material; in the second phase, the group members will work together in planning new organizational efforts.

The facilitator gives each participant six copies of the Reviewing Objectives and Strategies Sheet and instructs the participants that they may either work individually or consult freely with one another and that their task is to prepare as many objectives and strategies as they can, limiting themselves to present operations and ongoing tasks. The facilitator states that the emphasis of the activity is on quantity of ideas rather than on technicalities and reminds the group members that an objective is simply a statement of intention, whereas strategies are statements of steps that one will take to reach the objective. (Thirty minutes.)

10. After thirty minutes, the participants are directed to tape their Reviewing Objectives and Strategies Sheets to newsprint sheets and to post them around the room so that everyone can walk around and read them. (Ten minutes.)

11. The facilitator leads the group in compiling a listing of new areas in need of planning, using data from the group's list of organizational weaknesses, objectives generated from the activity just completed, and the group members' further reflections. A sheet of newsprint, titled "Changes We Want to Effect," is posted, and suggestions are listed on this. (Twenty minutes.)

12. The facilitator helps the group to discuss and select items from the list. As each item is examined, a written statement of objective, along with planned action steps, responsibilities, and resources is compiled and posted. (Thirty minutes.)

13. The group reviews the statements, summarizing and categorizing wherever possible. (The facilitator may suggest that the posted material be distributed in typewritten form as the work plan for the coming year.) The participants then identify any issues not raised thus far; these are written on newsprint and preserved as agenda for future staff meetings. (Twenty minutes.)

Variations

- If the group has difficulty in working through an issue during step 12, the facilitator can direct the participants to form three groups and announce that the task for each subgroup is to prepare three charts as follows:

- Chart I. State the issue or the problem.
   a. What do we do well?
   b. What do we do poorly?
- Chart II.
   a. Write a pessimistic statement that describes our approach to

   _____.

   b. Write an optimistic statement that describes our approach
      to _____.
- Chart III.
   a. What objectives must be established to move from the pessimistic statement to the optimistic one? List three to five objectives that are clear and measurable.
   b. What strategies must be followed to accomplish each objective? List as many as are needed and indicate the resources that are needed.
- If a block of time devoted to "thinking about the future" would be more productive than steps 7 or 9, the following procedure can be used:
   - The facilitator comments that even though the future is unpredictable, it can be useful to ask "what might happen" and "how would we cope?"
   - The facilitator divides the participants into three groups, distributes four sheets of newsprint and felt-tipped markers to each subgroup, and gives the following instructions:

      "Your subgroup's task for the next ten minutes is to identify four significant trends, internal or external to the organization, that could have an impact within five years on your operation. Consider the four trends as future problems with which your subgroup will have to grapple. Write a trend or problem at the top of each of the sheets of newsprint."

   - Each subgroup is directed to give two of its newsprint sheets to each of the other subgroups. Each subgroup now has four new problems with which to work. The facilitator then gives the following instructions:

      "Identify strategies to cope with each of the problems you have received. Be as imaginative as you wish, but do not assume that you will have unlimited resources of money or personnel. Write your solutions for each problem on the sheet of newsprint." (Forty minutes.)

- The facilitator suggests that, as each solution is presented, the members feel free to cheer and clap to show approval of a solution as well as to boo and hiss to show their disapproval.

- The activity and instructions can be modified to meet the needs of temporary task groups by having the task-group members review their efforts to date and their strategies for the accomplishment of their task.

Originally published in The 1982 Annual Handbook for Facilitators, Trainers, and Consultants.

Reviewing Objectives and Strategies Sheet

1. Objective: (What is your intention; what do you plan to
        achieve? What end result do you want?)

2. Strategies: (What action steps will be necessary to reach the
        objective? If you are not the person to take these
        steps, identify the person who is.)

        a.

        b.

        c.

        d.

3. Who will be responsible?

4. Resources needed: (If money or people or other resources are
                          needed for this item, indicate them here.)

Skill Building

13

Feedback Awareness: Skill Building for Supervisors

Robert William Lucas

Goals

- To enhance the participants' awareness of the impact of feedback.

- To offer principles and guidelines for giving and receiving feedback.

- To provide a vehicle for practice in giving and receiving feedback.

- To offer the participants an opportunity to discuss and identify feedback characteristics and techniques.

Group Size

Four to six subgroups of four participants each. This activity is designed for use with supervisors as participants.

Time Required

Two hours to two hours and fifteen minutes.

Materials

- A copy of the Feedback Awareness Theory Sheet for each of the participants.
- A copy of the Feedback Awareness Procedure Sheet for each of the participants.
- Two copies of the Feedback Awareness Communication Sheet for each of the participants.
- Several sheets of blank paper and a pencil for each participant.
- A clipboard or other portable writing surface for each participant.
- Five newsprint posters prepared in advance:
  - On the first poster:

    The importance of feedback to supervisors and subordinates
    The roles of the supervisor and the subordinate in the performance-feedback process
  - On the second poster:

    Tips for eliciting quality feedback from a subordinate
    Tips for discovering whether feedback given to a subordinate has been effective
  - On the third poster:

    Procedure
    Brainstorm ideas. One partner records. (5 min.)
    Choose best ideas. Other partner records. Monitor behavior. (10 min.)
    Fill out Feedback Awareness Communication Sheet. (5 min.)
    Share ideas with total group. (10 min.)
    People in outer chairs switch places.
    Repeat first four steps, using new topics. (30 min.)
  - On the fourth poster:

    Guidelines for Giving Feedback
    Be objective.
    Be specific.
    Write about changeable behavior.
    Describe how behavior affected you.
  - On the fifth poster:

    Guidelines for Receiving Feedback
    Keep an open mind.

Listen. Do not interrupt, justify, explain.
Paraphrase the feedback.
If necessary, ask for example or explanation.

- A newsprint flip chart and a felt-tipped marker.

- Masking tape for posting newsprint.

Physical Setting

A large room in which the subgroups can work without disturbing one another. There should be plenty of wall space for posting newsprint, and movable chairs must be provided.

During step 3 the chairs for each four-member subgroup should be arranged in two pairs as shown in Figure 1. (When the subgroups have been assembled, each participant is seated directly opposite another.)

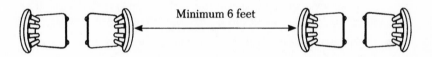

Figure 1. Arrangement of Chairs for One Subgroup

Process

1. The facilitator announces the goals of the activity, distributes copies of the theory sheet, and asks the participants to read this handout. (Ten minutes.)

2. The facilitator elicits and answers questions about the handout, clarifying the content as necessary. (Ten minutes.)

3. The participants are assembled into four-member subgroups, and each subgroup's chairs are arranged according to the configuration shown in Figure 1.

4. The facilitator posts the first, third, fourth, and fifth prepared newsprint posters. *(See Materials. Note that the second prepared newsprint poster is displayed later, after the participants have finished dealing with the topics on the first poster.)* Each participant is given a copy of the procedure sheet, two copies of the communication sheet, several sheets of blank paper, a pencil, and a clipboard or other portable writing surface. The facilitator reviews the content of both handouts while the participants follow on their copies and then elicits and answers questions about the content. (Ten to fifteen minutes.)

5. The facilitator instructs the participants to begin and uses the steps on the procedure poster to guide the participants. (One hour.)

6. After the steps described in the procedure sheet have been completed, the participants are instructed to distribute their completed communication sheets to the partners whose names appear on those sheets and to clarify written comments as necessary. The participants are reminded to use the guidelines for giving and receiving feedback. (Ten to twenty minutes.)

7. The facilitator reconvenes the total group and leads a discussion based on the following questions:

- How did you feel when you wrote comments about other people's communication techniques?

- How did you feel when you read the comments written about your own communication techniques?

- On the basis of your experience during this activity, what barriers can you identify as interfering with the feedback process? What might be done to remove some of those barriers or to reduce their impact?

- What have you learned about your own abilities to give and to receive feedback?

- How might you improve your abilities to give and to receive feedback?

- What will you do differently in the performance-feedback process in the future?

Variations

- The facilitator may ask the participants to concentrate on either giving or receiving feedback.

- After step 7 the participants may be asked to return to their subgroups. Within each subgroup two members role play a brief performance-feedback session while the remaining two members observe. Subsequently, the observers give feedback and all four members discuss the experience.

Originally published in The 1992 Annual: Developing Human Resources.

FEEDBACK AWARENESS THEORY SHEET

The following statements describe the appropriate way to give feedback to a subordinate. As you read each, think about whether it reflects your own behavior.

1. *Before I give feedback, I consider whether to do so publicly or privately.* I praise people in front of peers or coworkers, but I reprimand in private.

2. *Before giving feedback, I check my impressions of the behavior with others, doing so in a way that does not threaten or incriminate.* I understand that misperceptions on my part can lead to giving ineffective feedback.

3. *I provide timely feedback.* I give feedback as soon as possible after the behavior has occurred so that it has maximum impact for my subordinate.

4. *I avoid surprising my subordinates with performance feedback.* I tell them that I intend to provide regular feedback on their performance, and then I follow through.

5. *I am objective in describing behavior.* I base my comments on observation, not on conjecture. I describe the behavior fully before I offer personal thoughts or feelings about it.

6. *I state specific details, not generalities.* I avoid comments like "You did a good job on the monthly report." Instead, I say things like "Your monthly report was clear and concise, and the graph you included gave an excellent illustration of the changing trend in production."

7. *I direct feedback at behaviors that my subordinates can change.* I realize that it is *not* helpful to comment on a subordinate's stutter, for example, whereas it is helpful to comment on a subordinate's need to improve writing skills.

8. *After describing the behavior, I tell my subordinate what I think and how I feel about that behavior, describing its impact on me.* I recognize that comments about personal thoughts and feelings help my subordinate to put the feedback in perspective.

9. *After giving feedback, I verify that my subordinate has understood my message as I intended it.* I listen carefully to what my subordinate has heard; if the message has been misunderstood, I clarify as necessary.

10. *After I have given negative feedback, I give my subordinate time to make the desired change while I monitor the behavior in question.* I avoid constant negative feedback on a particular behavior because it is counterproductive and harmful. If the behavior improves, I praise my subordinate; if it does not improve, I consider performance-counseling alternatives.

FEEDBACK AWARENESS PROCEDURE SHEET

Procedure

1. You and your partner spend five minutes brainstorming ideas about the two topics listed on newsprint. One of you records ideas.

2. The two of you spend ten minutes discussing the brainstormed ideas and choosing the best ones. The other partner (the one who did not write previously) records final ideas. As you work, each of you monitors the other's use of the techniques listed on the Feedback Awareness Communication Sheet. Two minutes before the end of the discussion period, the facilitator announces the remaining time. Two minutes later you are told to stop working.

3. Each of you writes his or her name and the partner's name on one copy of the Feedback Awareness Communication Sheet and spends five minutes writing brief comments about the partner's communication techniques. Each strives to write feedback according to the "Guidelines for Giving Feedback" on this sheet. (Your facilitator will post these guidelines in abbreviated form for your convenience.) Until instructed otherwise, each of you keeps the completed communication sheet.

4. After five minutes the facilitator asks you to stop writing. The person who recorded final ideas shares them with the total group when instructed to do so. The other subgroups also share their ideas. As ideas are presented, the facilitator records them on newsprint, displays them, and leads a brief discussion about them.

5. The two people in the outer chairs (see the illustration below) switch places so that everyone has a new partner. The facilitator displays another newsprint poster with two new topics.

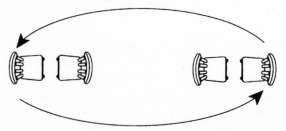

6. Steps 1 through 4 are completed again, this time centering on the new topics.

Guidelines for Giving Feedback

- Be objective in describing the behavior.
- State specific details, not generalities.
- Deal only with changeable behavior.
- Describe the impact of the behavior on you.

Guidelines for Receiving Feedback

- Keep an open mind; be willing to hear ways to improve.
- Listen without interrupting, justifying, or explaining.
- Paraphrase the feedback so that the person who gave it can determine whether you understood the intended message.
- If you do not understand, ask for an example or further explanation.

FEEDBACK AWARENESS COMMUNICATION SHEET

Instructions: Write your name and your partner's name in the blanks below. Answer the six questions, jotting down any specifics that might be useful to your partner. Then describe your partner's communication strengths and areas for development.

Your Name _____

Your Partner's Name _____

During the conversation, did your partner:

1. Use clear language?

2. Speak at a rate that you could easily follow and comprehend?

3. Use specific rather than general terms?

4. Avoid jargon?

5. Periodically verify that you understood?

6. Maintain good eye contact?

Communication Strengths:

Communication Areas for Development:

The Pfeiffer Book of Successful Leadership Development Tools © 2003 John Wiley & Sons, Inc. Published by Pfeiffer.

14

Delegation:
Using Time and Resources Effectively

Michael N. O'Malley and Catherine M.T. Lombardozzi

Goals

- To assist the participants in identifying barriers to delegation, the benefits of delegation, and which kinds of tasks can be delegated and which cannot.

- To present the participants with a method for delegating.

- To provide the participants with an opportunity to practice planning delegation in accordance with this method.

Group Size

Up to five subgroups of five or six participants each.

Time Required

Approximately two hours and fifteen minutes.

Materials

- A copy of the Delegation Theory Sheet for each participant.
- A copy of the Delegation Check List for each participant.

- A copy of the Delegation Record Sheet for each participant.
- Blank paper for each subgroup (for the recorder's use).
- A pencil for each participant.
- Newsprint and a felt-tipped marker.
- Masking tape for posting newsprint.

Physical Setting

A large room with a table and chairs for each subgroup.

Process

1. The facilitator introduces the goals of the activity.

2. The participants are asked to brainstorm definitions of delegation. As definitions are mentioned, the facilitator writes them on newsprint. After the participants have exhausted their ideas, the facilitator summarizes the definitions listed on newsprint and points out common elements in these definitions. The newsprint list remains on display so that the participants can refer to it later. (Ten minutes.)

3. The facilitator assembles the participants into subgroups of five or six members each, asks each subgroup to be seated at one of the tables, and explains that each subgroup's task is to discuss the reasons that people do not delegate and the benefits for those who do. The subgroups are instructed to appoint recorders to list these *barriers to delegation* and *benefits of delegation*. Each subgroup is given blank paper and a pencil for the recorder's use during this task. The facilitator further explains that in fifteen minutes each recorder will be asked to report the results of the discussion. Then the participants are instructed to begin. (Twenty minutes.)

4. The facilitator reassembles the total group and asks the recorders to take turns reporting the results of the subgroup discussions. As the barriers and benefits are announced, the facilitator records them in two separate lists on newsprint and posts the lists next to the one generated during step 2. (Fifteen minutes.)

5. Each participant is given a copy of the Delegation Theory Sheet and is asked to read this sheet. (Five minutes.)

6. The facilitator leads a brief discussion of the content of the theory sheet, clarifying as necessary and pointing out similarities and differences be-

tween that content and the information listed on the posted newsprint. (Ten minutes.)

7. Each participant is given a copy of the Delegation Check List and is asked to read this handout. (Five minutes.)

8. The facilitator elicits and answers questions about the content of the check list. (Five minutes.)

9. The facilitator gives everyone a copy of the Delegation Record Sheet and a pencil and asks each participant to think about his or her responsibilities and to list in the far-left column on the record sheet several tasks or projects that could be delegated but currently are not. It is clarified that the participants need not complete the other columns at this time. (Five minutes.)

10. The subgroups are reassembled and are told to be seated at their tables. The facilitator asks each subgroup to select one task or project from those listed by the subgroup members. Each subgroup is to plan the delegation of this task or project by asking questions based on the check list. To determine the appropriate subordinate for the task, each subgroup member is to consider which of his or her own subordinates would be best for the task and to present this subordinate's qualifications to the subgroup; then the subgroup members are to arrive at a consensus about who is best suited for the task. The facilitator instructs each subgroup to select a recorder to fill out the first four columns of a record sheet (all columns except "Progress Notes") in accordance with the subgroup's plan. Then the subgroups are instructed to begin. (Thirty minutes.)

11. The total group is reassembled, and the facilitator asks the following questions:

- What kind of task did you choose to delegate?

- What type of subordinate did you choose to do the work?

- What feelings did you experience in thinking about delegating the task to the particular person chosen?

- What discoveries did you make about the delegation process?

- How do your discoveries fit with what happens in your organization? How do they fit with the information about delegation in the theory sheet?

- How can you ensure that you will follow through on delegating the tasks you listed on your own personal copy of the record sheet?

(Twenty minutes.)

12. The facilitator suggests that each participant keep the handouts to refer to or use on the job. After making final comments, the facilitator concludes the activity.

Variations

- The participants may work individually to fill out their record sheets and then share with their fellow subgroup members what was easy or difficult about the task.

- After the check list is read, the participants may assemble into pairs (with one participant as manager and one as subordinate) to role play the planning and discussion phases of the delegation process, focusing on some task that could be accomplished during the session (planning a coffee break, rearranging the room, planning a follow-up session, and so forth).

- The facilitator may specify a particular task that he or she can delegate and may choose a volunteer (as subordinate) with whom to plan and discuss. The rest of the participants may observe the process by following the check list, reporting their observations, and giving feedback.

Originally published in The 1988 Annual: Developing Human Resources.

DELEGATION THEORY SHEET

Delegation is accomplishing organizational purposes through the proper deployment of people. Defined in this way, delegation is nearly synonymous with leadership. In fact, delegation involves skills that are requisite qualities of leaders. Setting goals, coaching, and recognizing performance are all elements of the delegation process and are essential attributes of leaders. Similarly, the aims of the delegation process and leadership are similar: to accomplish organizational ends while enhancing the abilities, confidence, and initiative of one's staff.

The benefits of delegation outweigh the potential drawbacks, yet many managers are hesitant to delegate in spite of the fact that most tasks can be delegated. Only responsibilities that demand personal attention, such as handling a performance problem, or duties inherent in the manager's job, such as setting his or her unit's goals, should not be delegated.

There are a myriad of reasons that managers use to justify not delegating. Few are legitimate reasons, and the usual consequence is impaired managerial functioning. Common reasons for not delegating include the following:

- Insufficient time;

- The perception that the job is too important to take risks;

- The manager's belief that he or she can do the job best;

- The fact that the manager enjoys doing certain jobs;

- A lack of confidence in subordinates;

- The desire to maintain control;

- Fear that a subordinate might do the job better than the manager; and

- Concern that the manager's boss will think that the manager is not working.

It is important to note that the extent to which delegation occurs reflects a manager's personality and sense of personal competence as well as his or her sense of subordinates' competence. Furthermore, a manager who does not delegate is not managing.

There is one additional reason that managers do not delegate: They may not know how. The process requires planning and patience; and, in general, it works best when the manager employs a participatory-management style. Consider the following two approaches to delegating the same task:

1. The manager communicates to the subordinate a need to inform the company's field sales staff about a new product by saying, "Copy this product fact sheet onto company letterhead and mail it to our two thousand sales personnel by next Friday."

2. The manager informs the subordinate what needs to be accomplished (notifying field sales personnel of a new product) and asks the subordinate to think about how this task could best be achieved. After the subordinate devises a plan, the manager and subordinate discuss it.

In the first example, the "delegation" offers the subordinate no room for growth or self-direction; the instructions are offensive in that they treat the subordinate as someone incapable of independent thought. In the second example, the subordinate's plan might offer no more than the obvious: copying the product fact sheet and doing a mass mailing. However, the climate engendered by the second example is qualitatively different from the one created in the first example; it includes the element of respect. The subordinate is trusted to develop a plan of his or her own.

The irony of a delegation process like the one in the second example is that the manager as well as the subordinate frequently learns from it. For example, the employee might know that the corporate magazine will be issued in time to include an announcement of the new product. This might be an alternative method of approaching the task that the manager had never considered.

The specific delegation process is conceived as having five phases:

1. *Preparation:* establishing the goals of the delegation, specifying the task that needs to be accomplished, and deciding who should accomplish it;

2. *Planning:* meeting with the chosen subordinate to describe the task and to ask the subordinate to devise a plan of action;

3. *Discussion:* reviewing the objectives of the task as well as the subordinate's plan of action, any potential obstacles, and ways to avoid or deal with these obstacles;

4. *Audit:* monitoring the progress of the delegation and making adjustments in response to unforeseen problems; and

5. *Appreciation:* accepting the completed task and acknowledging the subordinate's efforts.

When delegating, there are several important points to keep in mind:

1. Unless the manager can visualize and articulate what he or she wants in terms of results, the process will fail.

2. The manager must stretch the capabilities of his or her staff; repeatedly assigning the same jobs to the same people because they do them well does not foster development within the manager's unit.

3. The manager must let the chosen subordinate know how the assigned task fits into the unit's major objectives and to what extent the subordinate is empowered to act in the unit's behalf. Without this information, it is difficult for the subordinate to operate independently.

4. The delegation should never be revoked. Doing so undermines what a manager wishes to establish: initiative.

5. The manager should never accept unfinished or unsatisfactory work. Such acceptance communicates tolerance of low standards.

6. Completed work should be evaluated against the results that the manager wanted to achieve, not against the way in which the manager would have achieved them.

7. A satisfactory outcome should be recognized. Many delegations fail because hard work goes unappreciated and forgotten. At the very least, a successfully completed task should be rewarded with the chance to be given another challenging task at a future date.

DELEGATION CHECK LIST

Preparation Phase

Specify for yourself the goals of the delegation, what needs to be done, and by whom.

1. Specify the job to be delegated:
   - Results expected;
   - Materials, resources, and information needed;
   - Relevant policies and procedures to be considered;
   - Time frame for project; and
   - Others involved in project (suppliers, others doing parts of the work, and so forth).

2. Decide to whom the task will be delegated:
   - Consider subordinates' abilities, knowledge, interests, experience, attitudes, confidence, developmental goals, and so forth;
   - Consider subordinates' current work loads; and
   - Consider the types of tasks and/or projects that subordinates are currently working on.

Planning Phase

The subordinate who is chosen is briefed on the project to be completed and is asked to formulate a plan of action. A more lengthy follow-up meeting is scheduled.

1. Explain the reasons for delegation to this person.

2. Describe the project clearly (results expected and so forth), including how the project fits into the larger scheme of things. Ask the subordinate to prepare a plan of how the job could be accomplished and to specify what obstacles he or she anticipates as well as ways to avoid or deal with these obstacles.

3. Establish a meeting time to discuss the subordinate's ideas and determine how long the meeting will last.

4. Arrange for the meeting to take place in a nonthreatening location.

 The Pfeiffer Book of Successful Leadership Development Tools © 2003 John Wiley & Sons, Inc. Published by Pfeiffer.

Discussion Phase

Review the project objectives with the subordinate and discuss ideas on how he or she plans to proceed, what obstacles he or she anticipates, and how these obstacles can be avoided or dealt with.

1. Discuss the subordinate's plan of action and ways of overcoming potential obstacles.
2. Specify the resources that will be made available and make any necessary introductions to others who will be involved in the project.
3. Tell the subordinate how much authority you will confer.
4. Discuss how much follow-up to expect; establish checkpoints.
5. Emphasize the subordinate's responsibility for the outcomes.

Audit Phase

1. Monitor the progress of the delegation; make adjustments in response to unforeseen problems.
2. Make sure that needed materials, resources, and so forth are available to the subordinate.
3. Discuss problems and progress at designated checkpoints and/or as needed.
4. Offer encouragement; do not revoke the delegation or begin to perform certain elements of the task yourself.

Appreciation Phase

1. Accept the completed project and acknowledge the subordinate's efforts.
2. Do not accept unfinished, inaccurate, unprofessional, or off-target work.
3. Show an interest in the results; reward the subordinate for achievements.
4. Accept your own accountability. Do not blame the subordinate for less-than-satisfying results for which you may be responsible.
5. Review the delegation process and what has been learned.
6. Delegation record sheet.

DELEGATION RECORD SHEET

Task/Project	Expected Results	Person Delegated to	Checkpoints	Progress Notes

15

Constructive Discipline: Following Organizational Guidelines

Allen J. Schuh

Goals

- To help the participants to develop an understanding of the importance and complexity of discipline problems within an organization.
- To develop the participants' awareness of the guidelines that can be used to handle discipline problems.

Group Size

Up to ten trios.

Time Required

Approximately two hours.

Materials

- A copy of the Constructive Discipline Lecturette for each participant.
- A copy of the Constructive Discipline Data Sheet for each participant.
- Blank paper and a pencil for each arbitrator.
- A clipboard or other portable writing surface for each arbitrator.

Physical Setting

A room that is large enough to allow the trios to work without disturbing one another.

Process

1. The facilitator announces that the participants are to be involved in an activity that deals with constructive discipline within an organization. Each participant is given a copy of the Constructive Discipline Lecturette and is asked to read this handout. (Ten minutes.)

2. Questions about the content of the handout are elicited and answered. (Ten minutes.)

3. The facilitator assembles the participants into trios, distributes copies of the Constructive Discipline Data Sheet, and asks the participants to read this sheet. (Five minutes.)

4. Within each trio the following roles are assigned: *proponent, opponent,* and *arbitrator.* Each arbitrator is given blank paper, a pencil, and a clipboard or other portable writing surface. It is explained that each trio is to use the following procedure to analyze each of the five problems on the data sheet:

   - The proponent and opponent discuss the situation, the proponent supporting the position that the disciplinary action taken was appropriate and the opponent supporting the position that it was inappropriate.

   - The arbitrator listens carefully to this discussion, decides whether the disciplinary action was appropriate or inappropriate, and explains his or her rationale.

   - If the arbitrator determines that the action taken was inappropriate, all three members work to establish a better way to handle the situation. The arbitrator makes notes about the new disciplinary approach that is established.

5. The facilitator elicits and answers questions about the task, announces that each trio has forty-five minutes to complete its work, and instructs the participants to begin.

6. After forty-five minutes the facilitator asks the trios to stop their work. The total group is reconvened, and the arbitrators are asked to report their decisions and any new disciplinary approaches that were established. (Fifteen minutes.)

7. The facilitator leads a concluding discussion by asking the following questions:

- For those of you who served as proponents and opponents, how were you affected when you had to defend positions with which you disagreed?

- For those of you who served as arbitrators, how were you affected by having to choose between the two sides?

- How did the proponents and opponents react to the arbitrators' decisions?

- How often did disagreement result in your trio because the parties in a particular case problem had not followed the guidelines presented in the lecturette?

- What can be concluded about the disciplinary process in organizations?

- How does your experience with this activity relate to your back-home situation? How can you improve your back-home situation as a result of this activity?

Variations

- Within each trio the roles of proponent, opponent, and arbitrator may be switched for each case problem considered.

- The participants may be asked to use their own disciplinary problems as cases to be considered.

- The participants may be asked to use their own disciplinary problems for the purpose of contracting back-home efforts after step 7.

- Copies of the lecturette may be distributed after the trios have completed their task rather than before. Subsequently, the trios may be instructed to evaluate their decisions according to the guidelines presented in the lecturette.

Originally published in The 1984 Annual: Developing Human Resources.

CONSTRUCTIVE DISCIPLINE LECTURETTE

Discipline within an organization involves the administration of negative motivational techniques in response to rule infraction or other misconduct on the part of an employee.

Infraction of a rule occurs when an employee has been informed of a specific rule, knows that there are consequences for the inappropriate behavior in question, and then violates the rule by omission or commission.

It is generally accepted as reasonable, then, that employees know in advance what they are expected to do and what they are expected not to do. Forewarning tends to promote the desired behavior, and the burden of such forewarning generally rests with an employee's supervisor. When disciplinary action becomes necessary, this action should be constructive in that it should attempt to guide future behavior.

Certain types of misconduct that are not governed by written rules can also necessitate disciplinary action. An organization cannot and should not be expected to generate rules governing matters that are dictated by common sense or by some higher authority than that of the organization, such as state or Federal law. For example, no employee should require forewarning that he or she is not to burn down the company facility or physically assault a fellow employee.

Practical Guidelines for the Supervisor

1. The supervisor should build good relations before there are problems by being firm but fair and by ensuring that subordinates understand the rules of the organization.

2. If disciplinary action is called for, the employee's immediate supervisor should administer the action.

3. Disciplinary action should be administered as promptly as possible. However, the supervisor should take time to calm down if he or she is angry or emotionally upset so that the disciplinary action will be objective and fair. Also, extra time may be needed to obtain the facts about what happened. The supervisor must listen to the offender's side of the story.

4. The burden of proof is on the supervisor to show that a subordinate is guilty of an alleged offense. An employee should be presumed innocent until proven guilty. The amount or degree of evidence required varies with the seriousness of the charge; the more severe the charge, the more evidence

is needed to establish the guilt of the subordinate. If there is doubt as to an employee's guilt or innocence, arbitrators may be called in.

5. One of the main criteria used in administering disciplinary action is the concept of "just cause." In determining whether there is just cause for disciplining a subordinate, the supervisor must answer three questions:

- Can it be proven that the employee did, in fact, commit the improper act?

- Should the employee be punished for the behavior? The fact that the employee committed an infraction does not mean that he or she should be punished automatically. If industry custom, company tradition, past practice, or some other rationale can be given to explain or justify a specific behavior, it may be appropriate to waive the penalty for the infraction.

- Does the contemplated punishment fit the nature of the offense? When a violation occurs and does warrant punishment, the penalty assigned must be appropriate. This requirement prevents the exacting of severe penalties for minor infractions, such as the firing of an employee for coming to work late on one occasion. This provision is sometimes referred to as a "reasonableness criterion."

6. For moral as well as legal reasons, penalties must be exacted in a nondiscriminatory manner. In general, two employees should receive the same penalty for the same offense, although there are exceptions. To introduce flexibility into a disciplinary system, a range of penalties may be established for the same offense. Flexibility is both needed and justifiable. For example, if two employees arrive late for work, one may be verbally reprimanded and the other may be fired. This discrepancy in punishment could be justifiable if the verbally reprimanded employee had never been late for work before, whereas the fired employee had been formally warned repeatedly and had even been suspended recently for the same offense.

7. Strict consistency may not be entirely fair. Court judges and public administrators, who must strive for consistency in administering laws, use the term "strategic leniency" in circumstances in which some bending of the rules is wise. Such considerations as intent, provocation, inexperience, and temporary disability may justify more favorable treatment of one person than another. Of course, once an exception is made, the door is open to further appeals and to abuse. At this point it is important to recall the purpose of disciplining. If the subsequent behavior of the employees who know of the case will be improved by making an exception, then consistency should be

sacrificed. However, the supervisor who elects to sacrifice consistency should be prepared to make an exception for any subordinate in similar circumstances, and he or she should let the reasons for the exception be known so that it will not appear to be arbitrary favoritism. When handled in a way that is generally regarded as fair, adjusting disciplinary measures to individual circumstances actually can improve the effect that the discipline has on future behavior.

8. Rule infractions are generally grouped into two broad categories: minor or major offenses. No such classification could apply to all organizations and all situations, but examples of representative minor and major offenses are as follows:

Minor Offenses	Major Offenses
Loafing	Maliciously destroying any company property
Sleeping on the job	
Being absent without an excuse	Deliberately falsifying any company records
Gambling	
Engaging in horseplay	Physically fighting with a superior
Being habitually tardy	Carrying a concealed weapon
Producing defective work	Stealing money or equipment
Selling or canvassing on company property	Conducting oneself in a grossly immoral, indecent, or disgraceful manner
Failing to report an accidental injury	
Leaving the work area without authorization	Failing to obey safety rules
	Engaging in drug or alcohol abuse
Generating excessive scrap and waste	
Punching another employee's time card	

9. The main forms of organizational penalties, in the general order of their severity from mild to harsh, are as follows:

- Verbal reprimand
- Written warning
- Loss of privileges
- Fines
- Temporary suspension
- Demotion
- Permanent discharge

Violations of a minor offense are usually subject to a progressive penalty system; the second incident carries a stronger penalty than the first, and the third incident warrants an even stronger penalty. However, the first offense of a major infraction can bring immediate suspension or discharge. Loss of privileges, fines, and demotions are not commonly used within private business.

10. As a general rule, disciplinary action should be administered privately, but there may be exceptions.

11. After disciplinary action has been taken, the supervisor should attempt to assume and reestablish a normal attitude toward the disciplined subordinate. It is important that the supervisor express confidence in the subordinate's ability to improve.

12. An infraction should be erased from the offender's personnel record after one or two years. There is no justification for holding against an employee, in perpetuity, indiscretions of past years if the employee has reformed.

13. Sometimes there is a question as to whether an employee has actually committed an infraction of the rules. Consequently, an accused employee should always have the right to appeal to an authority higher than the immediate supervisor. A full hearing before higher authorities may be desirable to demonstrate to all parties that the accused person has been treated justly. The appeal system is also needed for situations in which the supervisor has not properly judged the merits or severity of a case. Still another possibility in serious cases may be the intervention of a union arbitrator or of a legal agency.

Constructive Discipline Data Sheet

Problem One

Stacy, the senior sales representative for the company, comes to work drunk one day. The sales manager sends Stacy home. The next morning Stacy comes in drunk, picks up a stapler, and throws it at the manager, who must be sent to the hospital for stitches and x-rays. The company discharges Stacy for insubordination, assault, and intoxication on the job.

Problem Two

The company has struggled to make it clear that absenteeism will not be tolerated. Within the past year, Terry, a highly skilled maintenance technician, has been absent without notice once or twice each month. Terry has worked for the company for six years and has a reputation for doing high-quality work, accepting almost any assignment unquestioningly, and working overtime when necessary. When confronted with the problem of the absences, Terry always promises to do better; however, the continuation of the problem led to a disciplinary layoff, and since then there still has been no improvement. Although quiet and uncommunicative, Terry is known to have family problems. There are six children, one of whom is always ill, and the home is run in a disorganized manner. The company reluctantly decides to discharge Terry because other employees are complaining.

Problem Three

The senior editor, Sandy, was assigned to a complicated project a year ago. Original estimates indicated that the project could be accomplished in six months. Sandy has been working diligently to complete the project and is deeply concerned that it is so far off schedule. For the past three months, the managing editor has noticed that Sandy has begun falsifying written reports about the progress that has been made. After the first incident, the managing editor discussed the situation with Sandy, emphasizing that the falsification must not take place again. After the second incident, the managing editor again discussed the situation with Sandy and wrote a formal reprimand to be placed in Sandy's personnel file. Finally, there is a third incident, after which the managing editor decides to remove Sandy from the project and to demote Sandy to the position of staff editor.

Problem Four

The general manager goes to the washroom and finds Dale, a machine operator, asleep on a bench. Without awakening Dale, the manager stuffs a dismissal notice in Dale's pocket. The manager returns from the washroom and discovers that the maintenance crew is repairing Dale's machine. The maintenance supervisor told Dale to "get lost" for a couple of hours.

Problem Five

The purchasing manager hears from a sales representative that Kim, the secretary in the purchasing department, is "selling" the manager's appointment time to sales representatives for gifts of liquor, theater tickets, and so forth. The informant, who says that the fee has been increasing recently, states, "We have to pay it because we can't afford to lose your account." The purchasing manager telephones the personnel department and asks that Kim be transferred to a new job "for personal reasons."

16

Vice President's In-Basket: A Management Activity

Annette N. Shelby

Goals

- To focus attention on the issues involved in setting priorities for communications in organizations.

- To increase awareness of the role of delegation in organizations.

Group Size

Four to twenty-five participants.

Time Required

Approximately three and one-half hours.

Materials

- A copy of the Vice President's In-Basket Background Sheet for each participant.

- A copy of the Vice President's In-Basket Organizational Chart Sheet for each participant.

- A copy of the Vice President's In-Basket Situation Sheet for each participant.

- A copy of the Vice President's In-Basket Calendar Sheet for each participant.
- One set of the fourteen Vice President's In-Basket Item Sheets for each participant.
- A copy of the Vice President's In-Basket Solution Sheet for each participant (optional).
- A pad of blank or ruled paper and a pencil for each participant.
- Fifteen paper clips for each participant.
- Newsprint and a felt-tipped marker.

Physical Setting

Tables on which the participants can spread out their materials, a chair for each participant, and space to conduct small-group discussions.

Process

1. The facilitator introduces the activity and states its goals. (Five minutes.)

2. The facilitator distributes all materials except the Vice President's In-Basket Solution Sheet to the participants and directs them to read the Vice President's In-Basket Background Sheet, Organizational Chart Sheet, and Situation Sheet before beginning to work. The facilitator tells the participants that they will have two hours to complete the activity and that they probably will not have time to finish everything in their in-baskets in that amount of time; therefore, they will need to make some choices about priorities and delegation. The facilitator announces the time at which the participants will be asked to stop working and to turn in their responses to the original materials. The facilitator then tells the participants to begin working, suggesting that it will save time if they clip responses to items as they go. (Five minutes.)

3. The participants work on their in-basket items for two hours. At the end of this time, the facilitator directs them to turn in their fourteen in-basket items with the response to each item paper clipped to it, whether they have finished all the items or not. (Two hours.)

4. The facilitator directs the participants to form subgroups of four or five members each and to discuss:

- Their thoughts and feelings as they worked through the activity.

- How they prioritized the items.
- How they decided which items they should attend to themselves and which should be delegated.

(Fifteen minutes.)

5. While the groups are conducting their discussions, the facilitator prepares the following chart on newsprint:

Item	Topic	Priority	Action	Reason
1	Internal Reporting Format			
2	Guidelines for Clarifying Material			
3	Rejection Letter Memo			
4	Rejection Letter Form			
5	Request from Eric Short			
6	Speech Outline			
7	Writing Checklist			
8	Clarifying Employee Benefits			
9	Note from Lorraine			
10	Newspaper Article			
11	Memo on Ad Meetings			
12	Annual Report Format			
13	Letters of Condolence			
14	Exhibit on Gross Revenues			

6. At the end of the discussion period, the facilitator reassembles the entire group and examines the disposition of each item, summarizing the group's discussions and writing in the priority, action step, and reasons offered by the participants on the newsprint chart. The Vice President's In-Basket Solution Sheet may be distributed at this time. If the following points are not made by the participants, the facilitator may advance them:

- The first working day after the trip will be Tuesday, May 26.
- Some requests have been on Hick's desk since the first week in May.

- Lorraine Short will not be able to type anything before Tracy leaves.
- Some requests (e.g., art work) require lead time.

(Twenty minutes.)

7. The facilitator concludes with a discussion of the following questions:

- How did your personal style of working help or hinder you during this activity? Did you handle work that was easiest for you or most essential for the company?

- What other options are available besides "Do, Delegate, or Dump" (e.g., working on the airplane, mailing in work from New York, calling the office between meetings)?

- What is the difference between delegating to a peer and delegating to a subordinate?

- How can the most important factors affecting priorities in this activity be summarized? What were the highest priority items? (The facilitator may give participants the Vice President's In-Basket Solution Sheet at this point.)

- How can this activity help the participants in their back-home work roles?

(Fifteen to thirty minutes.)

Variations

- In-basket items can be added or deleted to lengthen or shorten the activity.
- The background situation and in-basket items can be modified or rewritten to reflect the work situation of the participants.
- The participants can pair off after step 7 to reassess priorities.
- The subgroups can be asked to reach consensus on priorities for the items.
- Responses can be collected during step 3 in order to assess the participants' skills in business communication.

Originally published in The 1983 Annual Handbook for Facilitators, Trainers, and Consultants.

VICE PRESIDENT'S IN-BASKET BACKGROUND SHEET

The Acme Company is rapidly becoming an energy conglomerate. Begun as a partnership between Paul and Harold Anderson (brothers), the company incorporated in 1985. Although the Andersons retain only 25 percent of the company's stock, company policy and procedure remain under their tight control.

Originally an oil-exploration company, Acme has pumped resources into shale oil and coal development, setting up separate corporate divisions for each.

A major thrust now is in strip mining of both coal and shale. Acme's projected plans to strip-mine five hundred miles in Colorado and three hundred miles in Alabama have environmentalists angered, and they have filed lawsuits in both states.

"Sixty Minutes," a TV news program, ran a special last Sunday on what it called Acme's "excessive profits" and "rape of the environment."

Yesterday, an explosion at a test site near Steamboat Springs, Colorado, claimed forty-two lives.

Coal miners in Alabama's underground mines are threatening to go on strike next month.

VICE PRESIDENT'S IN-BASKET ORGANIZATIONAL CHART SHEET

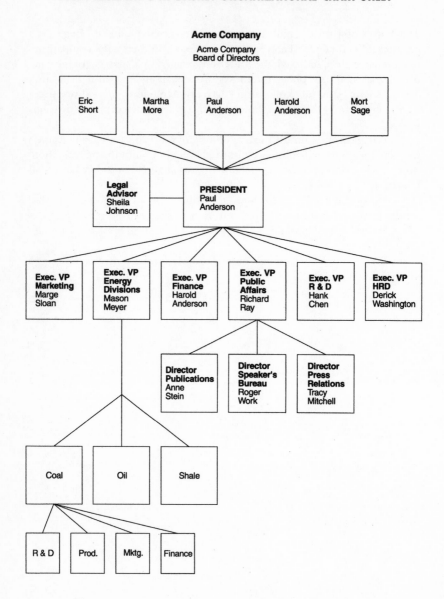

Acme Company

Acme Company
Board of Directors

| Eric Short | Martha More | Paul Anderson | Harold Anderson | Mort Sage |

Legal Advisor Sheila Johnson

PRESIDENT Paul Anderson

Exec. VP Marketing Marge Sloan

Exec. VP Energy Divisions Mason Meyer

Exec. VP Finance Harold Anderson

Exec. VP Public Affairs Richard Ray

Exec. VP R & D Hank Chen

Exec. VP HRD Derick Washington

Director Publications Anne Stein

Director Speaker's Bureau Roger Work

Director Press Relations Tracy Mitchell

Coal

Oil

Shale

R & D

Prod.

Mktg.

Finance

VICE PRESIDENT'S IN-BASKET SITUATION SHEET

Assignment

You are Tracy Mitchell. At 7 a.m. this morning (May 19), Paul Anderson phoned with the news that Richard Ray is in critical condition at Memorial Hospital following a massive coronary.

You (Tracy) are to take over immediately as Acting Vice President for Public Affairs.

You are to continue your liaison responsibility with the press and, Mr. Anderson reminded you, you are to sit in on the meetings in New York City this week to discuss plans for a new corporate advertising campaign. Although the campaign is primarily the responsibility of the marketing division, Mr. Anderson wants you to be involved because of your sensitivity to the public-relations implications. This is most important because of recent negative news coverage and the impending strike.

You are scheduled to fly to New York at 10:30 this morning. You cannot count on leaving New York before noon on Friday.

You have just arrived at the office (8 a.m.). By pushing it, you will have about two hours in the office.

Note: All typing and other secretarial work is channeled through Lorraine Jones. Neither Mr. Ray nor you has a personal secretary.

VICE PRESIDENT'S IN-BASKET CALENDAR SHEET

MAY					Friday	Saturday
					1	2
Sunday	Monday	Tuesday	Wednesday	Thursday		
3	4	5	6	7	8	9
10	11	12	13	14	15	16
17	18	19	20	21	22	23
24	25 MEMORIAL DAY HOLIDAY	26	27	28	29	30
31						

VICE PRESIDENT'S IN-BASKET
ITEM SHEET 1

Office Memorandum

TO: Richard Ray   DATE: May 1, 19___

FROM: Mason Meyer: *mm*

SUBJECT: *Internal Reporting Format*

With the expansion of our energy divisions, we need to standarize formats for our internal reporting. Paul suggested that I ask for your suggestions.

VICE PRESIDENT'S IN-BASKET
ITEM SHEET 2

Office Memorandum

TO: Richard Ray   DATE: May 6, 19___

FROM: Paul Anderson *PA*

SUBJECT: *Guidelines for Clarifying Material*

Rick, I'm calling on your communication expertise again!

OSHA has ordered that we rewrite mining procedures so that miners will be able to understand the safety instructions more easily. Currently, they are written in engineering terminology.

You'll be glad to know that I'm not asking you to do the rewriting; I feel that's best done at the job site. However, I do want you to draft some guidelines for simplifying material, which I'll ask Mason Meyer to distribute under my signature to all managers and line supervisors. They will do the actual rewriting.

VICE PRESIDENT'S IN-BASKET
ITEM SHEET 3

Office Memorandum

TO: Richard Ray   DATE: May 12, 19___

FROM: Derick Washington 𝒟𝒲

SUBJECT: *Rejection Letter*

    I need your help. The (attached) letter that we send to applicants we don't intend to hire sounds pretty harsh.

    Since PR is your "bag," Would you give the letter a once-over? Thanks.

VICE PRESIDENT'S IN-BASKET
ITEM SHEET 4

Date:

Dear Applicant:

    We have received your application for a position here at Acme. Unfortunately, we cannot hire you at this time. We know how tough the job market is these days and we do wish you the best of luck in finding employment.

Yours truly,

Derick Washington

Derick Washington
Vice President
Human Resources Development

VICE PRESIDENT'S IN-BASKET
ITEM SHEET 5

486 High Forest
Mulga, OH 33221
May 11, 19___

Richard Ray
Executive Vice President
Public Affairs
Acme Company
11312 Macon Square
Cambridge, IL 24613

Dear Rick:

I received a copy of the last annual report and want to compliment you on its production. The only thing that bothered me was that I felt it was a little too worker-oriented. It seems to me that we are interested in getting more investors. You had pictures of miners. But that's just my own reaction.

The reason that I am writing is to ask a personal favor of you. As you know, I recently have been re-elected as president of the Rotary Club here in Mulga, and we are celebrating National Industry Week, May 25–29. Could you send someone to speak at our Rotary-Friend Luncheon on May 26th?

Thank you for your attention to this matter. I hope that you can send someone.

Yours truly,

Eric Short

Eric Short

ES: an

VICE PRESIDENT'S IN-BASKET
ITEM SHEET 6

Office Memorandum

TO: Richard Ray   DATE: May 19, 19___

FROM: Paul Anderson *PA*

SUBJECT: *Speech Outline*

I received an invitation today to speak at the Chicago Press Club on
May 29. (Somebody must have died.)

Could you get a bare bones outline to me by noon on the 21st so
I can send it to research? Time is short!

I've listed a few ideas below, but feel free to add your own.

> Address environmental concerns
> We need to justify profits
> Take free-enterprise stance
> The work progress is key
> Should we talk about balance of payments?
> What about governmental regulation?

VICE PRESIDENT'S IN-BASKET
ITEM SHEET 7

Office Memorandum

TO: Richard Ray   DATE: May 12, 19___

FROM: Paul Anderson *PA*

SUBJECT: *Writing Check List*

I continue to be appalled at the poor quality of writing at Acme. Because you're our "in-house communication expert," please draw up a checklist that managers can use to give feedback to subordinates on writing problems.

Make the list short, simple, and easy to use, but make it comprehensive enough to be worthwhile.

VICE PRESIDENT'S IN-BASKET
ITEM SHEET 8

Office Memorandum

TO: Richard Ray   *DW*   DATE: May 4, 19___

FROM: Derick Washington

SUBJECT: *Clarifying Employee Benefits*

A recent survey shows that 58 percent of Acme's employees do not understand the company's benefit package. What are your ideas on how to correct this?

cc: Sheila Johnson

VICE PRESIDENT'S IN-BASKET
ITEM SHEET 9

Mr. Ray —   5/18

I have a dentist's appt.
Tuesday, the 19th, and will
not be in the office before noon.

Lorraine Jones

VICE PRESIDENT'S IN-BASKET
ITEM SHEET 10

From the Desk of
Paul Anderson

Tracy—
You'll have
to handle
this— Let me see a draft before you
leave town—
Paul A.

Rick— The
press is pushing for a
response. Let me see a
draft a.s.a.p.
Express regret, tell them we're
investigating, and generally
smooth the waters.
Paul A.

(STEAMBOAT SPRINGS, COLO-RADO—Yesterday about 5:00 p.m., an explosion claimed the lives of forty-two miners in nearby Brat's gulch. Survivors blamed the lack of safety precautions for the explosion. According to one miner, who does not wish to be identified, the company stored flammable chemicals nearby the construction site. A spark from the drilling rig ignited the chemicals. Spokespeople for Acme Company, owner of the drilling operation, could not be reached for comment.

VICE PRESIDENT'S IN-BASKET
ITEM SHEET 11

From the Desk of
Paul Anderson

Rick —
I've asked Tracy to
sit in on the ad meetings
in NYC this week.
Tracy will be out of
the office Tuesday through
Friday. Paul   5/18

VICE PRESIDENT'S IN-BASKET
ITEM SHEET 12

Office Memorandum

TO: Richard Ray   DATE: May 18, 19___

FROM: Paul Anderson *PA*

SUBJECT: *Annual Report Format*

Rick, thumb through several annual reports from other companies
and give me some feedback about formats we may wish to consider using
this year.

I think our research library should have copies of several reports.

VICE PRESIDENT'S IN-BASKET
ITEM SHEET 13

From the Desk of
Paul Anderson

Tracy—
While you're working on
that press release on the
mine explosion, you may
as well draft some letters
of condolence to the families.
Thanks!
Paul

VICE PRESIDENT'S IN-BASKET
ITEM SHEET 14

From the Desk of
Paul Anderson

Rick—

Prepare a preliminary sketch for an exhibit on the following data on gross revenues. This is to be used in Congressional testimony on the 27th (May). How about giving me two alternatives?

Data: Over the past five years, gross revenues increased from $1.5 million in 19__ to $2.3 million in 19__, $4.5 million in 19__, $5.9 million in 19__, and $7.1 million in 19__.

Vice President's In-Basket Solution Sheet

Using the Calendar:

1. Note carefully the dates and times that you will be out of town.

2. What are the implications of Lorraine Jones being out of the office until noon?

3. Note the dates of requests and the lead time needed to complete the materials (for example, the art work).

Setting Priorities:

1. *Speech Outline* (#6). The president asked for this material. Time does not allow you to put it off. You are not safe delegating it to Roger Work because his position is likely to be administrative.

2. *Letter to Eric Short* (#5). You may delegate the task of finding a speaker to Roger Work, but you need to write to Eric Short to tell him you have done so. A carbon copy to Paul Anderson would be advisable in case Roger fails to follow through. Because Eric is on the Board of Directors, he is too important not to give special attention to his request.

3. *Sketches* (#14). The president asked for sketches, and you have a time constraint. To delegate might be dangerous; although actual art work will be produced by someone else from your sketches, you need to provide lead time.

4. *Press Release* (#10). The president wants a copy on his desk before you leave town.

5. *Letters of Condolence* (#13). Time is a critical factor here, and you may not be able to trust anyone else with the "tone" of the letter.

Delegating Responsibilities:

1. Numbers 1, 2, 3, 4, 7, 8, and 12 probably can be delegated to others. However, you must ultimately take responsibility for their work. You must decide whether you want to see the work before it goes out and whether this will be possible. You need to build in some checkpoints.

2. Delegating work for which the president of the company is holding you personally responsible may not be a good idea.

3. You must be careful about delegating too much to any one individual. That person also has other work to do, and yours may not receive top priority.

4. Some items can be taken to New York.

5. You must leave very clear instructions for Lorraine Jones.

Throwing Away:

Items 9 and 11 should be thrown away.

17

Under Pressure: Managing Time Effectively

Glenn H. Varney

Goals

- To focus attention on the HR/OD issues involved in setting priorities under pressure of deadlines.
- To increase awareness of the role of empowering others in organizations.
- To examine one's time-management skills.

Group Size

Up to thirty participants who are practicing human resource professionals or consultants.

Time Required

Two hours and ten minutes.

Materials

- One copy of the Under Pressure Background Sheet for each of the participants.
- One copy of the Under Pressure Decision/Action Form for each of the participants.

- One set of the fifteen Under Pressure Items for each of the participants.
- A pad of paper, a pencil, and fifteen paper clips for each participant.
- A newsprint poster prepared in advance with the information from the Under Pressure Decision/Action Form:

Item	Topic	Priority	Time Allotted	Who Will Handle the Item?	What Will Be Done with the Item?	Reasons?
1	Bill Bother					
2	Glades Brown					
3	Charles					
4	Outline					
5	Mike Pike					
6	Henry McDonald					
7	Dale Blake					
8	Roulf Shouve					
9	Mary					
10	Chris					
11	Batfield					
12	Robin Smith					
13	Hardy Push					
14	Ben Drake					
15	Terry Piper					

Legend: "A" priority = Handle Before the Meeting
"B" priority = Handle Today After the Meeting
"C" priority = Handle Tomorrow
"D" priority = Delegate

- One copy of the Under Pressure Suggested Response Sheet for the facilitator's use.

- A newsprint flip chart and a felt-tipped marker.
- Masking tape for posting newsprint.

Physical Setting

Tables on which participants can spread out their materials, a chair for each participant, and space to conduct small-group discussions.

Process

1. The facilitator introduces the activity and its goals. (Five minutes.)
2. Each participant is given the following materials:
   - A copy of the Under Pressure Background Sheet.
   - A copy of the Under Pressure Decision/Action Form.
   - A set of the fifteen Under Pressure Items.
   - A pad of paper, a pencil, and fifteen paper clips.

   (Five minutes.)
3. The participants are instructed to read the Under Pressure Background Sheet before beginning to work. The facilitator tells the participants that they will have one hour to complete the activity and that they probably will not have time to finish everything in their in-baskets in that amount of time; therefore, they will need to make some choices about priorities and delegation. The facilitator announces the time at which the participants will be expected to have finished setting priorities and delegating tasks. The facilitator then tells the participants to begin working, suggesting that it will save time if they clip notes to the items as they go along indicating how they plan to handle them. (Sixty-five minutes.)
4. At the end of one hour, the facilitator calls time and directs the participants to form subgroups of four or five members each. Each subgroup is instructed to discuss the following topics:
   - Their thoughts and feelings as they worked through the activity.
   - Their criteria for deciding priorities and the importance assigned to each item.
   - How they decided which items they should attend to themselves and which should be delegated.

   (Twenty minutes.)

5. At the end of the discussion period, the facilitator reassembles the total group and posts the newsprint poster listing the in-basket items to be handled. The group uses majority rule to designate each item as "A," "B," "C," or "D" priority and to indicate whether the item should be handled personally or delegated. The facilitator explains that each item will be assigned a priority, as listed on the newsprint poster. "A" priority indicates that the item should be handled before the meeting; "B" priority indicates that the item should be handled today after the meeting; "C" priority indicates that the item should be handled tomorrow; and "D" priority indicates that the item should be delegated. In addition, the group provides an estimate of the time required to accomplish that item. (Fifteen minutes.)

6. The facilitator leads the group in a concluding discussion based on the following questions:

- How did your personal style of working help or hinder you during this activity? Did you handle work that was easiest for you or most essential for the company?

- What other options are available besides do it, delegate it, or file it?

- How can the most important factors in managing time effectively be summarized?

- What can you now do differently in prioritizing and delegating?

(Twenty minutes.)

Variations

- Items can be added or deleted to lengthen or shorten the activity.

- The background situation and items can be modified or rewritten to reflect the work situation of the participants.

- The facilitator may elect to establish pairs or teams, rather than having participants work alone.

- Participants can work together on actual responses to memos, phone calls, and visits.

Originally published in The 1996 Annual: Volume 2, Consulting.

UNDER PRESSURE BACKGROUND SHEET

Instructions: The case you are about to study places you into a typical day in the life of an internal organization development (OD) consultant. Using your experience and knowledge of OD, you are challenged to address the various issues that face you. Fifteen situations need your attention. You are to study each situation and decide what action needs to be taken. Use the attached decision/action form to record what you decide to do. Keep in mind that you must try to satisfy your clients' needs without stepping beyond ethical boundaries.

The Rankton Company is a one-billion dollar division of a major company. The company produces auto replacement parts for international markets. The Rankton Division was acquired by the owner two years ago. At the time of the acquisition, Rankton had two new plants under construction in small-town communities. Both facilities were designed as world-class plants, using self-directed work team concepts. The new owners were attracted to Rankton because of these two innovative plants, as well as the fact that Rankton had a forward-looking management team.

The Organization Development Department was also considered a valuable asset by the new owners. The OD department is organized as follows:

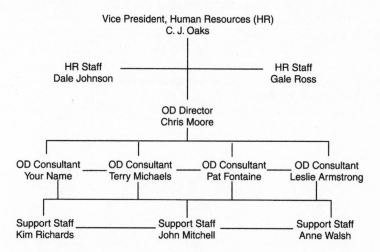

Organization Development at the Rankton Company is designed to offer organization-change consulting to twenty-one plants and a variety of staff departments. The Organization Development Department was organized six years ago with only one person; it expanded to its present size a year ago when you were hired. The culture of Rankton is considered to be unique and forward looking because of the participative style of the leadership. Many problems facing the auto-parts industry are affecting Rankton; however, Rankton has addressed these problems and is achieving considerable success in meeting competition.

You have just arrived back in your office at 10:15 a.m. on Monday, December 4th, following a meeting with your team leader, OD Director Chris Moore. The purpose of the meeting was to report the results of a weekend team-building session you conducted with nine members of the Engineering Department. You started this team-building session at 12:00 noon on Friday and ended Sunday at 4:00 p.m. In the middle of your desk is a stack of messages, correspondence, and fax messages. You have about an hour and fifteen minutes before your next meeting and you must get through the stack on your desk and still allow time to plan for your 11:30 a.m. presentation to the six maintenance supervisors in your largest plant. You want to increase their awareness of what the OD Department does. The outline for this presentation is Item 4.

You have thoroughly enjoyed your work at Rankton and have a good reputation for success. This morning, however, you feel tired and a bit frustrated because the weekend team building resulted in some harsh words being said. You feel that you may have let things get out of control during the day on Sunday.

Nevertheless, you realize you have a lot to do today, so you start through the stack on your desk. **Keep in mind you must make decisions and take action. Record what you decide to do with each item (1–15) on the Under Pressure Decision/Action Form.**

Under Pressure Decision/Action Form

Instructions: Following is a list of the items you must consider. Rank each with "A," "B," "C," or "D" priority, decide whether to handle it yourself or delegate it, and list briefly your reasons. Then estimate the time needed in order to complete each item.

Item	Topic	Priority	Time Allotted	Who Will Handle the Item?	What Will Be Done with the Item?	Reasons?
1	Bill Bother					
2	Glades Brown					
3	Charles					
4	Outline					
5	Mike Pike					
6	Henry McDonald					
7	Dale Blake					
8	Roulf Shouve					
9	Mary					
10	Chris					
11	Batfield					
12	Robin Smith					
13	Hardy Push					
14	Ben Drake					
15	Terry Piper					

Legend: "A" priority = Handle Before the Meeting
"B" priority = Handle Today After the Meeting
"C" priority = Handle Tomorrow
"D" priority = Delegate

UNDER PRESSURE ITEM 1

```
For    You              Urgent ☐

Date   12/1        Time  4:00 pm

       While You Were Out
M      Bill Bother

Of     Audio-Visual Dept.        ·

Phone   ext. 2323
        AREA CODE    NUMBER   EXTENSION

   Telephoned ☐          Please Call ☒
   Came To See You ☐     Will Call Again ☐
   Returned Your Call ☐ Wants To See You ☐

Message
You forgot to include definition

of the word "Intervention" on

the transparency you had us

prepare for you.

Signed_____
```

Note: This refers to an overhead transparency that describes what your department can do to help clients. You need this transparency for your 11:30 a.m. meeting.

UNDER PRESSURE ITEM 2

<u>Memorandum</u>

TO: You

FROM: Glades $\mathcal{GB}$ Brown, Director of Financial Planning

DATE: December 3rd

RE: Team Building

I have heard that team building is a valuable way to improve the effectiveness and productivity of departments such as mine. I have decided to hold a team-building session on December 8th and wondered if you would facilitate this meeting for me?

Please let me know as soon as possible if you are available. If you are not, I know a person who has facilitated similar sessions for a group at my church who could probably help us.

/dk

UNDER PRESSURE ITEM 3

I just looked over the data
generated as a result of
the survey we conducted last week
and feel that we have really made
substantial progress. This really
pleased me.

Just wanted to see if you agree. I' ve
attached the data. Let me know what
you think.

Charles
Nov. 28

MEASURES

	Pre-test	Follow-up
Task	3.1	3.21
Process	3.8	3.89
Interpersonal	3.33	3.48
Leadership	2.8	3.1
Performance	3.81	3.83
Total	3.36	3.50

Scale: 1-5
1 = Very Low
5 = Very High

UNDER PRESSURE ITEM 4

Outline

1) Introduction
2) What is OD?
3) Role of the OD Consultant

Supportive

Integrative

Persuasive

Analytical

Agreeable

4) Steps in the transformation process
5) Analytical Models

Sociotechnical

Force Field

Emergent Group Behavior

6) Interventions
7) Results from projects

Note: You need to put the finishing touches on the outline for your 11:30 a.m. presentation to a group of six maintenance supervisors from your largest plant. You are concerned about their level of awareness regarding what the OD department does. Look over the attached outline. Does it look OK? Is it too technical? What needs to be changed to meet the situation.

Under Pressure Item 5

```
┌─────────────────────────────────────┐
│  For    You              │ Urgent ☐   │
│                                       │
│  Date   12/4       Time  8:00 am      │
│                                       │
│       While You Were Out              │
│  M    Mike Pike                       │
│                                       │
│  Of   Engineering Dept.               │
│                                       │
│  Phone   ext. 2124                    │
│       AREA CODE   NUMBER   EXTENSION  │
│  ┌─────────────────────────────────┐ │
│  │  Telephoned ☐      Please Call ☐ │ │
│  │  Came To See You ☐  Will Call Again ☐ │
│  │  Returned Your Call ☐ Wants To See You ☒ │
│  └─────────────────────────────────┘ │
│  Message                              │
│   What the hell did you               │
│   say to Betty that upset             │
│   her so much?                        │
│                                       │
│                                       │
│  Signed_____  │
└─────────────────────────────────────┘
```

Note: Betty is a member of the Engineering Department that attended the weekend team-building session. She came to you during the session almost in tears begging you to please not ask her to participate. She said it embarrassed her to talk in front of the group. You agreed to back off. Mike Pike is an aggressive boss who "bores in" when he sees a problem and probably asked Betty what was going on.

Under Pressure Item 6

TO: Chris Moore, OD Director

FROM: Henry McDonald, C.F.O. *Henry McDonald*

DATE: 3 December

RE: Organization Development

My purpose in writing you is to express my view of the work being performed by your department so that you will have the benefit of this information as you complete your budgeting for next year.

Quite frankly I have always viewed what your department does as a "frill" because it does not, in any way that I can see, contribute to the "bottom line." From all the reports I have heard most of what you do I would classify as "soft management."

To be more specific somehow you have aroused several of my department heads and have piqued their interest in conducting meetings they call "team building." I refer, for example, to Glades Brown who has scheduled December 8th for team building with one of your staff. She is sold on the idea and no amount of persuasion on my part seems to change her mind.

I want you to give me a report that shows me just how much this type of effort contributes to reducing costs and making us more efficient. Please have this to me by December 6th.

cc: "Your Name"
/jk

FAX TRANSMITTAL SHEET

Rankton Corporation
Forward Plant

Confidential

To: "Your Name"

From: Dale Blake, Plant Manager

Re: Pat Barnes

Please send Pat Barnes' Myers-Briggs test results to me today
We are considering Pat for a promotion and this information
will help us in our decision.

Note: The Myers-Briggs test is a personality inventory that
was used in a team-building meeting with a production
coordinator in the Forward Plant.

UNDER PRESSURE ITEM 8

Creative Design Changes Group, Ltd.
400 Front Level Rd.
New York, NY 10001
216-888-8818

Mr./Ms. "Your Name"
OD Consultant
Rankton Company

Dear Mr./Ms. "Your Name"

We have heard great things about your company's work in QWL. We are specialists in quality-of-work-life (QWL) installation, and we have a five-step installation process that guarantees success.

An associate of mine and I will be in your area on December 5th and would like to stop by to show you what we can offer your organization.

If we don't hear from you, we'll plan to stop by at 11:30 a.m. Please let us know if this conflicts with your schedule.

Sincerely,

Rolf Shouve
Senior Partner
/st

Note: Ranton has two well-developed self-directed work sites to which these consultants probably are referring.

MESSAGE:

Francis Jones from the Local Chapter of the M.I.S. Society called and would like you to address the group at the January 7th meeting on the subject of "Selling Staff on System Change." Needs an answer today.

Mary

Under Pressure Item 10

You promised to look over the
attached survey that I want
to use to measure "employee attitude"
in my 200-person plant. I need your
comments today.

Thanks,
Plant Manager

OPINION SURVEY

The purpose of this survey is to collect your opinions on a number of things
going on around the plant. Please give us your honest opinion by checking the
box that most closely represents your viewpoint. When you are finished, put this
in the envelope provided and give it to your supervisor.

	I agree with the statement.	I disagree with the statement.
1) The quality of work life here is good.	☐	☐
2) My pay is good.	☐	☐
3) My benefits are fine.	☐	☐
4) I have a good supervisor.	☐	☐
5) The productivity of the plant is high.	☐	☐
6) Cooperation among my fellow workers is good.	☐	☐
7) Working conditions are good.	☐	☐
8) The plant is well managed.	☐	☐
9) I have a future here.	☐	☐
10) We make the best products in the business.	☐	☐

You may sign your name if you wish.

UNDER PRESSURE ITEM 11

Call Batfield plant manager!

Note: This is a penciled note to yourself from your morning meeting with the OD Director. The Batfield plant manager wants to talk about installing self-directed work teams as a way to eliminate one "full layer" of management. You need to call him before 11:30 a.m. The reason that the self-directed work teams and other quality tools meet opposition is that they are seen as another form of downsizing. You want to explain how self-directed work teams work in the two successful plants, and perhaps offer tours of those plants. What approach will you use when you talk to him about it?

UNDER PRESSURE ITEM 12

Situation: It is 10:45 a.m. Robin Smith appears at your door and asks for a "minute" of your time to interpret the results of the Teamwork Survey data (attached) that you sent last week.

You explain that you have only a few minutes but will be glad to assist. Robin sits down; what do you say?

Section I—SUMMARY DATA

Overall Results
Team N = 11

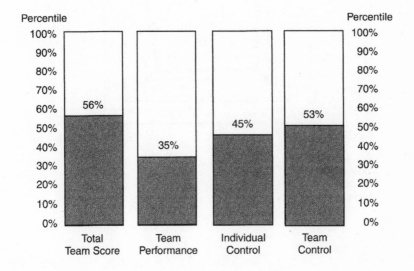

Section II—SUMMARY DATA

Effectiveness Profile

TASK 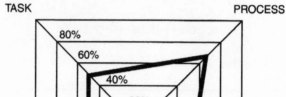 PROCESS

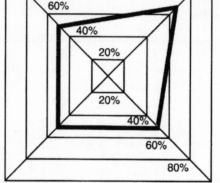

LEADERSHIP INTERPERSONAL

Task = 51%
Process = 63%
Interpersonal = 49%
Leadership = 49%

The Pfeiffer Book of Successful Leadership Development Tools © 2003 John Wiley & Sons, Inc. Published by Pfeiffer.

Under Pressure Item 13

```
For    You              Urgent ☐

Date   12/4        Time  8:30 am
       While You Were Out
M      Hardy Push

Of     Marketing

Phone  ext. 2262
       AREA CODE    NUMBER    EXTENSION

   Telephoned ☐        Please Call ☒
   Came To See You ☐   Will Call Again ☐
   Returned Your Call ☐ Wants To See You ☒

Message
Could you have the conflict-
resolution plan ("model") to me
by noon today?


Signed_____
```

Note: Hardy Push had previously requested help in managing a conflict situation between two members of his department. You need to quickly sketch out an approach he can use to resolve the problem and get it to him before you leave at 11:30 a.m.

UNDER PRESSURE ITEM 14

For   You | Urgent ☐

Date   Time

While You Were Out

M   Ben Drake

Of Drake and Drake Employment

Phone   1-800-800-1000
AREA CODE   NUMBER   EXTENSION

Telephoned ☐   Please Call ☒
Came To See You ☐   Will Call Again ☐
Returned Your Call ☐ Wants To See You ☐

Message

Please call a.s.a.p. Has

interesting response from

IVT Corp.

Signed_____

Note: Ben Drake called you about two months ago about a position with IVT Corporation. You expressed interest, sent your resume, and two weeks ago spent a day interviewing for the position of Director of Organization Effectiveness. The position pays about 25% more than you are currently earning.

UNDER PRESSURE ITEM 15

Situation: The phone rings while you are in your office. It's 11:00 a.m. The person on the line is the Vice President of Manufacturing, Terry Piper, who wants to know why people are so resistant to new ideas and changes being made in several of the plants. Terry asks, "Isn't there some program or training that can be used to break down this resistance?"

UNDER PRESSURE SUGGESTED RESPONSE SHEET

Item	Topic	Priority	Time Allotted	Who Will Handle the Item?	What Will Be Done with the Item?	Reasons?
1	Bill Bother	A	5 min.	Me	Call with definition	Need for meeting; it's in my head
2	Glades Brown	B	10 min.	Me	Call after meeting	Importance of the department
3	Charles	C	5 min.	Me	Call and set up meeting to discuss	Completed— just needs reaction
4	Outline	A	10 min.	Me	Immediate action (if it needs to be retyped)	Language change
5	Mike Pike	B	10 min.	Me	Call	Already over; can call after meeting; ethically can't divulge this kind of information if trust is to be upheld.
6	Henry McDonald	A	5 min.	Me and delegate	Call OD Director and get staff working on data collection	C.F.O. needs to back the OD department
7	Dale Blake	B	5 min.	Delegate	If policy is to share information, send it; if not, call and explain why	Information is needed for promotion; if it's an ethical issue, it needs to be explained
8	Roulf Shouve	B	5 min.	Delegate	Staff to call and schedule at a convenient time	Fit into my schedule without being too reactive

Item	Topic	Priority	Time Allotted	Who Will Handle the Item?	What Will Be Done with the Item?	Reasons?
9	Mary	B	5 min.	Delegate	Have staff call and give an answer	I've already talked to Mary and can call personally another time
10	Chris	B	15 min.	Me	Read after the meeting and make comments	I promised
11	Batfield	A	10 min.	Me	Call	Per OD Director, need to call before the meeting
12	Robin Smith	A	10 min.	Me	Explain what it means and set another time to talk after the meeting	The person is there!
13	Hardy Push	A	15 min.	Me and delegate	Before 11:30, sketch out and have staff deliver with note	Previous request; important for department
14	Ben Drake	B*	10 min.	Me	Call after meeting	Need to keep this job for now
15	Terry Piper	A	10 min.	Me	Give a quick answer and set up a later meeting or agree to send information	Important person to have behind us

Legend: "A" priority = Handle Before the Meeting
"B" priority = Handle Today After the Meeting
"C" priority = Handle Tomorrow
"D" priority = Delegate

* Or C, depending on how interested I am

18

Interviewing: Gathering Pertinent Information

Kenneth L. Murrell

Goals

- To help the participants to become familiar with the interviewing process from the interviewer's perspective.

- To allow the participants to practice developing criteria that a job candidate must meet based on the nature and duties of the job.

- To assist the participants in developing ways to elicit pertinent information from job candidates.

Group Size

Three to ten trios.

Time Required

One hour and forty-five minutes.

Materials

- Blank paper and a pencil for each participant.
- A newsprint flip chart and a felt-tipped marker or a chalkboard and chalk.

Physical Setting

Any room in which the trios can work without disturbing one another. Writing surfaces should be provided for the participants.

Process

1. The facilitator delivers a lecturette on the process of interviewing from the interviewer's perspective. It is emphasized that before any interviews take place, the interviewer must determine the following:

   - The exact nature and duties of the job in question;

   - The skills and characteristics that a person must have in order to succeed in the job; and

   - Ways to elicit pertinent information from job candidates. (Ten minutes.)

2. The facilitator briefly explains the activity and its goals. The participants brainstorm a list of jobs while the facilitator records these jobs on newsprint or a chalkboard. Then they select one job from the list to serve as the focus of the interviews to be conducted. (Ten minutes.)

3. Blank paper and pencils are distributed. Concentrating on the chosen job, the participants use brainstorming to make the three determinations emphasized in step 1. During this process the facilitator records the results on newsprint or a chalkboard, inviting the participants to refer to the information throughout the activity. In addition, the participants are encouraged to jot down questions that should be asked of a candidate for the chosen job; it is explained that these questions are for their own use during the activity. (Twenty minutes.)

4. Trios are formed. Within each trio one member assumes each of the following roles: interviewer, job candidate, and observer. The participants are cautioned to maintain their roles throughout the interviewing process. The interviewer conducts the interview in accordance with information established during steps 1 through 3; the job candidate responds as required; and the observer makes notes regarding the interviewer's success at finding out what he or she needs to know about the candidate. After the interview the observer provides feedback about the interviewer's performance. (Fifteen minutes.)

5. Within each trio each participant assumes a different role; new interviews are conducted; and the new observer provides feedback. (Fifteen minutes.)

6. Step 5 is repeated, with each participant again playing a different role. (Fifteen minutes.)

7. The total group is reconvened for a concluding discussion. Questions that may be helpful during this discussion are as follows:

- How did you go about devising questions related to job criteria?

- What types of questions and techniques seemed to be helpful in eliciting pertinent information? Which were not so successful?

- When you served as a job candidate, which question or experience carried the greatest impact for you?

- What conclusions can be drawn about the interview process and the skills that are necessary for the interviewer?

- How does this activity compare with your own experience as an interviewer? as a job candidate?

- What is one interviewing skill that you can transfer to your own work environment? In what way might this skill be helpful to you?

Variations

- New trios may be formed for each round of interviewing.

- Each trio may choose a job on which to focus.

- The participants may be given sample job descriptions from which to derive their interviewing questions.

Originally published in A Handbook of Structured Experiences for Human Relations Training, Volume IX *(1983).*

19

Meeting Management:
Coping with Dysfunctional Behaviors

Patrick Doyle and C.R. Tindal

Goals

- To enable the participants to identify dysfunctional behaviors in meetings.

- To allow the participants to plan and test coping strategies for dealing with such behaviors in meetings.

Group Size

Two to six subgroups of three or four members each.

Time Required

Approximately one hour for up to four subgroups. One and one-half hours for five or six subgroups.

Materials

- A copy of the Meeting Management Work Sheet for each participant.

- One copy of the Meeting Management Suggested Rankings Sheet for every participant.

- A pencil for each participant.

- A clipboard or other writing surface for each participant.
- Newsprint and a felt-tipped marker.

Physical Setting

A room sufficiently large for the subgroups to interact independently and for a summary session involving all participants.

Process

1. The facilitator explains the goals and the process of the activity.

2. The facilitator divides the participants into subgroups of three or four members each and distributes a copy of the Meeting Management Work Sheet, a pencil, and a clipboard to each participant.

3. The facilitator directs the participants to work individually to examine each of the meeting situations described, assess the three suggested responses by the meeting chairperson, and then rank the various suggested responses. (Ten minutes.)

4. The facilitator directs each subgroup to attempt to achieve consensus on the ranking of the responses for each meeting situation. (Thirty minutes.)

5. The total group is reassembled, and each subgroup reports its rankings of the responses. The facilitator lists these rankings on newsprint. (Five to ten minutes.)

6. A copy of the Meeting Management Suggested Rankings Sheet is distributed to each participant, and the participants are given a few minutes to review these rankings and the explanatory notes. During this interval, the facilitator can chart on newsprint the suggested rankings compared to the group rankings. (Ten minutes.)

7. The facilitator leads a discussion of the most appropriate methods of handling dysfunctional behaviors in meetings by asking the following questions:

   - Which of these dysfunctional behaviors did you recognize? in yourself? in others? What reactions did you have to being in the chair role and deciding how to deal with the dysfunctional behaviors? What influenced your choices?

   - What, if any, dysfunctional behaviors occurred in your subgroup as you worked toward consensus? How did the subgroup deal with them?

- How are these behaviors representative of your experience in meetings? How are the chairperson's responses characteristic of what you have heard? What new insights do you now have for conducting productive meetings?

- What are some insights or methods you can take away from this activity? How do you envision yourself using them? What do you think the results will be?

Variations

- Each subgroup can be given a few minutes after step 5 to modify its rankings in light of the suggestions that have been offered by the other subgroups.

- The participants (or subgroups) can generate their own responses and evaluate them, either with or without referring to the possible responses now found on the work sheet or to the suggested rankings.

- The facilitator can create a competitive situation by singling out the subgroup that comes closest to the suggested rankings.

Originally published in The 1986 Annual: Developing Human Resources.

MEETING MANAGEMENT WORK SHEET

Participants in meetings generally exhibit a variety of behaviors, many of which are disruptive or dysfunctional. If the other participants in such meetings knew how best to respond to dysfunctional behavior, they presumably could minimize its impact and thereby derive more benefit from the meeting. In this activity, you will be presented with a number of meeting situations that have reached a critical point—critical in that the effectiveness of the meeting could depend on the response to the disruptive behavior. You will be offered three possible responses to each situation.

The purpose of this activity is to encourage you to consider alternative methods of responding to dysfunctional behavior in meetings and the likely impact of various responses.

Instructions: Described below is a committee meeting in which a number of "typical" dysfunctional behaviors arise. Three possible responses to each are presented. Examine each situation carefully and then rank the alternative responses in order of appropriateness (with 1 being the *most* generally appropriate and 3 being the *least* appropriate).

The Committee

The seven situations that follow all involve the management committee of a hospital, composed of the following members:

Stacy Spence, Executive Director (Chairperson of the committee)
Robin Bowman, Personnel Manager
Kip Troy, Finance Officer
Casey Brown, Manager of Auxiliary Services
George Jones, Manager of Information Services
Fred Hill, Supervisor of Maintenance
Sharon Dixon, Director of Nursing
Jody Graves, Public Relations Officer

Meeting Incidents

Situation One:

A meeting has been called to discuss the shortage of staff in the housekeeping division of the hospital. As Casey Brown, manager of auxiliary services, begins to make a presentation on the need for an increase in the cleaning and maintenance staff, Kip Troy (finance officer) interjects: "I don't see any point to this meeting since there simply aren't any additional funds available!"

Possible responses by the chairperson:

Group Ranking	Individual Ranking	
_____	_____	a. "If you really believe that, Kip, why did you come to this meeting?"
_____	_____	b. "How do the rest of you feel about proceeding with this meeting in light of Kip's statement?"
_____	_____	c. "That's precisely why you were asked to this meeting, Kip, because only you can identify potential sources of funding if the group decides that this staffing need must be met."

Situation Two:

As the meeting progresses, the chairperson notices that Casey keeps referring to an error in the last monthly financial report generated by Kip's office. The error was corrected and the matter is irrelevant to the present discussion.

Possible responses by the chairperson:

Group Ranking	Individual Ranking	
_____	_____	a. "As you know, Casey, that error was corrected very promptly, and I'm sure you'll agree that Kip is by far the best qualified person to advise us on the financial issue we face today."
_____	_____	b. "Casey, could you explain to the group why you think that point is relevant to this meeting?"
_____	_____	c. "Casey, if you have an axe to grind, please keep it out of this meeting."

Situation Three:

Later in the meeting, the supervisor of the maintenance crew, Fred Hill, states that the understaffing is causing a serious cleaning problem and that he doesn't want this group to sweep the problem under the rug. You notice that this is the fourth pun from Fred in the past ten minutes.

Possible responses by the chairperson:

Group   Individual
Ranking   Ranking

_____ _____ a. "Fred, while we appreciate your humor, we do need your expertise in solving this problem."

_____ _____ b. "If you keep this up, Fred, I'll have to call you on the carpet."

_____ _____ c. "Fred, will you please cut out the jokes so that we can get on with the meeting?"

Situation Four:

The chairperson notices that Jody Graves (public relations officer), who first brought to the committee the increasing public complaints about the dirty condition of the hospital, has remained silent throughout the meeting.

Possible responses by the chairperson:

Group   Individual
Ranking   Ranking

_____ _____ a. "Jody, you're the one who first brought this problem to my attention; what do you have to say about it?"

_____ _____ b. "Jody, in what ways does this discussion relate to your responsibilities?"

_____ _____ c. "You are very quiet today, Jody; don't you have anything to say?"

Situation Five:

Every time that Sharon Dixon, director of nursing, has been asked for her views, she has stressed the need for more information and further study of the situation—an approach she tends to take with almost every topic.

Possible responses by the chairperson:

Group　　Individual
Ranking　Ranking

_____　_____　a. "Sharon, this matter has been studied to death;
　　　　　　　　　　　it's time to make a decision."

_____　_____　b. "Sharon, where, specifically, do you think we
　　　　　　　　　　　need more information?"

_____　_____　c. "While your questions certainly have helped us
　　　　　　　　　　　to appreciate the background of this matter,
　　　　　　　　　　　Sharon, I believe that the time now has come
　　　　　　　　　　　to make a decision."

Situation Six:

George Jones, director of information services, arrived quite late and now announces that he must leave for another meeting (concerning the acquisition of new computer equipment) in five minutes.

Possible responses by the chairperson:

Group　　Individual
Ranking　Ranking

_____　_____　a. "Inasmuch as you just got here, George, don't
　　　　　　　　　　　you think you should stay awhile?"

_____　_____　b. "For heaven's sake, George, why are you in-
　　　　　　　　　　　volved in overlapping meetings?"

_____　_____　c. "George, perhaps we should discuss this later,
　　　　　　　　　　　to ensure that this problem doesn't happen
　　　　　　　　　　　again."

Situation Seven:

During the meeting, Robin frequently has been off topic and not very attentive. Robin is now whispering to Kip about matters not on the agenda.

Possible responses by the chairperson:

Group Ranking	Individual Ranking	
_____	_____	a. Pause in mid-sentence and look at Robin without comment, perhaps adding "Robin, I guess you have something to say here" or "Robin, perhaps the whole group could benefit from your remarks."
_____	_____	b. "Robin, could you please direct your attention to the matter under discussion?"
_____	_____	c. "What do you see as the personnel implications of this point, Robin?"

Meeting Management Suggested Rankings Sheet

The following are suggested rankings for the responses to each situation from the Meeting Management Work Sheet. These rankings are generalized; the appropriateness of any particular response may vary with the situation.

Situation One:

One common dysfunctional behavior faced by a new committee is the behavior described in situation one—that of the saboteur. In some instances, an individual may have been placed on a committee (or sent to a meeting) specifically to play this role.

Suggested
Ranking

___3___ a. The first response is a negative confrontation. You are playing hardball, but on the saboteur's ground. Such a response will serve only to accomplish the objective of the saboteur by provoking an angry exchange that will detract from the purpose of the meeting.

___2___ b. Although less confrontational, the second response may still divide the committee.

___1___ c. The third response has several benefits. It keeps Kip psychologically included in the group and, thus, does not create any division in the group at this point. If Kip's remark had stemmed from a lack of confidence in dealing with the other members, this response could affirm Kip's value to the committee. This response also would be helpful if Kip's basic point was valid. The discussion should proceed on the basis of some awareness of financial reality.

Situation Two:

The behavior described in this situation is referred to as sniping. It frequently is caused by difficulties between individuals that have arisen outside the committee's deliberations (although, in this instance, the sniping could have been prompted by the behavior described in situation one). Whatever its cause, this behavior must be addressed.

Suggested
Ranking

___1___ a. Consideration also must be given to the person who has been the target of the sniper. Kip should be reassured that it is not necessary to defend oneself from such a tactic and that an unwarranted attack on a team member will be dealt with openly. The first response meets these needs and also gives Casey an opportunity to make peace by agreeing with the chairperson.

___2___ b. The second response gives Casey an opportunity to back off while establishing the precedent that snipers will be asked to explain or justify their remarks.

___3___ c. The third response is the most inappropriate. It puts Casey down very bluntly and may cause Casey to withdraw from further participation in the meeting.

Situation Three:

This situation describes the comedian or clown at work. The comedian can make a valuable contribution, often by relieving stress when matters become unnecessarily intense. However, unless such behavior is confined to the appropriate circumstances, the comedian can be a distraction and even an irritation.

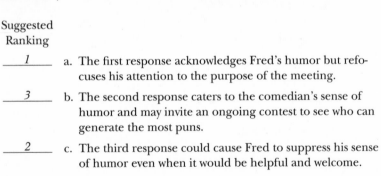

Suggested
Ranking

___1___ a. The first response acknowledges Fred's humor but refocuses his attention to the purpose of the meeting.

___3___ b. The second response caters to the comedian's sense of humor and may invite an ongoing contest to see who can generate the most puns.

___2___ c. The third response could cause Fred to suppress his sense of humor even when it would be helpful and welcome.

Situation Four:

This situation depicts the "silent partner" on the committee. There may be many reasons for such behavior, but if it continues the committee is deprived of the contribution of that member.

Suggested
Ranking

_____3_____   a. Although the first statement may be true, it leaves the silent individual at a disadvantage and usually results in defensive behavior and/or continued silence.

_____1_____   b. The second response provides Jody with an opportunity to contribute without feeling criticized.

_____2_____   c. The third response is too vague and general and may trigger an unexpected or unhelpful response. For example, Jody might have replied, "Sorry, I was just wondering how long this meeting would last."

Situation Five:

Sharon Dixon's behavior has been called "paralysis by analysis." This type of behavior often is practiced by a "denier," a person who attempts to avoid taking sides or admitting that a problem exists, so as to be spared the need to make a decision or exert influence.

Suggested
Ranking

_____3_____   a. The first response enables the individual to withdraw even more from the group and, as a result, to have limited or no commitment to the solution finally reached.

_____2_____   b. Although the second response may elicit further information, it also encourages further use of the delaying tactic. (Respondents who believe that Sharon may have been stereotyped may rank this response as #1.)

_____1_____   c. The third response acknowledges Sharon's concerns but also focuses the group on the decision-making task. It does not diminish Sharon's potential contribution but directs her toward the completion of the group's task.

Situation Six:

The behavior in this situation is usually associated with the "attention grab-ber." In this particular instance, George may be trying to impress the other group members with his importance.

Suggested
Ranking

___2___ a. The first response lends legitimacy to George's late arrival. In so doing, it diminishes the importance of the committee for the others present. If delivered sarcastically, this response also is a criticism of George. It may be deserved, but it will not solve the problem.

___3___ b. The second response is more emotional than considered. It invites a lengthy reply from George about how busy (important) he is.

___1___ c. The third response is the best of the three presented. It avoids creating stress or confrontation by not placing blame. It does, however, acknowledge that this situation is unacceptable and calls for action in the form of later dis-cussion between the chairperson and George.

Situation Seven:

The behavior in this situation often is associated with "sidetracking." An indi-vidual can deliberately introduce a "red herring" or can simply be, for whatever reasons, lacking the mental discipline to stay focused on the relevant topics.

Suggested
Ranking

___1___ a. The first response is an example of an effective use of silence.

___3___ b. The second response disciplines Robin, but also may inhibit the openness of the group if others interpret the chairperson's comment as stifling informal discussion and interaction.

___2___ c. The third response reinforces Robin's behavior by making Robin the center of attention in a supportive manner.

Part 3
Inventories, Questionnaires, and Surveys

If you want to become a better leader, it's best to begin with an accurate picture of who you are, what you value, how you're perceived by others, and what you honestly assume to be the proper relationship of leaders and followers. If you want to take a leadership role in a particular organization, it's also helpful to understand what kind of behavior the organization values—or fears.

And, of course, if an organization sets out consciously to change the leadership style of its managers, such information is indispensable.

The instruments in this section are tools that provide insight into the beliefs, practices, and leadership styles of individuals and organizations. They can be used in workshops to set the stage for more focused and meaningful discussions. They can be administered in the early stages of a leadership-development initiative to generate data about the present condition of a company, a department, or a group of leaders at a particular level. They can be used by individuals seeking to clarify their own beliefs about leadership or the way their behavior is viewed by subordinates, peers, and others.

Each survey includes the background information necessary to understand it, use it, and interpret it. Scoring sheets and scales are provided, as are data provided by the survey's authors about its reliability and validity. You are free to reproduce the questionnaires and to employ them for training purposes as you see fit.

We present these seven instruments as the best the Pfeiffer *Annuals* have to offer for gathering the sort of information that trainers, consultants, and participants are likely to find useful in leadership-development efforts. The surveys approach the subject from several different angles, so choose instruments to meet particular needs. The descriptions below are only thumbnail guides to the nature of each inventory and the purposes it might serve.

- Strategic Leadership Styles Instrument: Identifies both the leadership styles currently practiced in an organization and the styles that individual managers would like to adopt.

- The Supervisory and Leadership Beliefs Questionnaire: Managers examine their own beliefs about employees and the way they should be led.

- Motivational Analysis of Organizations—Behavior (MAO-B): What motivates your own behavior at work? Which of six factors influence the values and fears that drive you?

- Motivational Analysis of Organizations—Climate (MAO-C): Which of the same six factors motivate the prevailing behavior that determines your organization's climate?

- Managerial Work-Values Scale: Identify and measure the things you value about a job or a working environment. Are you in the right job and the right company to assume a leadership role?

- Patterns of Effective Supervisory Behavior: Describe the behavior of the most and least effective bosses you've had in your career. What does that tell you about the kind of leader you want to be?

- The Leadership Dimensions Survey: Subordinates or peers rank your leadership ability on four dimensions.

1

Strategic Leadership Styles Instrument

Gaylord Reagan

Leadership styles are not static. They can be changed
to serve the needs of an individual, group, or organization. A small investment of time and energy to identify and then to consider the significance of a strategic
leadership style can return big dividends. Productive
individuals, groups, and organizations that willingly
make this investment and accept responsibility for
shaping their own futures refuse to go on "doing what
comes naturally."

THE INSTRUMENT

Theoretical Framework

Consultant Lawrence M. Miller (1989) writes:

> All living things . . . exhibit patterns or cycles of development, moving
> from periods of vitality and growth, to periods of decay and disintegra-
> tion. The pattern of business growth and decline—and the behavior of

This instrument is based on *Barbarians to Bureaucrats: Corporate Life Cycle Strategies—Lessons from the Rise and Fall of Civilizations* by Lawrence M. Miller (1989). New York: Crain Publishers, Inc.

leaders—follows this same course . . . . It is natural for leaders in every stage to rely on responses they find most comfortable and to fail when they do not adopt innovative responses . . . . [The history] of corporations demonstrates this relationship, between the behavior of leaders and the cycle of growth and decline. (p. 1)

Based on this observation, Miller constructs "a theory of corporate life cycles," which explains the natural stages of evolution experienced by organizations and the people who lead them as they confront day-to-day challenges. Miller also identifies a series of leadership styles that dominate each of the six stages of organizational life.

In designing the Strategic Leadership Styles Instrument, the author separated Miller's Builder and Explorer styles, added the Synergist style, and sequenced the resulting styles as follows:

1. *Prophet:* A visionary who creates breakthroughs and has the human energy to pursue them. The Prophet adheres to a set of values and has high standards. In pursuing goals, the Prophet tends to rely on the support of a small circle of true believers.

2. *Barbarian:* A conqueror who commands the organization and pursues rapid growth. The Barbarian takes the Prophet's vision and begins implementing it in a direct, pragmatic, action-oriented, and forceful manner. Adherents of this style are self-confident and personally involved, and they demand complete loyalty from others.

3. *Builder:* A developer of structures required for successful organizational growth. Builders increase the efficiency of the Barbarian's early efforts. They focus on expansion, quantity, quality, and diversification, and they initiate the shift from command to collaboration.

4. *Explorer:* A developer of skills required for successful organizational growth. Explorers increase the efficiency of the Barbarian's early efforts. They focus on expansion, quantity, quality, diversification, and competition.

5. *Synergist:* A leader who helps the organization successfully balance expansion and the structures required to sustain that growth.

6. *Administrator:* An integrator of systems and structures to help organizations successfully shift their focus from expansion to safe and routine operation. The Administrator stresses perfecting financial and management practices but does not become involved with production operations.

7. *Bureaucrat:* An imposer of tight controls. Unlike the Prophet, the Bureaucrat has no interest in creativity; and unlike the Barbarian, no interest in

growth. To improve performance the Bureaucrat relies on strategic planning, cost cutting, and acquiring (not inventing) new products or services.

8. *Aristocrat:* An alienated inheritor of others' results. Aristocrats do no work and produce only organizational disintegration. They also tend to be autocratic. They communicate poorly, tolerate warfare among internal fiefdoms, seek to acquire symbols of power, and avoid making decisions.

Reliability and Validity

The Strategic Leadership Styles Instrument is designed to be used as an action-research tool rather than as a rigorous data-gathering instrument. Applied in this manner, the instrument has demonstrated a high level of face validity when administered to groups ranging from executive managers to nonmanagement personnel.

Administration

The following suggestions will be helpful to the facilitator who administers the instrument:

1. Before respondents complete the instrument, discuss briefly the concept of organizational life cycles. Miller (1989) describes a process whereby all living things, including organizations, move through a series of developmental cycles. These cycles begin with vitality and growth but can end with decay and disintegration. Miller's model also describes the challenges confronted by leaders as their organizations pass through these cycles. Miller contends that by breaking this cyclical pattern, leaders can help their organizations grow and develop.

2. Distribute copies of the Strategic Leadership Styles Instrument and read the instructions aloud as the respondents follow.

3. Instruct the respondents to read all eight phrases in a group before assigning ranking numbers. Make sure they understand that assigning "8" indicates that the phrase most accurately describes the respondent's behavior or beliefs and that "1" indicates the least accurate phrase. Respondents should select their "8" phrases first, then their "1" phrases, then assign the intermediate rankings ("2" through "7") to the remaining phrases.

4. Ask respondents to wait to score the instrument until everyone has completed the rankings.

Scoring

Each respondent should be given a copy of the Strategic Leadership Styles Instrument Scoring Sheet. Each respondent should complete the scoring sheet by transferring the ranking numbers from the instrument to the corresponding blanks on the scoring sheet. Then the five numbers in each category should be totaled. Respondents should then proceed to their scoring grids. Each respondent circles the appropriate score below each of the eight styles. A line should then be drawn on the grid to connect the circled numbers.

Interpretation and Processing

The percentiles on the left side of the scoring grid offer respondents a means for assessing the strength of their relative preferences for the eight styles. The descriptors across the bottom of the grid help respondents assess the impact of their styles on their organizations; that is, they indicate whether their preferred styles fall into the command, collaboration, or disintegration area or some combination of those areas. Respondents should try to determine how their preferences match the current and future needs of their organizations.

It is sometimes useful for the facilitator to prepare a large copy of the scoring grid on newsprint. In this case, the facilitator polls the individual respondents and posts their individual scores for each of the eight styles, drawing a line to connect each individual's scores. The various patterns can form the basis for a discussion. It may also be useful to compute average scores for each of the eight styles and provide the respondents with group norms.

The facilitator distributes the Strategic Leadership Styles Interpretation Sheet, which gives brief descriptions of the eight leadership styles. It also offers suggestions to respondents whose supervisors exemplify the different styles and to supervisors whose employees demonstrate preferences for the various styles.

The facilitator divides the respondents into small groups (four or five members in each group). If intact work groups are present, they should constitute the small groups. The Strategic Leadership Styles Instrument Discussion Guide is distributed, and the facilitator instructs the groups to use the guide to stimulate discussion and then to prepare individual action plans.

Uses of the Instrument

Strategic Leadership Styles Instrument is designed to accomplish the following objectives:

1. To help individual respondents to examine their relative preferences for strategic leadership styles associated with Miller's developmental cycles;

2. To help respondents to differentiate the impact of the eight leadership styles on their organizations;

3. To facilitate discussion among members of intact work groups about their collective style pattern;

4. To initiate discussions about the appropriateness of individual or group leadership style preferences within the context of an organization's short- and long-term viability; and

5. To stimulate planning designed to increase individual and group use of appropriate leadership styles.

Selected Bibliography and References

Clifford, D.K, Jr. (1985). *The winning performance: How America's high-growth midsize companies succeed.* New York: Bantam.

Collins, E.G.C. (Ed.). (1983). *Executive success: Making it in management.* New York: John Wiley & Sons.

Hickman, C.R., & Silva, M.A. (1984). *Creating excellence: Managing corporate culture, strategy, and change in the new age.* New York: New American Library.

Kilmann, R.H. (1989). *Managing beyond the quick fix: A completely integrated program for creating and maintaining organizational success.* San Francisco: Jossey-Bass.

Kouzes, J.M., & Posner, B.Z. (1989). *The leadership challenge: How to get extraordinary things done in organizations.* San Francisco: Jossey-Bass.

Maccoby, M. (1988). *Why work: Leading the new generation.* New York: Simon & Schuster.

Manz, C.C., & Sims, H.P., Jr. (1989). *Super leadership: Leading others to lead themselves.* Upper Saddle River, NJ: Prentice-Hall.

Miller, L.M. (1989). *Barbarians to bureaucrats: Corporate life cycle strategies-lessons from the rise and fall of civilizations.* New York: Clarkson N. Potter.

Steers, R.M. (1977). *Organizational effectiveness: A behavioral view.* Santa Monica, CA: Goodyear.

Tichy, N.M., & Devanna, M.A. (1986). *The transformational leader.* New York: John Wiley & Sons.

Waterman, R.H., Jr. (1987). *The renewal factor: How the best get and keep the competitive edge.* New York: Bantam.

Originally published in The 1993 Annual: Developing Human Resources.

STRATEGIC LEADERSHIP STYLES INSTRUMENT

Gaylord Reagan

Instructions: Within each of the five groups of statements (Group A through Group E), read all eight statements; then write the number "8" in the space preceding the statement that most accurately describes you, your behavior, or your beliefs with regard to your organization. Next write the number "1" in the space preceding the statement that least accurately describes you or your behavior or beliefs. Finally, use the numbers "2" through "7" to indicate the best intermediate rankings for the remaining statements. Then proceed to the next group and repeat the process. Rank all statements (leave none blank), and use each ranking number only once within each group of statements.

Group A

_____ 1. My ideas are long range and visionary.

_____ 2. My top priority is survival, and my mission is clear and urgent.

_____ 3. I enjoy actually making products or delivering services.

_____ 4. I am a convincing and enthusiastic communicator.

_____ 5. I seek to balance opposing forces.

_____ 6. Thus far, my career has taken place mainly in staff areas rather than production areas.

_____ 7. In meetings, my remarks review what has already happened.

_____ 8. I have not personally developed a new product or service in a long time.

Group B

_____ 9. I am willing to make sacrifices to see my ideas realized.

_____ 10. I do not like analyzing numbers and trends prior to acting.

_____ 11. I like measuring the results of my work.

_____ 12. Sometimes I feel as though I work for my customers or clients rather than for this organization.

_____ 13. I openly discuss the philosophy and values behind my decisions.

_____ 14. I consider myself to be an expert at procedures, processes, and systems.

_____ 15. I do not see my job as including the development of new products or services.

_____ 16. I concentrate on strategic planning rather than actually producing products or services.

Group C

_____ 17. I tend to withdraw for long periods to think about ideas.

_____ 18. I am in charge and am very comfortable making decisions.

_____ 19. I make decisions quickly, take action, and see the results.

_____ 20. I like to keep score and am competitive by nature.

_____ 21. I am hard on performance but soft on people.

_____ 22. Order, consistency, and smooth operations are high priorities for me.

_____ 23. Views of the organization are more important than those of its customers.

_____ 24. A person in my position has a right to enjoy exclusive perks.

Group D

_____ 25. Other people see me as being a bit different.

_____ 26. Other people say I am authoritarian and do not consult them on decisions.

_____ 27. I am not a visionary and do not devote a lot of time to dreaming.

_____ 28. I believe this organization should place a greater emphasis on expansion.

_____ 29. I stress teamwork and constant improvement of products and services.

_____ 30. I focus more on the present than on the future.

_____ 31. I believe that tighter controls will solve many of the organization's problems.

_____ 32. Only I and a few others really understand the organization's strategy.

Group E

_____ 33. I am neither well organized nor overly interested in details.

_____ 34. I am action oriented and do not like careful planning.

_____ 35. I do not like wasting time doing things through committees.

_____ 36. I feel that the organization gets bogged down in paperwork.

_____ 37. I believe in the value of organizational flexibility.

_____ 38. I place heavy emphasis on control and discipline.

_____ 39. I spend more time with staff personnel than production personnel.

_____ 40. Many times I cannot trust people to do what is right.

STRATEGIC LEADERSHIP STYLES INSTRUMENT SCORING SHEET

Instructions: Transfer the number you assigned to each statement in the Strategic Leadership Styles Instrument to the corresponding blank on this sheet. Then add the numbers under each category and write the total in the blank provided.

1. Prophet Category:

Statement 1.   _____

Statement 9.   _____

Statement 17.   _____

Statement 25.   _____

Statement 33.   _____

Total =   _____

This is your *Prophet* score. Prophets are visionaries who create breakthroughs and the human energy needed to propel organizations forward.

2. Barbarian Category:

Statement 2.   _____

Statement 10.   _____

Statement 18.   _____

Statement 26.   _____

Statement 34.   _____

Total =   _____

This is your *Barbarian* score. Barbarians are leaders who thrive on crisis and conquest, who command organizations during periods of rapid change.

3. Builder Category:

Statement 3.   _____

Statement 11.   _____

Statement 19.   _____

Statement 27. _____

Statement 35. _____

Total = _____

This is your *Builder* score. Builders are developers of the specialized structures required for successful change and growth. They initiate the shift from command to collaboration.

4. Explorer Category:

Statement 4. _____

Statement 12. _____

Statement 20. _____

Statement 28. _____

Statement 36. _____

Total = _____

This is your *Explorer* score. Explorers are developers of the specialized skills required for successful change and growth. They complete the shift from command to collaboration.

5. Synergist Category:

Statement 5. _____

Statement 13. _____

Statement 21. _____

Statement 29. _____

Statement 37. _____

Total = _____

This is your *Synergist* score. Synergists are leaders who maintain a balance and continue the forward motion of a growing and complex organization by unifying and appreciating the diverse contributions of Prophets, Barbarians, Builders, Explorers, and Administrators.

6. Administrator Category:

Statement 6. _____

Statement 14. _____

Statement 22. _____

Statement 30. _____

Statement 38. _____

Total = _____

This is your *Administrator* score. Administrators create integrating systems and structures, and they shift the organization's focus from expansion toward security.

7. Bureaucrat Category:

Statement 7. _____

Statement 15. _____

Statement 23. _____

Statement 31. _____

Statement 39. _____

Total = _____

This is your *Bureaucrat* score. Bureaucrats impose tight controls that inhibit the creativity of Prophets and the risk-taking habits of Barbarians.

8. Aristocrat Category:

Statement 8. _____

Statement 16. _____

Statement 24. _____

Statement 32. _____

Statement 40. _____

Total = _____

This is your *Aristocrat* score. Aristocrats are those who inherit success and are alienated from those who do the actual work. They often cause rebellion and disintegration.

STRATEGIC LEADERSHIP STYLES INSTRUMENT SCORING GRID

Instructions: On the grid below, circle your scores for each of the eight leadership styles shown at the top. Then connect the circles with a line to form a graph of your comparative style preferences.

Prophet	Barbarian	Builder	Explorer	Synergist	Admin-istrator	Bureaucrat	Aristocrat
40	40	40	40	40	40	40	40
39	39	39	39	39	39	39	39
38	38	38	38	38	38	38	38
37	37	37	37	37	37	37	37
36	36	36	36	36	36	36	36
35	35	35	35	35	35	35	35
34	34	34	34	34	34	34	34
33	33	33	33	33	33	33	33
32	32	32	32	32	32	32	32
31	31	31	31	31	31	31	31
30	30	30	30	30	30	30	30
29	29	29	29	29	29	29	29
28	28	28	28	28	28	28	28
27	27	27	27	27	27	27	27
26	26	26	26	26	26	26	26
25	25	25	25	25	25	25	25
24	24	24	24	24	24	24	24
23	23	23	23	23	23	23	23
22	22	22	22	22	22	22	22
21	21	21	21	21	21	21	21
20	20	20	20	20	20	20	20
19	19	19	19	19	19	19	19
18	18	18	18	18	18	18	18
17	17	17	17	17	17	17	17
16	16	16	16	16	16	16	16
15	15	15	15	15	15	15	15
14	14	14	14	14	14	14	14
13	13	13	13	13	13	13	13
12	12	12	12	12	12	12	12
11	11	11	11	11	11	11	11
10	10	10	10	10	10	10	10
9	9	9	9	9	9	9	9
8	8	8	8	8	8	8	8
7	7	7	7	7	7	7	7
6	6	6	6	6	6	6	6
5	5	5	5	5	5	5	5

└── COMMAND ──┘ └────── COLLABORATION ──────┘ └ DISINTEGRATION ┘

STRATEGIC LEADERSHIP STYLES INSTRUMENT
INTERPRETATION SHEET

This interpretation sheet gives a brief description of the eight strategic leadership styles. Now that you have determined which leadership style or styles you generally use, you should be able to recognize the styles used by others in your organization. Under each description listed below, you will find some suggestions about how to work with both managers and subordinates who exhibit that style. You may find it useful to share the suggestions under your own leadership style with your manager and your subordinates.

1. **Prophets** are at their best when organizations are getting started or are entering a period of major restructuring and renewal. Prophets hold—and engender in others—a strong belief in new products and services. They have high standards and do not believe in the abilities of people outside their own small group. They make decisions by themselves; and although they may listen to others, they are not likely to make effective use of participative decision making. They tend to have many ideas that can confuse other people, because they have little use for either structure or systems. They tend to change on a whim.

   If you work for a Prophet:

   - Do not expect him or her to provide specific objectives or instructions. Ask to discuss your objectives and then write your own, based on your discussion.

   - Do not expect him or her to follow up on details of your work. Discuss the larger goals toward which you are working.

   - Seek out him or her for advice and ideas.

   - Be tolerant of his or her latest ideas, even if they seem illogical and inconsistent. Do not confront Prophets about their apparent lack of direction; instead, ask leading questions that will help them shape their brainstorms into practical courses of action.

   - Realize that Prophets do not expect you to share their characteristics. In fact, they often appreciate having people around who organize and accomplish their ideas for them.

If Prophets work for you:

- Recognize them for their creative abilities, and reinforce and encourage those talents. Do not demand that they be well organized or conform to standard procedures.

- Listen to them. They need to know that their visionary ideas are important to you. Let them know that within your organization there is room and opportunity for the implementation of their ideas.

- Help Prophets distinguish between their regular jobs and their creative activities. Prophets may need to justify their salaries with mundane work.

- Protect them from Bureaucrats. Remember that in mature organizations Prophets are all too often ignored or eliminated.

- Have patience. Prophets work not for this quarter's results, but for the impact they can have over the long run. Their view is very long range. Insisting on immediate results destroys their creativity.

2. **Barbarians** excel when organizations are struggling to survive or to broaden their base or attempting to diversify. Barbarians see themselves as being in life-or-death struggles to accomplish the Prophet's objectives. High control and direct action appeal to Barbarians, who like to personally lead the troops into battle. They want others to join the team or move out of the way. Barbarians prefer to establish a few simple systems and structures while stressing a high degree of task flexibility.

If you work for a Barbarian:

- Be prepared for action. Barbarians expect you to act quickly and not to engage in lengthy or detailed planning exercises. Go to the heart of the matter and take action.

- Do not expect to be involved in long meetings or consensus decision making. Barbarians will make the decisions and you will carry them out.

- When Barbarians ask for your input, be completely honest and direct. Do not beat around the bush or give lengthy explanations.

- Go to Barbarians; do not wait for them to come to you. If you want a Barbarian to give you a promotion or different job or if you have an idea, you must seek out him or her and discuss your needs in a straightforward manner.

If Barbarians work for you:

- Be sure that their assignments are appropriate for command and single-minded action.

- Leave no confusion about Barbarians' areas of responsibility and what you expect of them. If you do not establish limits for them, they may run down the road so fast that you will have trouble getting things back under control.

- Take advantage of Barbarians' greatest talents; working in turnaround situations and managing organization units that are growing fast and need quick decisions. If your organization is in decline and needs a revolution, Barbarians—if put in charge—can inject excitement and urgency and can renew the vision.

- Help Barbarians make the transition to the next management stage by encouraging them to involve their people more, to delegate more, and to consider longer-range factors and outcomes.

3. **Builders** are most valuable when successful organizations are confronted by many opportunities for growth and diversification. Builders believe in their organization's products and services. They are interested in the means of production, although they focus their energies on making those means more efficient. They are detail oriented and are concerned with short-range numbers. They initiate their organization's leadership shift from "command" to "collaboration."

If you work for a Builder:

- Offer clear, specific, written objectives. Builders hate surprises and believe that you should have a blueprint for your activities.

- Realize that Builders are not the world's greatest communicators. You can help them by initiating needed communication. Do not expect them to do so.

- Do not expect a great deal of positive reinforcement. Builders take satisfaction from the quality and volume of the products that go out the door and they expect that you will, too.

- Realize that Builders appreciate creativity within bounds. They want better ways to get things accomplished. Builders are more interested in "how" than in "what" or "why."

If Builders work for you:

- Be sure that your measurement and feedback are not based entirely on the short term. Builders already tend toward that direction. You need to help them learn to think in the long term.

- Help them to understand the need for involving people below them in decision making.

- Remember that Builders respond to rewards for improving processes ("how") more than for results ("what").

- Do not burden Builders with too much central-staff help. They like to run their own operations with the greatest possible degree of autonomy. Hold Builders accountable for improvements. Offer help but do not impose it.

4. **Explorers** are similar to Builders, but Explorers place their emphasis on increasing the efficiency of the skills used to produce the organization's products and services. They are the organizational members most in touch with customers. They are highly competitive and enjoy keeping score. Interpersonal relationships are important to Explorers, and they are enthusiastic and intuitive. On the other hand, they hate paperwork and do little or no managing.

If you work for an Explorer:

- You will win points for producing results and gaining new business—things an Explorer understands most.

- Tell him or her about your plans. Explorers want to know that their employees have high objectives and expectations.

- Do not tell him or her what cannot be done or what should have been done. Keep your level of enthusiasm high, and frame your comments in a positive context.

If Explorers work for you:

- Remember that they appear to need your approval more than others do, because they are "out in the wilderness" most of the time. When they come back to the office, they need your praise; let them have it.

- When they seem overly optimistic about their own performance, do not shoot them down. Instead, help them develop more realistic expectations and projections.

- When they want you to spend more time in the field with customers than you can afford, work with them on making the best use of their time.

- When they do not have the best relations with those whose support they need in production, help them understand the importance of these members of their team. Explorers often have difficulty along this line.

5. **Synergists** do not favor a single leadership style. Instead, they incorporate the different styles of leadership required to succeed throughout an organization's life cycle. Synergists seek social unity, balance, teamwork, and continuous improvement of products and services (total quality management). To achieve these goals and foster development of the production process, they emphasize positive behavioral reinforcement by using symbols, participative decision making, interpersonal skills, and high levels of technical competence.

If you work for a Synergist:

- Be sensitive to his or her need to blend and balance the characteristics of Prophets, Barbarians, Builders, Explorers, and Administrators.

- Do not expect consistency. Demonstrate flexibility in your own approach to problems.

- Demonstrate ability in teamwork, participation, delegation, and constant improvement of products and services.

- Appreciate the Synergist's need for emphasizing both the material and spiritual aspects of the organization.

If Synergists work for you:

- Reward them for achieving a balance between the preservation of creativity and the need for order.

- Realize that Synergists may want you to increase the amount of time that you spend with personnel in production areas instead of staff areas. Although this is generally a good idea, there is still a need to take care of the administrative aspects of the organization.

6. **Administrators** contribute most when organizations have entered a secure stage, are financially successful, are developing broader markets for their products and services, and are developing more complex internal structure. Administrators believe in efficiency and in maximizing the financial side of the organization. To this end, they stress perfecting management-control systems and tend to take the organization's products and services for granted. They are not effective in dealing with people. They make decisions based on data and spend lots of time seeking "correct" answers. Under Administrators, line managers lose power while staff gains it.

If you work for an Administrator:

- Realize that he or she is more likely to reward you for conforming than for creating.

- Understand his or her essential need for administrative control and discipline. When that control becomes stifling, you must help the Administrator to recognize your situation.

- Recognize who you are and what your ambitions are. If you always work for an Administrator, you can develop the same characteristics, which may or may not be the best for you.

If Administrators work for you:

- Remember that Administrators are good at taking care of details; reward them for that. Also help them to see the larger picture, direction, trends, and reasons. Keep them in touch with what is important to the organization.

- Help Administrators to see their jobs as serving those whose performance should be enhanced by their systems: the Builders and Explorers.

7. **Bureaucrats** are most visible in diversified organizations, where primary products and services are viewed as being mature "cash cows." For Bureaucrats, growth occurs through acquiring younger organizations and cost cutting. Bureaucrats confront no problems that cannot be overcome through sound financial management and controls. They place little emphasis on creativity and are more concerned with numbers than people. Bureaucrats like written reports, and they cultivate the flow of paper. They seek to increase autocratic command throughout their organization, often resulting in overorganization, overspecialization, and a lack of trust between levels.

If you work for a Bureaucrat:

- Remember that the Bureaucrat tends to focus on performance that fits the system, without asking whether it is the right performance. Help him or her by asking questions that will lead to a consideration of more creative responses.

- As a Bureaucrat needs order and conformity, do not make him or her nervous by being "weird." It is difficult to work for a nervous boss, particularly if you are the one who makes the boss nervous.

- Serve as a buffer for your subordinates. Manage them to produce creative responses without interference from your Bureaucratic supervisor. Do not make your own problem your subordinates' problem.

If Bureaucrats work for you:

- Remember that Bureaucrats are better in staff jobs, not line jobs.

- Make sure that they do not spin a web of stifling systems and structure around others.

- As Bureaucrats constantly complain about others who are violating the sanctity of their systems, learn to ask, "So what?"

- Reward them for developing and managing the most efficient administrative processes. Define "efficient" as meaning the fewest possible staff requiring the least amount of time from line managers.

8. **Aristocrats** are generally most evident when the organization's primary products and services are declining because of a lack of attention, investment, and creativity; when organizational components are being eliminated and divested; and when cash is desperately needed. At these times cynicism permeates all parts and levels of the organization. Aristocrats increasingly surround themselves with expensive tokens of their positions ("perks") and view their primary mission as preventing further organizational erosion. They have an aloof management style and do not like making decisions. If forced to do so, they generally use a highly autocratic style. Their organizations are burdened with excessive layers of management, poor communication, little clarity of mission, low motivation, lots of internal warfare, and ineffective formal structures.

If you work for an Aristocrat:

- Quit.

- If you cannot quit, consider the Aristocrat's objectives but create your own independently. Hope that the Aristocrat's successor appreciates your efforts.

If Aristocrats work for you:

- Encourage them to leave.

- If they will not quit, ask them specific questions about their efforts to improve the organization, the quality of their products and services, and their plans for creative developments. Let them know that their jobs depend on a change in behavior.

STRATEGIC LEADERSHIP STYLES INSTRUMENT DISCUSSION GUIDE

Use the following questions to stimulate a discussion in your group:

1. Which of the eight leadership styles do your scores on the Strategic Leadership Styles Instrument suggest that you are most likely to use? In what ways are these styles important to your work?

2. What are your key subordinates' leadership styles? What behaviors could you use to improve your relationships with those people? What behaviors should you avoid using?

3. What are your key peers' leadership styles? What behaviors could you use to improve your relationships with those people? What behaviors should you avoid using?

4. What is your supervisor's leadership style? What behaviors could you use to improve your relationship with that person? What behaviors should you avoid using?

5. What suggestions would you give to the following people about how to relate to you better and what to avoid doing?

   a. Your supervisor

   b. Your peers

   c. Your subordinates

6. Which leadership styles are most needed in your organization if it is to adapt successfully to its changing environment? Which behaviors may need to be de-emphasized?

7. To what extent do the behaviors of your leadership style fit with those most needed by your organization? In other words, is your leadership behavior part of the solution or part of the problem? In what ways?

2

The Supervisory and Leadership Beliefs Questionnaire

T. Venkateswara Rao

One of the most important tasks of a manager is to manage human resources. Effective management of human resources requires understanding the capabilities of subordinates, assigning them appropriate tasks, helping them to acquire new capabilities, maintaining their motivation level, and structuring the work so that people can derive some satisfaction from doing it. As one goes up the managerial ladder, he or she is required to spend an increasing amount of time interacting with people. These interactions may be on the shop floor, in group meetings, in face-to-face encounters with one other person, through telephone conversations, or in formal or informal gatherings. Many managers spend more than 50 percent of their time interacting with their subordinates.

The effectiveness of the manager depends on both the content of the interaction and the manager's style. The manager's technical competence, functional knowledge, skills, and information are very important in determining his or her effectiveness in managing subordinates. A capable manager is

Adapted from T.V. Rao, "Supervisory and Leadership Styles." In U. Pareek, T.V. Rao, & D.M. Pestonjee, *Behavioural Processes in Organisations*. New Delhi, India: Oxford & IBH, 1981.

able to influence a subordinate by providing technical guidance and clear directions when needed. However, if the manager is not sensitive to the emotional needs of subordinates and does not use the appropriate styles of supervision and leadership, there is a great danger of crippling the growth of the subordinates. For example, an authoritarian manager may arouse strong negative reactions by continually dictating terms to capable subordinates but may do extremely well with subordinates who are dependent and who are just beginning to learn their roles. Similarly, a democratic manager may be liked by capable subordinates but seen as incompetent by dependent subordinates. It is necessary, therefore, for managers to interact differently with different people.

MAJOR SUPERVISORY FUNCTIONS

The objective of supervision is to ensure that subordinates do what they are supposed to do. The manager can accomplish this through:

1. Continually striving to understand the style of operation and needs of each subordinate;

2. Continually evaluating the activities of each subordinate in terms of results and the goals toward which that subordinate is working;

3. Guiding subordinates in planning activities;

4. Evaluating the outcomes of activities;

5. Helping to plan future activities on the basis of past experiences; and

6. Rewarding subordinates for satisfactory or superior work.

Understanding the Needs of Subordinates

An effective supervisor understands how individual subordinates are motivated and what their needs are. Such understanding helps in assessing their tasks and performance and then later in guiding future activities.

Continual Evaluation

To guide subordinates effectively, a supervisor must observe their activities. Because a manager may have a very limited amount of time to observe all subordinates, a mechanism should be developed for obtaining and maintaining information about their various activities. Periodic discussions with individual subordinates can be helpful in obtaining such information.

Guidance in Planning Activities

Supervision also involves helping subordinates to plan their activities. This may include providing information and helping to set goals and priorities.

Providing Rewards

Managing also has a motivational aspect: rewarding workers when they accomplish something worthwhile. When a supervisor fails to do this, employees' motivational levels drop. Rewards need not always be monetary; receiving greater responsibility or a verbal expression of appreciation can be highly rewarding to subordinates.

STYLES OF SUPERVISION

Although every supervisor is unique in some way, certain supervisory styles are characteristic of the majority of managers. Any manager may incorporate more than one of these styles into his or her own, depending on the situation.

Authoritarian and Democratic Styles

Lippitt and White (1943) identify two types of leaders: authoritarian and democratic. The authoritarian leader determines all policies and strategies, decides on the composition and tasks of the work teams, is personal in giving praise and criticism, and maintains some personal distance from employees. In contrast, the democratic leader ensures that policies and strategies are determined by the group, gives technical advice whenever the group needs it, allows freedom to group members to choose their work teams, tries to be objective in providing rewards and punishments, and participates in discussions.

When Lippitt and White compared these two styles of management in their experimental studies, they found that authoritarians produced (a) a greater quantity of work, (b) a greater amount of aggressiveness toward the leader, (c) less originality in work, (d) less work motivation, (e) more dependence, (f) less group feeling, and (g) more suppressed discontent.

Task-Oriented and Employee-Oriented Styles

Blake and Mouton (1964) developed the concept of task-oriented and people-oriented leadership. The following paragraphs explain the differences between these supervisory styles.

Task-Oriented Supervisor. A task-oriented supervisor emphasizes the task, often believes that ends are more important than means, and thinks that employees need to be supervised closely in order to accomplish their tasks. This type of supervisor becomes upset when tasks are not accomplished. The concern for task is so high that the human aspect is likely to be neglected in dealings with subordinates. This type of supervisor is likely to have difficulty in human relations and may appear to be a "tough" person. A task-oriented supervisor may frequently question or remind subordinates about their tasks, warn them about deadlines, or show a great deal of concern about details.

Employees who work with an excessively task-oriented supervisor often develop negative attitudes about their work and their supervisor. They may be motivated only by fear and may feel job dissatisfaction. They may develop shortcuts that, in the long run, affect the organization's performance.

Employee-Oriented Supervisor. In contrast, the employee-oriented supervisor believes that a concern for subordinates' needs and welfare promotes both the quality and quantity of work. This concern may be reflected in attempts to keep subordinates in good humor and in frequent inquiries about their problems (even those unrelated to work). In the extreme, this type of supervision also leads to inefficiency. Subordinates may perceive this type of supervisor as too lenient and may take advantage of the supervisor's concern.

The task-oriented and employee-oriented styles may not be present in pure forms, and one manager may demonstrate combinations of the two styles. The effectiveness of the styles also may depend on factors such as the nature of the task or the nature of the subordinate.

Subsequent work by Fiedler (1967) indicated that the effectiveness of task-oriented or people-oriented styles is contingent on situational factors such as the power of the leader, acceptance of the supervisor by subordinates, and the way in which the tasks are structured.

Benevolent, Critical, and Self-Dispensing Styles

Another way of looking at supervisory and leadership styles (Rao & Satia, 1978) has been used in various countries with satisfactory results. This classification was influenced by McClelland's (1975) work on institution builders and institutional managers and by Stewart's concept of psychosocial maturity

(McClelland, 1975). In this concept, leadership or supervisory styles stem from three mutually exclusive orientations: benevolent, critical, and self-dispensing.

Benevolent Supervisor. This type protects subordinates, continually tells them what they should and should not do, and comes to their rescue whenever needed. Such supervisors cater to subordinates' needs for security and generally are liked by their employees. They are effective as long as they are physically present. In their absence, workers may experience a lack of direction and motivation. Such supervisors tend to have dependent followers, and initiative-taking behavior may not be reinforced.

Critical Supervisor. This type takes a critical approach to employees and does not tolerate mistakes, low-quality work, undisciplined behavior, or individual peculiarities. Finding mistakes, criticizing subordinates, and making them feel incompetent are characteristic behaviors of critical managers. Subordinates may produce acceptable work out of fear, but they do not like this type of manager.

Self-Dispensing Supervisor. This type has confidence in the subordinates, helps them to set broad goals, and allows them to work on their own. Guidance is provided only when requested by subordinates. Competent workers who have this kind of supervision are likely to feel confident about their work. They are free to work both independently and interdependently with their colleagues.

Institutional Supervisor

Closely related to the self-dispensing supervisor is what McClelland and Burnham (1976) refer to as an institutional supervisor, because this type is involved in developing the department or unit. Such supervisors are also called institution builders, because they ensure the growth and development of their units and subordinates by incorporating processes that help people to give their best and to grow with the organization. McClelland and Burnham identify the following characteristics of institutional supervisors:

1. They are organization oriented and tend to join organizations and feel responsible for building them.

2. They are disciplined to work and enjoy their work.

3. They are willing to sacrifice some of their own self-interests for the welfare of the organization.

4. They have a keen sense of justice.

5. They have a low need for affiliation, a high need to influence others for social or organizational goals, and a disciplined or controlled way of expressing their power needs.

Such supervisors often aim at a self-dispensing style but are flexible in their use of styles. They are likely to create highly motivating work environments in their organizations.

IMPLICATIONS OF SUPERVISORY STYLES

No single supervisory style is universally effective. The effectiveness of the style depends on the employee, the nature of the task, and various other factors. If a new employee does not know much about the work, a benevolent supervisor is helpful; a critical supervisor may be frightening; and a self-dispensing supervisor may cause bewilderment. On the other hand, a capable employee may feel most comfortable with a self-dispensing style of supervision and resent a benevolent supervisor who continually gives unwanted advice.

Employees with low self-discipline probably could be developed best by critical supervision, at least on an intermittent basis. Continual use of critical supervision, however, is unlikely to be effective. Flexibility and perceptiveness about when to use each style are useful attributes for leaders or supervisors.

Leadership Styles and Motivational Climate

The effectiveness of any leadership lies in the kind of climate that is created in the organization. Supervisors may find the following suggestions helpful in creating a proper motivational climate.

1. *Create a climate of independence and interdependence rather than dependence.* A self-dispensing supervisor promotes an independent and interdependent climate for subordinates and does not interfere unless it becomes necessary. The subordinates are trusted and given freedom to plan their own ways of doing their work. They are expected to solve problems and to ask for guidance only when it is needed. By providing freedom of work, encouraging initiative, and supporting experimentation and teamwork, a supervisor also helps to satisfy the subordinates' needs for belonging, affection, and security.

Some supervisors allow their subordinates to come to them continually for advice and guidance and, in the extreme case, may not allow them to do anything on their own. If every subordinate must check with the supervisor and obtain approval before taking any action, the supervisor is creating a climate of dependence and the subordinates will not be able to take any initiative. When problems arise, they may hesitate to look for solutions; and when something goes wrong, they may not accept responsibility. Learning from experience becomes difficult, because they have always turned to their supervisor for advice. Thus, the supervisor becomes burdened with responsibilities and problem solving. Not only are the supervisor's energies wasted, but so are those of the subordinates.

2. *Create a climate of competition through recognition of good work.* Employees look forward to being rewarded for good or innovative work. Financial rewards are not always necessary; even a word of appreciation has a great motivating value. Although appreciation given indiscriminately loses its value, a supervisor should not withhold appreciation until the formal appraisal reports. Many other ways of recognizing good work can be very rewarding. Giving praise in the presence of others, giving increased responsibility, and writing letters of commendation and recommendation can be used in addition to financial rewards. Such recognition and public acknowledgment help employees to value work and to derive a sense of satisfaction and a feeling of importance. These go a long way in motivating people to do better work. They even create a sense of competition among employees.

3. *Create a climate of approach and problem solving rather than avoidance.* Some supervisors approach problems with confidence, face them squarely, work out mechanisms to solve them (often with the help of others), and constantly work to overcome problems. They derive satisfaction from this struggle— even if the outcomes are not always positive—and they inspire subordinates to imitate their initiative.

Some supervisors, however, see everything as a headache and postpone solutions to problems or delegate them to someone else. Workers also are quick to imitate this avoidance.

4. *Create an ideal climate through personal example.* Just as supervisors are imitated in their approaches to problem solving, they are viewed as models for other work habits. In fact, the supervisor's styles may filter down the hierarchy and influence employees several grades below. Therefore, good supervision and good work habits make the supervisor's job easier in two ways: His or her own tasks are done more efficiently, and a climate is created for making the department or unit more efficient.

5. *Motivate people through guidance and counseling.* The foregoing discussions point out some general strategies that supervisors can use in creating the proper motivational climate for their subordinates. However, because individual workers have individual needs, individual counseling also can motivate subordinates. Within a group of workers, a supervisor may find very efficient workers, poor workers, problem creators, cooperative employees, and so on. Therefore, the supervisor should be sensitive to subordinates' individual differences.

RESEARCH FINDINGS FROM THE SUPERVISORY AND LEADERSHIP BELIEFS QUESTIONNAIRE

This instrument was administered to eighteen senior executives and was followed by a ninety-minute session on supervisory styles. Scores were fed back and the results discussed in the class. A week later, when the executives were retested, dominant styles remained the same for fifteen of the eighteen participants. Similarly, the least-dominant style did not change for fifteen of the eighteen participants. Thus, style stability seems to exist in 83 percent of the cases. The three participants whose dominant style changed reported that they were influenced by the feedback and subsequent discussions.

Jain (1982) used this instrument to study the supervisory beliefs of six district collectors (Indian administrative service officers), who were also rated by their subordinates (N = 70) with the same instrument. The average scores of the perceptions of the subordinates differed from the self-assessments of the district collectors in only two of the six cases. This indicates that self-assessments of supervisory beliefs do tend to reflect the styles perceived by others. The self-dispensing style in this questionnaire should be considered close to the nurturant task-leadership style outlined by Sinha (1980). Sinha's research indicates that such a style leads to greater group productivity, satisfaction of group members, and work involvement.

ADMINISTERING THE INSTRUMENT

The Supervisory and Leadership Beliefs Questionnaire should be used for training purposes only. The instrument could be used for a short session (ninety minutes) on supervision and leadership or as part of a one-day workshop on supervisory/leadership styles. It is advisable to administer the questionnaire before any theoretical input is made. Scoring and interpretation should follow the theoretical input. Interpretation should focus on style flexibility and the need to use different styles with different employees, depending on the situations; however, the overall target should be the self-dispensing style. For a full-day workshop, role plays and simulation activities may be useful.

Scoring and Interpretation

The three scores obtained from this instrument are for benevolent, critical, and self-dispensing supervisory (or leadership) styles. The score of each style is obtained by transferring the points from the instrument to the scoring sheet and totaling each column on the scoring sheet. The sum of the three totals should equal 18. The column with the greatest total indicates the dominant supervisory orientation of the respondent. Scores above 9 normally indicate stronger style orientations, and scores near 0 indicate a lack of that supervisory orientation. For example, a benevolent score of 10, a critical score of 3, and a self-dispensing score of 5 would indicate that the respondent has a fairly strong benevolent orientation and less tendency to use the other two.

Scores are indicative of the strength of the beliefs or orientations underlying each style. However, a supervisor who was strongly oriented toward a certain style would probably use that style. Beliefs lead to behavior, although situations can create gaps between beliefs and behavior.

When one style strongly dominates a profile, style flexibility may be weak. In such a case, it is important for the respondent to examine his or her dominant style and the extent to which his or her flexibility is being hampered.

A higher self-dispensing score is desirable, particularly for managers who work in organizations with competent human resources. High critical scores may hinder human resource development and institutional development. The benevolent style is useful when the task is less structured, when the subordinate or the unit is new, or when the employees have high needs for dependence.

References

Blake, R.R., & Mouton, J.S. (1964). *The managerial grid.* Houston, TX: Gulf.

Fiedler, F.E. (1967). *A theory of leadership effectiveness.* New York: McGraw-Hill.

Jain, U. (1982). *Life styles of Indian managers: An exploratory study of the images, experiences and impact of collectors in their districts.* Unpublished fellow program dissertation, Indian Institute of Management, Ahmedabad, India.

Lippitt, R., & White, R.N. (1943). The social climate of children's groups. In R.G. Baker, J.S. Kounin, & H.F. Wright (Eds.), *Child behavior and development.* New York: McGraw-Hill.

McClelland, D.C. (1975). *Power: The inner experience.* New York: Irvington.

McClelland, D.C., & Burnham, D.H. (1976). Power is the great motivator. *Harvard Business Review, 54*(2), 100–110.

Sinha, J.B.P. (1980). *The nurturant task leader.* New Delhi, India: Concept Publishing.

Originally published in The 1986 Annual: Developing Human Resources.

THE SUPERVISORY AND LEADERSHIP BELIEFS QUESTIONNAIRE

T. Venkateswara Rao

Instructions: This instrument contains three sets of statements, and each set contains three statements. You are to distribute six points among the three items in each set. Distribute these points according to how strongly you agree with each statement. For example, if you strongly agree with the first statement and strongly disagree with the other two, the six points should be assigned to the first statement and zero points should be assigned to the other two. You may assign three points to one statement, two to another, and one to the remaining statement, or any similar combination. The assignment of points is governed simply by the degree to which you agree with each statement.

In these statements, the term "employees" refers to those employees who report to you or for whom you conduct the appraisal. If you supervise a department that is divided into subunits, all members of your department are considered your employees.

1. (a) Employees are capable of working on their own, and there is no need to supervise them. They need to be helped only occasionally. _____

   (b) Employees are generally lazy and avoid work unless they are closely supervised. _____

   (c) Employees need to be guided and helped continually. They need an affectionate supervisor who understands them and continually tells them what to do and what not to do. _____

2. (a) A good supervisor gives a great deal of freedom to employees and has faith in them. _____

   (b) A good supervisor treats employees as a parent would: continually advising them and telling them what to do and what not to do. _____

   (c) A good supervisor keeps a close eye on employees and makes them feel that they should be careful because they are being watched. _____

3. (a) How well employees work depends a great deal
on how well their supervisor provides continual
guidance. _____

   (b) How well employees work depends a great deal
on how strict their supervisor is with them. _____

   (c) How well employees work depends a great deal on
how much their supervisor trusts them, gives them
freedom to experiment, and helps them to learn
from their mistakes. _____

THE SUPERVISORY AND LEADERSHIP BELIEFS
QUESTIONNAIRE SCORING SHEET

Instructions: Transfer the points you have assigned to each statement to the appropriate blank below. Then total each column.

Item	Score	Item	Score	Item	Score
1 (c)	_____	1 (b)	_____	1 (a)	_____
2 (b)	_____	2 (c)	_____	2 (a)	_____
3 (a)	_____	3 (b)	_____	3 (c)	_____
Total	_____	Total	_____	Total	_____

Highest score here indicates a **Benevolent** supervisory orientation.

Highest score here indicates a **Critical** supervisory orientation.

Highest score here indicates a **Self-Dispensing** supervisory orientation.

3

Motivational Analysis of Organizations — Behavior (MAO-B)

Udai Pareek

A person's behavior is the result of several factors or motives. A knowledge of the typical, primary motivators of the behavior of people in a work setting can help managers and consultants to deal more effectively with those people. The first step in developing such knowledge is to become aware of one's own patterns of organizational behavior and to identify one's own primary motives. The Motivational Analysis of Organizations—Behavior (MAO-B) instrument enables the respondents to identify which of six primary factors motivates their own behavior in their organizational settings. The instrument can be used in managerial and supervisory training, as part of a human resource development (HRD) or team-building program, and for personal growth and development.

RATIONALE FOR THE INSTRUMENT

Murray (1938) developed a long list of human motives or needs. Murray's work inspired further studies, which have produced different lists of significant behavioral motives. McClelland, Atkinson, Clark, and Lowell (1953) suggested three important motives (achievement, affiliation, and power) and also suggested elaborate methods for measuring them. McClelland subsequently demonstrated the importance of the achievement motive for entrepreneurship and marketing (McClelland, 1961; McClelland & Winter, 1971) and of power as a motivator in management (McClelland, 1975; McClelland & Burnham, 1976). He further attempted to identify a pattern of leadership motivation in which power plays a critical role (McClelland & Boyatzis, 1982). Litwin and Stringer (1968) used the three motives of achievement, affiliation, and power in their study of organizational climates and found these motives useful for the study of organizational behavior.

Although McClelland's study of achievement and affiliation motives showed them to be rather simple variables, he found the motive of power to be a complex one. As he suggested during his study of power (McClelland, 1975), the desire for power contains both an urge to control others and an urge to make an impact. McClelland called these variables personalized power and socialized power. Thus, McClelland seems to suggest three different elements in the power motive: the need to control others (personalized power), the need to make an impact on others, and the need to use power in doing something for other persons and groups—such as in organizations (socialized power). It is helpful to make clear distinctions among these three. Control seems to be focused around keeping track of developments according to an agreed-on plan to be informed about "how things are going." This seems to be an important need or motive in managerial behavior. The so-called socialized dimension of power (reflected in the use of power for the benefit of others) seems to be a separate need or motive. Pareek (1968a, 1968b) suggests that this need is important for social development and calls it the extension motive.

Another motive that is relevant for organizational behavior is that of dependence. Although it generally has been regarded as a negative force, McGregor (1966) recognized the positive value of dependence in management, and Kotter (1979) further drew attention to its importance. Levinson (1982) pointed out the importance of dependence in the development of managers. This need is acknowledged in the process of mentoring (Levinson, 1982), which has received considerable attention in the recent management literature (e.g., Kram, 1985).

Thus, six primary needs or motives that are relevant to an understanding of the behavior of people in organizations have been identified. These are as follows:

1. *Achievement:* Characterized by concern for excellence, competition with the standards of excellence set by others or by oneself, the setting of chal-

lenging goals for oneself, awareness of the hurdles that stand in the way of achieving those goals, and persistence in trying alternative paths to one's goals.

2. *Affiliation:* Characterized by a concern for establishing and maintaining close, personal relationships, a value on friendship, and a tendency to express one's emotions.

3. *Influence:* Characterized by concern with making an impact on others, a desire to make people do what one thinks is right, and an urge to change matters and (develop) people.

4. *Control:* Characterized by a concern for orderliness, a desire to be and stay informed, and an urge to monitor and take corrective action when needed.

5. *Extension:* Characterized by a concern for others; an interest in superordinate goals; and an urge to be useful to larger groups, including society.

6. *Dependence:* Characterized by seeking the help of others in one's own self-development, checking with significant others (those who are more knowledgeable than oneself or have higher status, experts, close associates, etc.), submitting ideas or proposals for approval, and having an urge to maintain an "approval" relationship.

All these needs or motives can be used in explaining the behavior of people in organizations. However, each of these motives can have two dimensions: approach and avoidance. Atkinson (1953) first suggested the concept of avoidance behavior in discussing the achievement motive. It was further elaborated by several authors (Birney & Burdick, 1969; Heckhausen, 1967), and "fear of failure" emerged as an important component of the achievement motive, distinct from "hope of success," the other component. Much research has been done on fear of failure, which has been found to be dysfunctional although related to the achievement motive. For example, Varga (1977) showed that hope of success versus fear of failure (approach versus avoidance) was the most important intervening variable in explaining who benefited from achievement-motivation training programs as measured by an increase in entrepreneurial activity. People who were high in achievement motivation but also had a high component of fear of failure failed to start new businesses, in contrast to those who had a high component of hope of success. The concept of approach versus avoidance also is applicable to components of other motivators.

The six motives of achievement, affiliation, influence, control, extension, and dependence have been used in studying the behavior of people in

Table 1. Approach and Avoidance Dimensions of Six Motives

Motives	Approach (Hope of)	Avoidance (Fear of)
Achievement	Success	Failure
Affiliation	Inclusion	Exclusion
Extension	Relevance	Irrelevance
Influence	Impact	Impotence
Control	Order	Chaos
Dependence	Growth	Loneliness

organizations, and no further important managerial motives have been identified. Table 1 summarizes the approach and avoidance dimensions of each of the six motives. The behavior of a manager or employee thus can be analyzed not only in terms of the six primary motives but also from the perspective of (positive) approach or (negative) avoidance, reflected by hope or fear.

An employee's effectiveness may result from the existence or lack of a particular motivator or from the extent of the approach or avoidance dimension of a particular motivator. The motive, however strong it may be, may be made ineffective by a high degree of fear, i.e., high avoidance behavior. Thus, a high score for a motive on the MAO-B instrument must be assessed in relation to the number of avoidance items in the total score. High avoidance clearly can reduce an individual's effectiveness.

THE INSTRUMENT

The Motivational Analysis of Organizations—Behavior (MAO-B) instrument was developed to study manager or employee behavior in an organization. The MAO-B contains sixty items, five for each dimension (approach and avoidance) of each of the six previously discussed motives.

Scoring

The total score for each dimension (approach and avoidance) of the six motives can range from 5 to 20. The respondent's operating effectiveness quotient (OEQ) for each of the six motive-specific aspects of behavior, defined by the net score of approach dimensions, can be obtained by using the formula

$$\frac{P-5}{P+V-10} \times 100.$$

"P" and "V" represent total scores for approach and avoidance dimensions, respectively, of a motive-specific behavior. Table 2 can be used to find the OEQ for each motive-related behavior.

Table 2. Operating Effectiveness Quotients

Avoidance Scores	Approach Scores															
	5	6	7	8	9	10	11	12	13	14	15	16	17	18	19	20
5	0	100	100	100	100	100	100	100	100	100	100	100	100	100	100	100
6	0	50	67	75	80	83	85	87	89	90	91	92	92	93	93	97
7	0	33	50	60	67	71	75	78	80	82	83	85	86	87	87	88
8	0	25	40	50	57	62	67	70	73	75	77	78	80	81	82	83
9	0	20	33	43	50	55	60	64	67	69	71	73	75	76	78	79
10	0	17	28	37	44	50	54	58	61	64	67	69	70	72	74	75
11	0	14	25	33	40	45	50	54	59	60	62	65	67	68	70	71
12	0	12	22	30	36	42	46	50	53	56	59	61	63	65	67	68
13	0	11	20	27	33	38	43	47	50	53	55	58	60	62	64	65
14	0	10	18	25	31	36	40	44	47	50	53	55	57	59	61	62
15	0	9	17	23	28	33	37	41	44	47	50	52	54	56	58	60
16	0	8	15	21	27	31	35	39	42	45	48	50	52	54	56	58
17	0	8	14	20	25	29	33	37	40	43	45	48	50	52	54	56
18	0	7	13	19	23	28	32	35	38	41	43	46	48	50	52	54
19	0	7	12	18	22	26	30	33	36	39	42	44	46	48	50	52
20	0	6	12	17	21	25	29	32	35	37	40	42	44	46	48	50

Reliability

The test-retest reliability coefficients for the six dimensions of role behavior (based on a sample of fifty, two months apart) are as follows:

MAO-B Variable	Reliability Coefficient	Level of Significance
Achievement	.61	.001
Affiliation	.61	.001
Influence	.58	.001
Control	.68	.001
Extension	.53	.001
Dependence	.45	.001

All of the coefficients are very high, significant at the .001 level. The instrument is thus a highly reliable one.

Internal Factors

The MAO-B scores of about five hundred employees of a large bank were factor analyzed, rotated by the varimax method. Only those factors with an eigenvalue of 1 or above were taken, extracting in all five factors.

The five factors showed that the MAO-B has one factor of personal responsibility, one factor reflecting fear of responsibility, two positive factors related to people (one of personal growth with the help of others and the other encompassing human concern), and one factor of integration and centralization of tasks. Achievement, influence, and control contributed to the personal responsibility factor, whereas dependence and affiliation emerged as independent factors. Extension motivation was distributed into the various factors. Three motives emerged in the behavior of employees; these can be called the achievement motive, the task motive, and the affiliation (or human relationship) motive.

Validity

The relationship between effective role behavior (as reflected by the operating effectiveness quotient) and some personality variables was found in a study of five hundred employees, a sample of the employees of a large multi-locational firm. The levels of significance of the correlations appear in Table 3.[1]

---

1. A minus sign indicates that the correlations were negative.

As can be seen from the table, all dimensions of effective role behavior are positively correlated with role efficacy (see Pareek, 1980a, 1980b). It can be said that people who experience higher role efficacy use more effective role behavior on all dimensions. The same is true of the two dimensions of locus of control, internality and externality (see Pareek, 1982). Two types of external locus of control were discovered using the scale by Levenson (1972, 1973): externality events caused by others and externality events caused by chance. The correlation values were significant in the expected direction for all dimensions of role-behavior effectiveness. However, the correlation between the control dimension and internality was not found to be significant. It can be concluded that, on the whole, people having a higher external locus of control show less effective role behavior, and those having a higher internal locus of control show more effective role behavior (except, perhaps, on the control dimension).

As can be seen in Table 3, effective role behavior had a significantly negative correlation with the total role-stress score (see Pareek, 1983). Of the total for role stress, four of six correlations were significant at the .001 level; for the "extension" dimension, the correlation was significant at .004; and for affiliation, it was at .002. The correlation value of both of these dimensions (which are of an interpersonal nature) with two role stresses (role isolation and role erosion) were not significant. The correlation value of role ambiguity and of role stagnation was not significant respectively with the extension and affiliation dimensions. In summary, people who use more effective role behavior in general experience less role stress. This is particularly true of work-oriented role behavior.

Table 3 also shows the values of correlation between effective role behavior and strategies for coping with stress (avoidance and approach strategies). Effectiveness (OEQ) for all dimensions of role behavior had significant negative correlation with avoidance strategies and significant positive correlation with approach strategies (except for the affiliation dimension, for which the value was not significant). For the avoidance strategies, the correlations were significant at .001 for achievement and influence; at .004 for control; at .014 for extension; and at .036 and .044 for affiliation and dependence. For the approach strategies, the values were significant at .002, .001, and .004 for achievement, influence, and control, respectively, and at .014 and .018 for dependence and extension. It can be concluded that people who demonstrate effective role behavior generally use approach strategies in coping with role stress.

Table 3. Level of Significance of Correlation Between Role Effectiveness Dimensions and Other Variables

Other Variables	Role Effectiveness Dimensions (– Indicates negative correlation)					
	Achievement	Influence	Control	Extension	Affiliation	Dependence
1. Role Efficacy	.001	.001	.001	.001	.01	.001
2. Internality	.001	.003	—	.045	.001	.001
3. Externality (Others)	−.001	−.001	−.005	−.080	−.002	.001
4. Externality (Chance)	−.001	−.001	−.001	.001	−.003	−.022
5. Externality (Total)	−.001	−.001	−.001	−.004	−.001	−.001
6. Role Stress	−.001	−.001	−.001	−.004	−.002	−.001
7. Coping Strategy (Avoidance)	−.001	−.001	−.004	−.014	−.036	−.044
8. Coping Strategy (Approach)	−.002	.001	.004	.018	—	.014

Norms

The mean values for the MAO-B scores of a sample of five hundred employees from four banks (Sen, 1982) for the approach and avoidance dimensions and the OEQ are shown in Table 4. These tentatively can be used as cutoff points for interpretation of the scores. However, norms should be developed for different groups. The mean values for different levels of employees, as well as different age groups, are shown in Table 5a and 5b.

ADMINISTERING THE MAO-B INSTRUMENT

The MAO-B instrument can be administered in a group. The participants should be told that the instrument is meant to provide a profile of motivational aspects of role behavior and that there are no right or wrong answers.

Table 4. Mean Values for a Sample of Five Hundred Bank Employees

Dimensions	Approach	Avoidance	OEQ
Achievement	16	10	68
Influence	14	10	65
Extension	15	13	56
Control	15	12	63
Affiliation	15	11	64
Dependence	15	11	65

If the instrument is used for HRD purposes, the instrument results can be used to help individuals and the group to plan for increased effectiveness in their roles.

If the instrument is used with students of management, they should be asked to respond to the instrument as they would if they were in managerial positions in an organization. The scores can then be discussed to show the motivational trends of the students.

The concepts underlying the instrument should be presented after the respondents have obtained profiles of their motivational tendencies.

Table 5. Mean Values for Levels and Age Groups

Dimension	Levels				Age Groups						
	Top Mngmt.	Senior Mngmt.	Super-visory	Tellers	<25	26–30	31–35	36–40	41–45	46–50	>50
Achievement	73	70	67	65	64	66	68	65	71	68	72
Influence	70	67	65	61	62	64	63	63	67	68	69
Extension	58	58	56	54	52	55	57	56	56	57	58
Control	68	65	62	60	59	61	61	62	64	65	66
Affiliation	67	64	62	66	61	65	64	66	64	64	66
Dependence	66	67	64	64	64	63	64	64	67	67	67

USE OF THE MAO-B INSTRUMENT

The MAO-B can be used for self-analysis, for individual counseling, and for organizational and human resource training and development. A respondent can examine his or her scores and then plan to reduce the avoidance behavior of a motive for which he or she received a low OEQ score by examining the related items on the instrument and inferring the behavioral implications. In counseling work, both the counselor and the client can complete the instrument from the client's perspective; then the counselor can help the client to plan new behavior.

In an HRD or OD training program, the participants can look at their profiles, request feedback from other participants, and then discuss in trios ways of increasing their effectiveness by reducing their avoidance behaviors for the relevant motives. The instrument also can be used in organization development and consulting work to obtain group profiles, to search for organizational factors to explain the profiles, to develop organizational strategies to improve the profiles, and to develop individual strategies to increase employees' operating effectiveness for the various motives.

References

Atkinson, J.W. (1953). The achievement motive and recall of interrupted and complete tasks. *Journal of Experimental Psychology, 46,* 381–390.

Birney, R.C., & Burdick, H. (1969). *Fear of failure.* New York: Van Nostrand Reinhold.

Heckhausen, H. (1967). *The anatomy of achievement motivation.* New York: Academic Press.

Kotter, J.P. (1979). Power, dependence, and effective management. In *Harvard Business Reviews on human relations.* New York: Harper & Row.

Kram, K.E. (1985). Creating conditions that encourage mentoring. In L.D. Goodstein & J.W. Pfeiffer (Eds.), *The 1985 annual: Developing human resources.* San Francisco, CA: Pfeiffer.

Levenson, H. (1972, August). *Distinctions within the concept of internal-external control: Development of a new scale.* Paper presented at the meeting of the American Psychological Association, Honolulu, Hawaii.

Levenson, H. (1973, August). *Reliability and validity of the I, P, and C scales: A multidimensional view of locus of control.* Paper presented at the American Psychological Association convention, Montreal, Canada.

Levinson, H. (1982). *Executive* (rev. ed.). Cambridge, MA: Harvard University Press.

Litwin, G.H., & Stringer, R.A. (1968). *Motivation and organizational climate.* Boston: Harvard Business School.

McClelland, D.C. (1961). *The achieving society.* New York: Van Nostrand Reinhold.

McClelland, D.C. (1975). *Power: The inner experience.* New York: Irvington.

McClelland, D.C., Atkinson, J.W., Clark, R.A., & Lowell, E.L. (1953). *The achievement motive.* New York: Appleton-Century-Crofts.

McClelland, D.C., & Boyatzis, R.E. (1982). Leadership motive pattern and long-term success in management. *Journal of Applied Psychology, 67*(6), 737–743.

McClelland, D.C., & Burnham, D. (1976). Power is the great motivator. *Harvard Business Review, 54*(2), 100–111.

McClelland, D.C., & Winter, D.G. (1971). *Motivating economic achievement.* New York: The Free Press.

McGregor, D. (1966). *Leadership and motivation.* Cambridge, MA: MIT Press.

Murray, H.A. (1938). *Explorations in personality.* New York: Oxford University Press.

Pareek, U. (1968a). A motivational paradigm of development. *Journal of Social Issues, 24*(2), 115–122.

Pareek, U. (1968b). Motivational patterns and planned social change. *International Social Science Journal, 20*(3), 464–413.

Pareek, U. (1980a). Dimensions of role efficacy. In J.W. Pfeiffer & J.E. Jones (Eds.), *The 1980 annual handbook for group facilitators.* San Francisco, CA: Pfeiffer.

Pareek, U. (1980b). Role efficacy scale. In J.W. Pfeiffer & J.E. Jones (Eds.), *The 1980 annual handbook for group facilitators.* San Francisco, CA: Pfeiffer.

Pareek, U. (1982). Internal and external control. In J.W. Pfeiffer & L.D. Goodstein (Eds.), *The 1982 annual for facilitators, trainers, and consultants.* San Francisco, CA: Pfeiffer.

Pareek, U. (1983). Organizational role stress scale. In L.D. Goodstein & J.W. Pfeiffer (Eds.), *The 1983 annual for facilitators, trainers, and consultants.* San Francisco, CA: Pfeiffer.

Sen, P.C. (1982). *A study of personal and organizational correlates of role stress and coping strategies in some public sector banks.* Unpublished doctoral dissertation, Gujarat University.

Varga, K. (1977). Who gains from achievement motivation training? *Vikalpa, 2*(3), 187–199.

Originally published in The 1986 Annual: Developing Human Resources.

Motivational Analysis of Organizations — Behavior (MAO-B)

Udai Pareek

Instructions: This inventory can help you to understand how different motivations can affect your behavior and your performance at work. There are no "right" or "wrong" responses; the inventory will reflect your own perceptions of how you act at work, so you will gain the most value from it if you answer honestly. Do not spend too much time on any one item; generally, your first reaction is the most accurate.

For each of the statements, refer to the following scale and decide which number represents how often you engage in the behavior or have the feeling described. Then write that number in the blank to the left of the statement.

Rarely/ Never	Sometimes/ Occasionally	Often/ Frequently	Usually/ Always
1	2	3	4

_____ 1. I enjoy working on moderately difficult (challenging) tasks and goals.

_____ 2. I am overly emotional.

_____ 3. I am forceful in my arguments.

_____ 4. I refer matters to my superiors.

_____ 5. I keep close track of things (monitor action).

_____ 6. I make contributions to charity and help those in need.

_____ 7. I set easy goals and achieve them.

_____ 8. I relate very well to people.

_____ 9. I am preoccupied with my own ideas and am a poor listener.

_____ 10. I follow my ideals.

_____ 11. I demand conformity from the people who work for or with me.

_____ 12. I take steps to develop the people who work for me.

_____ 13. I strive to exceed performance/targets.

_____ 14. I ascribe more importance to personal relationships than to organizational matters.

The Pfeiffer Book of Successful Leadership Development Tools © 2003 John Wiley & Sons, Inc. Published by Pfeiffer.

Rarely/ Never 1	Sometimes/ Occasionally 2	Often/ Frequently 3	Usually/ Always 4

_____ 15. I build on the ideas of my subordinates or others.

_____ 16. I seek the approval of my superiors.

_____ 17. I ensure that things are done according to plan.

_____ 18. I consider the difficulties of others even at the expense of the task.

_____ 19. I am afraid of making mistakes.

_____ 20. I share my feelings with others.

_____ 21. I enjoy arguing and winning arguments.

_____ 22. I have genuine respect for experienced people.

_____ 23. I admonish people for not completing tasks.

_____ 24. I go out of my way to help the people who work for me.

_____ 25. I search for new ways to overcome difficulties.

_____ 26. I have difficulty in expressing negative feelings to others.

_____ 27. I set myself as an example and model for others.

_____ 28. I hesitate to make hard decisions.

_____ 29. I define roles and procedures for the people who work for me.

_____ 30. I undergo personal inconvenience for the sake of others.

_____ 31. I am more conscious of my limitations or weaknesses than of my strengths.

_____ 32. I take interest in matters of personal concern to the people who work for me.

_____ 33. I am *laissez faire* in my leadership style (do not care how things happen).

_____ 34. I learn from those who are senior to me.

_____ 35. I centralize most tasks to ensure that things are done properly.

_____ 36. I have empathy and understanding for the people who work for me.

Rarely/ Never 1	Sometimes/ Occasionally 2	Often/ Frequently 3	Usually/ Always 4

_____ 37. I want to know how well I have been doing and I use feedback to improve myself.

_____ 38. I avoid conflict in the interest of group feelings.

_____ 39. I provide new suggestions and ideas.

_____ 40. I try to please others.

_____ 41. I explain systems and procedures clearly to the people who work for me.

_____ 42. I tend to take responsibility for others' work in order to help them.

_____ 43. I show low self-confidence.

_____ 44. I recognize and respond to the feelings of others.

_____ 45. I receive credit for work done in a team.

_____ 46. I seek help from those who know the subject.

_____ 47. In case of difficulties, I rush to correct things.

_____ 48. I develop teamwork among the people who work for me.

_____ 49. I work effectively under pressure of deadlines.

_____ 50. I am uneasy and less productive when working alone.

_____ 51. I give credit and recognition to others.

_____ 52. I look for support for my actions and proposals.

_____ 53. I enjoy positions of authority.

_____ 54. I hesitate to take strong actions because of human considerations.

_____ 55. I complain about difficulties and problems.

_____ 56. I take the initiative in making friends with my colleagues.

_____ 57. I am quite conscious of status symbols such as furniture, size of office, etc.

_____ 58. I like to solicit ideas from others.

_____ 59. I tend to form small groups to influence decisions.

_____ 60. I like to accept responsibility in the group's work.

MOTIVATIONAL ANALYSIS OF ORGANIZATIONS — BEHAVIOR (MAO-B) SCORING SHEET

Instructions: Transfer your responses from the MAO-B inventory to the appropriate spaces on this sheet. If you entered the number 2 in the blank to the left of item 1, enter a 2 in the blank after the number 1 below; if you entered a 4 as your response to item 13, enter a 4 in the blank to the right of the number 13 below, and so on until you have entered all your responses in the spaces below.

A	B	C	D	E	F
1. ___	3. ___	5. ___	10. ___	12. ___	8. ___
13. ___	15. ___	17. ___	22. ___	24. ___	20. ___
25. ___	27. ___	29. ___	34. ___	36. ___	32. ___
37. ___	39. ___	41. ___	46. ___	48. ___	44. ___
49. ___	51. ___	53. ___	58. ___	60. ___	56. ___

A	B	C	D	E	F
Total ___	Total ___	Total ___	Total ___	Total ___	Total ___

a	b	c	d	e	f
7. ___	9. ___	11. ___	4. ___	6. ___	2. ___
19. ___	21. ___	23. ___	16. ___	18. ___	14. ___
31. ___	33. ___	35. ___	28. ___	30. ___	26. ___
43. ___	45. ___	47. ___	40. ___	42. ___	38. ___
55. ___	57. ___	59. ___	52. ___	54. ___	50. ___

a	b	c	d	e	f
Total ___	Total ___	Total ___	Total ___	Total ___	Total ___

Now sum the numbers that you have entered in each vertical column and enter the totals in the blanks provided. These totals are your scores for the approach-avoidance dimensions of each of the six primary motivators of people's behavior on the job. Transfer these totals to the appropriate blanks in the two middle columns on the next page.

Achievement	A (approach) ____	a (avoidance) ____	OEQ ____
Influence	B (approach) ____	b (avoidance) ____	OEQ ____
Control	C (approach) ____	c (avoidance) ____	OEQ ____
Dependence	D (approach) ____	d (avoidance) ____	OEQ ____
Extension	E (approach) ____	e (avoidance) ____	OEQ ____
Affiliation	F (approach) ____	f (avoidance) ____	OEQ ____

To compute your operating effectiveness quotient (OEQ) for each motivator, find the value for your approach (capital letter) score for the motivator along the top row of the table that follows, and then find your avoidance

Avoidance Scores	Approach Scores															
	5	6	7	8	9	10	11	12	13	14	15	16	17	18	19	20
5	0	100	100	100	100	100	100	100	100	100	100	100	100	100	100	100
6	0	50	67	75	80	83	85	87	89	90	91	92	92	93	93	97
7	0	33	50	60	67	71	75	78	80	82	83	85	86	87	87	88
8	0	25	40	50	57	62	67	70	73	75	77	78	80	81	82	83
9	0	20	33	43	50	55	60	64	67	69	71	73	75	76	78	79
10	0	17	28	37	44	50	54	58	61	64	67	69	70	72	74	75
11	0	14	25	33	40	45	50	54	59	60	62	65	67	68	70	71
12	0	12	22	30	36	42	46	50	53	56	59	61	63	65	67	68
13	0	11	20	27	33	38	43	47	50	53	55	58	60	62	64	65
14	0	10	18	25	31	36	40	44	47	50	53	55	57	59	61	62
15	0	9	17	23	28	33	37	41	44	47	50	52	54	56	58	60
16	0	8	15	21	27	31	35	39	42	45	48	50	52	54	56	58
17	0	8	14	20	25	29	33	37	40	43	45	48	50	52	54	56
18	0	7	13	19	23	28	32	35	38	41	43	46	48	50	52	54
19	0	7	12	18	22	26	30	33	36	39	42	44	46	48	50	52
20	0	6	12	17	21	25	29	32	35	37	40	42	44	46	48	50

(lowercase letter) score for that motivator in the left column. The number in the cell that intersects the column and row is your OEQ score for the motivator. Transfer that score to the tally marked "OEQ" on the previous page. Do this for each motivator.

When you have completed this process for all of your scores, you will have a numerical picture of what typically motivates your behavior at work, whether you respond positively (approach) or negatively (avoidance) to each of the six typical motivators, and how your responses to each motivator influence your operating effectiveness.

Motivational Analysis of Organizations — Climate (MAO-C)

Udai Pareek

Most organizations have a structure (division of work into units and establishment of linkages among units) and systems (specific ways of managing the major functions of the organization, such as finance, production, marketing, personnel, information, and the relationship with the external environment). Most also have norms (accepted patterns of behavior), values, and traditions; and these three elements constitute the organizational culture. The main actors in the organization are its top leaders; they and the other employees have their own individual needs in addition to those of the organization. All of these organizational components—structure, systems, culture, leader behavior, and psychological needs of employees—interact with one another and create what can be called organizational climate.

Organizational climate can only be discussed in terms of how it is perceived or felt by organizational members. Consequently, a climate may be perceived as hostile or supportive, as conducive to achievement or stifling, and so on. Hellriegel and Slocum (1974, p. 225)—adapting the concepts suggested by Beer (1971); Campbell, Dunnette, Lawler, and Weick (1970); Dachler (1973); and Schneider (1973)—defined organizational climate as "a set of attributes which can be perceived about a particular organization and/or its subsystems, and that may be induced from the way that an organization and/or its subsystems deal with their members and environment."

Although most authors have used organizational climate as a descriptive concept, some have used it for classifying organizations into categories. For example, Burns and Stalker (1961) describe organic versus mechanical climates, whereas Likert (1967) proposes four types of climates: exploitive, benevolent, consultative, and participative. Such frameworks generally use described categories. Only one framework, proposed by Litwin and Stringer (1968), emphasizes the effect of organizational climate on the motivation of its members. In a rigorous study Litwin and Stringer simulated three different climates (each fostering, respectively, achievement, affiliation, and power motives) and monitored the effects of these climates on productivity. Because climate affects people's motivation (for example, Likert, 1967), a framework based on motivation seems to be quite relevant in studying organizational climate.

SIX MOTIVES CONNECTED WITH ORGANIZATIONAL CLIMATE

Six motives are particularly appropriate in developing a framework that facilitates analysis of the connection between organizational climate and motivation:[1]

1. *Achievement.* This motive is characterized by concern for excellence, competition in terms of the standards set by others or by oneself, the setting of challenging goals for oneself, awareness of the obstacles that might be encountered in attempting to achieve these goals, and persistence in trying alternative paths to one's goals.

2. *Affiliation.* Affiliation is characterized by a concern for establishing and maintaining close, personal relationships; an emphasis on friendship; and a tendency to express one's emotions.

3. *Expert influence.* This motive is characterized by a concern for making an impact on others, a desire to make people do what one thinks is right, and an urge to change situations and to develop people.

4. *Control.* Control is characterized by a concern for orderliness, a desire to be and stay informed, an urge to monitor events and to take corrective action when needed, and a need to display personal power.

---

1. These six motives are also discussed in "Motivational Analysis of Organizations—Behavior (MAO-B)" by U. Pareek, 1986, in J.W. Pfeiffer & L.D. Goodstein (Eds.), *The 1986 Annual: Developing Human Resources* (pp. 121-133), San Francisco, CA: Pfeiffer.

5. *Extension.* Extension is characterized by a concern for others; an interest in superordinate goals; and an urge to be relevant and useful to large groups, including society.

6. *Dependency.* This motive is characterized by a desire for the assistance of others in developing oneself, a need to check with significant others (those who are more knowledgeable or have higher status, experts, close associates, and so on), a tendency to submit ideas or proposals for approval, and an urge to maintain a relationship based on the other person's approval.

TWELVE DIMENSIONS OF ORGANIZATIONAL CLIMATE

Likert (1967) proposed six dimensions of organizational climate (leadership, motivation, communication, decisions, goals, and control), while Litwin and Stringer (1968) proposed seven dimensions (conformity, responsibility, standards, rewards, organizational clarity, warmth and support, and leadership). A review of their studies and those of others indicates that twelve processes or dimensions of organizational climate relate specifically to motivation:

1. *Orientation.* The dominant orientation of an organization is the main concern of its members, and this dimension is an important determinant of climate. If the dominant orientation or concern is to adhere to established rules, the climate will be characterized by control; on the other hand, if the orientation is to excel, the climate will be characterized by achievement.

2. *Interpersonal relationships.* An organization's interpersonal-relations processes are reflected in the way in which informal groups are formed, and these processes affect climate. For example, if groups are formed for the purpose of protecting their own interests, cliques may develop and a climate of control may result; similarly, if people tend to develop informal relationships with their supervisors, a climate of dependency may result.

3. *Supervision.* Supervisory practices contribute significantly to climate. If supervisors focus on helping their subordinates to improve personal skills and chances of advancement, a climate characterized by the extension motive may result; if supervisors are more concerned with maintaining good relations with their subordinates, a climate characterized by the affiliation motive may result.

4. *Problem management.* Problems can be seen as challenges or as irritants. They can be solved by the supervisor or jointly by the supervisor and the

subordinate(s) concerned, or they can be referred to a higher level. These different perspectives and ways of handling problems contribute to the creation of an organization's climate.

5. *Management of mistakes.* Supervisors' attitudes toward subordinate mistakes develop the organizational orientation, which is generally one of annoyance or concern or tolerance. An organization's approach to mistakes influences the climate.

6. *Conflict management.* Conflicts may be seen as embarrassing annoyances to be covered up or as problems to be solved. The process of dealing with conflicts has as significant an effect on climate as that of handling problems or mistakes.

7. *Communication.* Communication, another important determinant of climate, is concerned with the flow of information: its direction (top-down, bottom-up, horizontal), its dispersement (selectively or to everyone concerned), its mode (formal or informal), and its type (instructions or feedback on the state of affairs).

8. *Decision making.* An organization's approach to decision making can be focused on maintaining good relations or on achieving results. In addition, the issue of who makes decisions is important: people high in the hierarchy, experts, or those involved in the matters about which decisions are made. These elements of decision making are relevant to the establishment of a particular climate.

9. *Trust.* The degree of trust or its absence among various members and groups in the organization affects climate. The issue of who is trusted by management and to what degree is also relevant.

10. *Management of rewards.* Rewards reinforce specific behaviors, thereby arousing and sustaining specific motives. Consequently, what is rewarded in an organization influences the motivational climate.

11. *Risk taking.* How people respond to risks and whose help is sought in situations involving risk are important determinants of climate.

12. *Innovation and change.* Who initiates change, how change and innovation are perceived, and how change is implemented are all critical in establishing climate.

The way in which these twelve dimensions of climate operate in an organization indicates the underlying motive of top management and the principal motive that is likely to be generated and sustained within the organization's population. When the twelve dimensions are combined with the six motives discussed previously, a matrix is formed that can be useful in diagnosing the motivational climate of an organization.

THE INSTRUMENT

The Motivational Analysis of Organizations—Climate (MAO-C) instrument was developed to study organizational climate, specifically with regard to motivation. The instrument employs the twelve dimensions of organizational climate and the six motives previously described. It consists of twelve categories, each of which includes six statements; each of the twelve categories corresponds to one of the twelve climatic dimensions, and each of the six statements represents one of the six motives. Respondents work individually to rank order the six statements within each separate category according to their perceptions of how much each statement is like the situation in their organization (or unit, branch, division, or department within the organization).

Scoring and Interpretation

Usually organizational-climate instruments require respondents to rate organizational processes, and respondents tend to assign ratings in the middle of the scale provided for this purpose. The MAO-C, in contrast, is based on rankings so that the respondent cannot escape in the "golden middle."

After completing the instrument, the respondent refers to the scoring key to discover which motives are indicated by his or her responses and then transfers rankings of motives to the matrix. Then the respondent adds the numbers in each vertical column of the matrix and writes the totals in the appropriate blanks; each of these totals is the score for the related motive or motivational climate. These scores can range from 12 to 72. Next the respondent refers to the conversion table, locates the total for each motive, and writes the corresponding MAO-C index number in the blank provided. The indexes can range from 0 to 100. The following formula was used to arrive at the index for each motive:

$$\text{Index} = \frac{(S - 12) \times 100}{60}$$

For each horizontal row on the matrix representing a dimension of organizational climate, the dominant motive (the one with the highest number in the row) and the backup motive (the one with the next-highest number) are noted in the blanks provided (see the two vertical columns on the extreme right of the matrix). The dominant and backup columns are helpful in diagnosing and in planning action to improve the motivational climate of the organization or unit involved. Finally, the respondent determines which motives appear most often in the dominant and backup columns and writes these motives in the blanks provided for *overall dominant motive* and *overall backup motive*.

An organization may total all respondents' index numbers for each motive and then average the numbers for an overall organizational index of each; or the total of the numbers in each vertical column of the individual respondents' matrices can be added and averaged and the index number written, using the conversion table. The advantage of the index is to show the relative strength of the climate with regard to the motives; the cutoff point is 50. If the index number for a particular dimension is greater than 50, the climate is relatively strong in that dimension; if the index number is less than 50, the climate is relatively weak in that dimension. The index also helps in comparing organizations or units within an organization.

Reliability

Retest reliability of the MAO-C has been reported by Sen (1982) and by Surti (1982).

Validity

Validity studies have not been done for the MAO-C. However, indirect evidence of the instrument's validity has been provided as a result of other research on organizational climate. Research on organizational climate as an independent measure and measures of organizational effectiveness share enough in common to warrant some generalizations. Hellriegel and Slocum (1974) have summarized these generalizations as a significant relationship between climate and both job satisfaction and performance.

Deci (1980) suggested three different kinds of environments as being associated with three different attributional patterns. A "responsive and informational" environment (in the terms of the MAO-C, one that is characterized by achievement and expert influence) has been linked with internality; a "controlling and demanding" environment (one characterized by control and dependency) has been linked with externality; and a "nonresponsive and capricious" environment has been linked with "impersonality."

Organizational environments and climate seem to influence the development of internality. Baumgartel, Rajan, and Newman (1985), using four indices of organizational environment (freedom-growth, human relations, performance pressure, and personal benefit) found clear evidence of the influence of organizational environments on locus of control. They concluded that internality could be developed by creating educational and work environments characterized by freedom to set personal performance goals, opportunity for personal growth, and opportunity to influence important events or conditions.

A regression analysis of data from 320 professional women, using role efficacy as a variable, showed that of the fourteen variables that finally emerged in the regression, organizational climate alone explained about 34 percent of the variance, thereby exhibiting a great effect on role efficacy (Surti, 1982).

Theoretically (see, for example, Litwin & Stringer, 1968), one might predict a negative relationship between organizational effectiveness and climates characterized by affiliation, dependence, and control. Litwin and Stringer (1968) found that an authoritarian climate (referred to in the MAO-C as a "control" climate) produced low job satisfaction and low performance. A climate characterized by achievement, extension, and expert influence might be assumed to be related to higher job satisfaction and performance. Using Litwin and Stringer's instrument, Cawsey (reported in Hellriegel & Slocum, 1974) found higher job satisfaction among insurance personnel who perceived the motivational climate as one of achievement.

One study reported on the administration of the MAO-C to 392 executives of a manufacturing firm (Khanna, 1986). Each executive was instructed to complete the MAO-C by evaluating the climate or culture of his or her specific unit or department (as opposed to that of the entire organization). Correlations were noted between the six perceived motives or motivational climates and measures of organizational effectiveness (consisting of consensus, legitimization, the need for independence, self-control, job involvement, innovation, organizational commitment, organizational attachment, and job satisfaction). The climates were also correlated with total satisfaction, that is, satisfaction with work and with the organization as a whole. No significant correlation was found between the climates and the need for independence, self-control, and innovation. With regard to job involvement, the only positive correlation significant at the .05 level was with an achievement climate.

In the same study there were positive correlations (significant at the .01 level) between five other aspects of organizational effectiveness (organizational commitment, organizational attachment, job satisfaction, total satisfaction, and total effectiveness) and an achievement climate, and there was a negative correlation between these five aspects and a control climate. An extension climate correlated positively with organizational commitment at the .05 level and with job satisfaction, total satisfaction, and total effectiveness at the .01 level. A dependence climate showed no relationship with any measure. An affiliation climate had a negative correlation with job satisfaction at the .05 level and with total satisfaction and total effectiveness at the .01 level. A climate perceived as characterized by expert influence had only one positive correlation (at the .05 level) with organizational attachment. All correlations were in the predicted direction, although more correlations were expected with climates characterized by dependence and expert influence.

Negative correlations might be predicted between role stress and climates perceived as characterized by achievement, extension, and expert influence; and positive correlations might be predicted between role stress and climates characterized by affiliation, dependence, and control. Khanna (1986) correlated climate scores with ten aspects of role stress and total role stress (as reported in Pareek, 1983). Specific correlations between role stress and the various climates were as follows:

- No significant correlation with a climate characterized by expert influence;

- Two positive correlations with an affiliation climate (role erosion at the .01 level and personal inadequacy at the .05 level);

- One positive correlation with a dependency climate (role stagnation at the .01 level);

- Six negative correlations with an extension climate (at the .05 level for interrole distance, role overload, and role isolation, and at the .01 level for role-expectation conflict, self-role distance, resource inadequacy, and total role stress);

- Negative correlations with an achievement climate at the .01 level for all aspects of role stress except interrole distance and personal inadequacy; and

- Positive correlations with a control climate at the .01 level for all aspects of role stress except personal inadequacy.

Similar results were reported by Sen (1982) and Surti (1982). All of these results were in the predicted directions.

In summary, organizational climate has an enormous influence on organizational effectiveness, role efficacy, and role stress. An achievement climate seems to contribute to effectiveness, satisfaction, and a sense of internality; a climate characterized by expert influence seems to contribute to organizational attachment; and a climate characterized by extension seems to contribute to organizational commitment. All of these climates foster relatively low levels of

Motive	Type of Organization
Achievement	Industrial and business organizations
Expert influence	University departments and scientific organizations
Control	Bureaucracies such as governmental departments and agencies
Dependency	Traditional or autocratic organizations
Extension	Community-service organizations
Affiliation	Clubs

Figure 1. Connections Between Dominant Motives and Types of Organizations

role stress. A control climate seems to lower role efficacy, job satisfaction, organizational commitment, organizational attachment, and total effectiveness and to foster relatively high levels of role stress. An affiliation climate tends to lower both satisfaction and effectiveness and increase role erosion and feelings of personal inadequacy.

Effectiveness Profiles

The completed matrix provides scores for all six motives tested by the MAO-C. The highest of these scores represents the perceived dominant motive within an organization. The general connections between dominant motives and particular types of organizations are shown in Figure 1.

A combination of an organization's highest or "dominant" score and its second-highest or "backup" score results in a basic characterization of that organization's climate. When the six motives are combined in patterns of dominant and secondary or backup styles, thirty organizational profiles are possible. Brief descriptions of these thirty profiles are provided in the following paragraphs. In each description the first motive noted represents the organization's dominant motive, and the second represents its secondary or backup motive. Some of these profiles are based on studies that have been conducted; others need to be studied to validate the concept. In general, climates dominated by achievement, expert power, and extension are conducive to the achievement of results, whereas climates dominated by control, dependency, and affiliation retard the achievement of results.

1. *Achievement-Expert influence.* Employees are involved in and highly stimulated by challenging tasks, and the specialists within the organization dominate in determining these tasks. The organization rewards specialization.

2. *Achievement-Control.* Most employees are involved in challenging tasks, but they face a lot of constraints attributable to rigid procedures and an inflexible hierarchy.

3. *Achievement-Dependency.* In spite of an emphasis on high achievement that is shared by most employees, there is a tendency to postpone critical decisions for the approval of a higher authority. The organization discourages making such decisions without approval from a higher level, resulting in a sense of frustration.

4. *Achievement-Extension.* Employees work on challenging tasks and devote equal attention to the social relevance of these tasks. The organization has a highly developed sense of social responsibility as well as a strong sense of its responsibility to fulfill employee needs.

5. *Achievement-Affiliation.* While employees work on challenging goals, they also form strong groups based on common interests or other factors. The organization pays a lot of attention to maintaining good relations among these cliques.

6. *Expert influence-Achievement.* The organization places a high value on specialization. The specialists influence most decisions, and they emphasize high work quality and unique contributions.

7. *Expert influence-Control.* The organization is controlled by experts who employ cumbersome procedures. The result is generally a lack of job satisfaction and low to moderate (rather than high) output.

8. *Expert influence-Dependency.* The organization has a rigid hierarchy dominated by experts. Decisions are made only at the upper levels of the hierarchy, and bright employees are highly dissatisfied.

9. *Expert influence-Extension.* Specialists play the major roles in the organization, working in a planned way on socially relevant matters. The organization pays attention to the employees' needs and welfare.

10. *Expert influence-Affiliation.* Although the organization is dominated by experts, strong groups are formed on the basis of common interests or other factors. Because primary attention is placed on maintaining a friendly climate, results usually suffer.

11. *Control-Achievement.* The organization is bureaucratic, is run in accordance with detailed procedures, and has a clear hierarchy. Quality of work is emphasized, but most employees with an achievement orientation feel frustrated. This climate is sometimes found in public-sector organizations.

12. *Control-Expert influence.* The organization is a bureaucracy in which specialists' opinions are valued but rules are treated as more important.

13. *Control-Dependency.* A bureaucracy and a rigid hierarchy dominate the organization. Because actions are generally referred to levels above for approval, decisions are usually delayed. It is more important to follow rules and regulations than to achieve results. The senior employees protect those subordinates who do not make any procedural mistakes. Most government offices function in this way.

14. *Control-Extension.* Although the organization is hierarchical, it emphasizes social concern and attends to the needs and welfare of its employees.

15. *Control-Affiliation.* The organization is hierarchical but places more emphasis on good relations among employees than on results. Informal groups based on relationships are seen as important. Some voluntary organizations are of this type.

16. *Dependency-Achievement.* Respect for those in positions of power is emphasized, and so is achievement. Freedom is granted to employees, with the exception that key decisions are controlled by those in power. Many family-owned organizations have such a climate.

17. *Dependency-Expert influence.* The organization has a hierarchy, with decisions made by those at higher levels. Experts play an important role in the various aspects of organizational life.

18. *Dependency-Control.* The organization has clear-cut channels of communication and is controlled by a few people who ultimately make all decisions.

19. *Dependency-Extension.* A few people dominate and control the organization and demand respect from all other members. However, they take care of the members' needs; and the organization works in socially relevant areas.

20. *Dependency-Affiliation.* The top managers control the organization and employ their own "in-group" members, who are extremely loyal to these managers.

21. *Extension-Achievement.* The organization strives to be relevant to society and emphasizes the achievement of results. People are selected for their competence and are given freedom in doing their work.

22. *Extension-Expert influence.* Social consciousness is emphasized by the organization, and experts influence all major decisions.

23. *Extension-Control.* The organization's goals have to do with serving a larger cause; but the structure is bureaucratic, with rules and regulations that are to be followed strictly.

24. *Extension-Dependency.* The business of the organization is community service (for example, education, health, or development). Emphasis is placed on conformity to the policies laid down by the top person or team, to whom all final decisions are referred.

25. *Extension-Affiliation.* The organization's business is community service, and members with similar backgrounds (ideology, specialization, and so on) form strong linkages with one another.

26. *Affiliation-Achievement.* The organization places great importance on relationships and draws people with similar backgrounds. Although the organization values achievement of results and excellence in performance, rewards are given mainly on the basis of an employee's relationship with the person or persons who are in a position to give such rewards.

27. *Affiliation-Expert influence.* The organization consists mainly of experts, emphasizes good relations, and either employs people of similar backgrounds or has cliques based on common links.

28. *Affiliation-Control.* Although the organization is concerned with maintaining good relations among members, its form is bureaucratic. (For example, a club with strict rules and procedures might be in this category.)

29. *Affiliation-Dependency.* The organization values the maintenance of friendly relations among members, and one or two people make most decisions. Employees are rewarded on the basis of their closeness to the top person(s).

30. *Affiliation-Extension.* The organization's main goal is to maintain good relations among members, and its work involves socially relevant issues. (The Lions Club and similar organizations might be in this category.)

Use of the Instrument

The MAO-C can be used to diagnose organizational climate from the standpoint of motivation. The focus of the instrument can be perceptions of the overall organizational climate or of individual units, divisions, branches, or departments within the organization. After the instrument has been administered, the respondents may individually use a rating scale to evaluate the operating effectiveness of the climate that has been analyzed. Then the administrator may lead a discussion on the basic characteristics of the different effectiveness profiles represented in the group (see the previous section). Subsequently, the respondents may discuss their individual scores and ratings and then arrive at a consensus regarding the diagnosis and evaluation of the climate, which of the twelve dimensions of organizational climate need improvement, why particular dimensions are weak, and what steps may need to be taken in response.

Another approach is to discuss individual rankings and to develop a consensus regarding the desired rankings of motives and what might be done to affect the perceived climate accordingly. Any specific action ideas that are developed may be presented to top management for discussion, approval, and commitment. Then the agreed-on action steps may be carried out and followed up with monthly reviews to determine the success of implementation.

References

Baumgartel, H.J., Rajan, P.S.S., & Newman, J. (1985). Educational environments and attributions of causality: Some exploratory research findings. *Quality of Work Life, 2*(56), 309–328.

Beer, M. (1971, September). *Organizational climate: A viewpoint from the change agent.* Paper presented at the American Psychological Association Convention, Washington, D.C.

Burns, T., & Stalker, G. (1961). *The management of innovation.* London: Tavistock.

Campbell, J.P., Dunnette, M.D., Lawler, E.E., III, & Weick, K.E., Jr. (1970). *Managerial behavior, performance, and effectiveness.* New York: McGraw-Hill.

Dachler, H.P. (1973). *Work motivation and the concept of organizational climate.* Paper presented at the 10th Annual Eastern Academy of Management Meeting, Philadelphia, PA.

Deci, E.L. (1980). *The psychology of self-determination.* Lexington, MA: Lexington Books.

Hellriegel, D., & Slocum, J.W. (1974). Organizational climate: Measures, research and contingencies. *Academy of Management Journal, 17*(2), 255–280.

Khanna, B.B. (1986). *Relationship between organizational climate and organizational role stress and their impact upon organizational effectiveness: A case study.* Unpublished doctoral dissertation, Banaras Hindu University, Varanasi, India.

Likert, R. (1967). *The human organization.* New York: McGraw-Hill.

Litwin, G., & Stringer, R. (1968). *Motivation and organizational climate.* Cambridge, MA: Harvard University Press.

Pareek, U. (1983). Organizational role stress. In L.D. Goodstein & J.W. Pfeiffer (Eds.), *The 1983 annual for facilitators, trainers, and consultants* (pp. 115–123). San Francisco, CA: Pfeiffer.

Pareek, U. (1986). Motivational analysis of organizations—behavior (MAO-B). In J.W. Pfeiffer & L.D. Goodstein (Eds.), *The 1986 annual: Developing human resources* (pp. 121–133). San Francisco, CA: Pfeiffer.

Schneider, B. (1973). *The perceived environment: Organizational climate.* Paper presented at the meeting of the Midwest Psychological Association.

Sen, P.C. (1982). *Personal and organizational correlates of role stress and coping strategies in some public sector banks.* Unpublished doctoral dissertation, University of Gujarat, Ahmedabad, India.

Surti, K. (1982). *Some psychological correlates of role stress and coping styles in working women.* Unpublished doctoral dissertation, University of Gujarat, Ahmedabad, India.

Originally published in The 1989 Annual: Developing Human Resources.

Motivational Analysis of Organizations — Climate (MAO-C)

Udai Pareek

Name _____   Title _____

Instructions: Completing this inventory will allow you to evaluate the climate or culture of your organization (or your unit or department, if the administrator of this inventory instructs you to interpret the inventory in this way). Below are twelve categories representing twelve dimensions of organizational climate, and within each category are six statements. You are to rank the statements in each category from *6* (*most* like the situation in your organization or unit) to *1* (*least* like the situation in your organization or unit). *Do not give the same rank to more than one statement.*

Rank   **1. Orientation**

_____   a. People here are mainly concerned with following established rules and procedures.

_____   b. The main concern of people here is to help one another develop greater skills and thereby advance in the organization.

_____   c. Achieving or surpassing seems to be people's main concern here.

_____   d. Consolidating one's own personal position and influence seems to be the main concern here.

_____   e. The dominant concern here is to maintain friendly relations with others.

_____   f. The main concern here is to develop people's competence and expertise.

Rank   **2. Interpersonal Relationships**

_____   a. In this organization most informal groups are formed around experts.

_____   b. The atmosphere here is very friendly, and people spend enough time in informal social relations.

_____   c. In this organization strong cliques protect their own interests.

_____   d. Businesslike relationships prevail here; people are warm, but they get together primarily to ensure excellence in performance.

_____   e. People here have strong associations mostly with their supervisors and look to them for suggestions and guidance.

_____   f. People here have a high concern for one another and tend to help one another spontaneously when such help is needed.

Rank   3. **Supervision**

_____   a. The purpose of supervision here is usually to check for mistakes and to "catch" the person making the mistake.

_____   b. Supervisors here strongly prefer that their subordinates ask them for instructions and suggestions.

_____   c. Supervisors here take pains to see that their subordinates improve personal skills and chances of advancement.

_____   d. Supervisors here reward outstanding achievement.

_____   e. In influencing their subordinates, supervisors here try to use their expertise and competence rather than their formal authority.

_____   f. Supervisors here are more concerned with maintaining good relations with their subordinates than with emphasizing duties and performance.

Rank   4. **Problem Management**

_____   a. People here take problems as challenges and try to find better solutions than anyone else.

_____   b. When problems are faced here, experts are consulted and play an important role in solving these problems.

_____   c. In dealing with problems, people here mostly consult their friends.

_____   d. When working on solutions to problems, people here keep in mind the needs of organizational members as well as society at large.

_____   e. People here usually refer problems to their superiors and look to their superiors for solutions.

_____   f. Problems here are usually solved by supervisors; subordinates are not involved.

Rank   5. **Management of Mistakes**

_____   a. When people here make mistakes, they are not rejected; instead, their friends show them much understanding and warmth.

_____   b. Here the philosophy is that the supervisor can make no mistake and the subordinate dare not make one.

_____   c. Usually people here are able to acknowledge and analyze their mistakes because they can expect to receive help and support from others.

_____   d. When a subordinate makes a mistake here, the supervisor treats it as a learning experience that can prevent failure and improve performance in the future.

_____   e. Subordinates here expect guidance from their supervisors in correcting or preventing mistakes.

_____   f. Here people seek the help of experts in analyzing and preventing mistakes.

Rank   6. **Conflict Management**

_____   a. Most interpersonal and interdepartmental conflicts here arise as a result of striving for higher performance; and in analyzing and resolving these conflicts, the overriding consideration is high productivity.

_____   b. Here conflicts are usually avoided or smoothed over to maintain the friendly atmosphere.

_____   c. Arbitration or third-party intervention (usually performed by experienced or senior people) is sought and used here.

_____   d. In a conflict situation here, those who are stronger force their points of view on others.

_____   e. In resolving conflicts here, appeal is made to principles, organizational ideals, and the larger good of the organization.

_____   f. Experts are consulted and their advice used in resolving conflicts here.

Rank 7. **Communication**

_____ a. After due consideration those in authority here issue instructions and expect them to be carried out.

_____ b. Most communication here is informal and friendly and arises from and contributes to warm relations.

_____ c. People here ask for information from those who are experts on the subject.

_____ d. Relevant information is made available to all who need it and can use it for the purpose of achieving high performance here.

_____ e. People here communicate information, suggestions, and even criticism to others out of concern for them.

_____ f. Communication is often selective here; people usually give or holdback crucial information as a form of control.

Rank 8. **Decision Making**

_____ a. While making decisions, people here make special attempts to maintain cordial relations with all concerned.

_____ b. Decisions are made at the top and communicated downward, and people here generally prefer this.

_____ c. People who have demonstrated high achievement have a big say in the decisions made here.

_____ d. Decisions here are generally made without involving subordinates.

_____ e. Decisions here are made and influenced by specialists and other knowledgeable people.

_____ f. Decisions are made here by keeping in mind the good of the employees and of society.

Rank 9. **Trust**

_____ a. Only a few people here are trusted by management, and they are quite influential.

_____ b. Trusting and friendly relations are highly valued here.

_____ c. Here high value is placed on trust between supervisor and subordinate.

_____ d. The specialists and the experts are highly trusted here.

_____ e. A general attitude of helping generates mutual trust here.

_____ f. Those who can achieve results are highly trusted here.

Rank 10. **Management of Rewards**

_____ a. Here the main things that are rewarded are excellence in performance and the accomplishment of tasks.

_____ b. Knowledge and expertise are recognized and rewarded here.

_____ c. Loyalty is rewarded more than anything else here.

_____ d. The people who are rewarded here are those who help their junior colleagues to achieve and develop.

_____ e. The ability to control subordinates and maintain discipline is afforded the greatest importance in rewarding supervisors here.

_____ f. The ability to get along well with others is highly rated and rewarded here.

Rank 11. **Risk Taking**

_____ a. When confronted by risky situations, supervisors here seek the guidance and support of friends.

_____ b. In risky situations supervisors here strongly emphasize discipline and obedience to orders.

_____ c. In risky situations supervisors here have a strong tendency to rely on expert specialists for their advice.

_____ d. Supervisors here generally go to their superiors for instructions in risky situations.

_____ e. In responding to risky situations, supervisors here show great concern for the people working in the organization.

_____ f. In responding to risky situations, supervisors here take calculated risks and strive above all to be more efficient or productive.

Rank   12. **Innovation and Change**

_____ a. Innovation or change here is initiated and implemented primarily by experts and specialists.

_____ b. Here innovation or change is primarily ordered by top management.

_____ c. Before initiating innovation or change, supervisors here generally go to their superiors for sanction and guidance.

_____ d. Those who initiate innovation or change here demonstrate a great concern for any possible adverse effects on others (in the organization or outside) and try to minimize these effects.

_____ e. Innovation or change here is mainly initiated and implemented through highly results-oriented individuals.

_____ f. Supervisors here seldom undertake innovations that disturb their existing friendships in the organization or earn the enmity of organizational members.

MOTIVATIONAL ANALYSIS OF ORGANIZATIONS — CLIMATE (MAO-C) MATRIX SHEET

Instructions: Organizations (and units, branches, divisions, or departments within organizations) tend to be perceived as driven by one or more of six specific motives. The *scoring key* will show you which motives are indicated by your responses on the MAO-C and, therefore, which motives you perceive as driving your organization or unit; then completing this *matrix sheet* will help you arrive at a profile of the general motivational climate of your organization or unit as you perceive it. For example, for the first category or dimension of organizational climate, *Orientation,* if you ranked item *a* as 4, you would look at the scoring key and learn that a indicates the *dependency* motive; then you would refer to this matrix sheet and find the horizontal row that corresponds to Orientation, locate the heading "Dependency," and write the number 4 under that heading in the Orientation row. Follow this process until you have transferred all six of your rankings for each of the twelve categories covered in the MAO-C.

Add the numbers in each vertical column of this matrix and write the totals in the blanks provided; each of these totals is your score for that particular motive. Then refer to the *conversion table,* locate your total for each motive, and write the corresponding MAO-C index number in the blank provided on this matrix sheet.

Next, for each horizontal row on the matrix, which represents a dimension of organizational climate, write the dominant motive (the one with the highest number in the row) and the backup motive (the one with the next-highest number) in the blanks provided (see the two vertical columns on the extreme right of the matrix). The dominant and backup columns are helpful in diagnosing and in planning action to improve the motivational climate of the organization or unit. Finally, determine which motives appear most often in the dominant and backup columns and write these motives in the blanks provided for *overall dominant motive* and *overall backup motive.*

Motives

Dimensions of Organizational Climate	Achievement	Expert Influence	Extension	Control	Dependency	Affiliation	Dominant (Abbreviate as necessary)	Backup (Abbreviate as necessary)
1. Orientation								
2. Interpersonal relationships							.	
3. Supervision								
4. Problem management								
5. Management of mistakes								
6. Conflict management								
7. Communication								
8. Decision making								
9. Trust								
10. Management of rewards								
11. Risk taking								
12. Innovation and change								
Total Scores							Overall Dominant Motive	Overall Backup Motive
MAO-C Index								

The Pfeiffer Book of Successful Leadership Development Tools © 2003 John Wiley & Sons, Inc. Published by Pfeiffer.

MOTIVATIONAL ANALYSIS OF ORGANIZATIONS — CLIMATE (MAO-C) SCORING KEY

Motives

Dimensions of Organizational Climate	Achievement	Expert Influence	Extension	Control	Dependency	Affiliation
1. Orientation	c	f	b	d	a	e
2. Interpersonal relationships	d	a	f	c	e	b
3. Supervision	d	e	c	a	b	f
4. Problem management	a	b	d	f	e	c
5. Management of mistakes	d	f	c	b	e	a
6. Conflict management	a	f	e	d	c	b
7. Communication	d	c	e	f	a	b
8. Decision making	c	e	f	d	b	a
9. Trust	f	d	e	a	c	b
10. Management of rewards	a	b	d	e	c	f
11. Risk taking	f	c	e	b	d	a
12. Innovation and change	e	a	d	b	c	f

Conversion Table

Score	Index	Score	Index	Score	Index	Score	Index	Score	Index
12	0	25	21	37	41	49	61	61	81
13	2	26	23	38	43	50	63	62	83
14	3	27	25	39	45	51	65	63	85
15	5	28	26	40	46	52	66	64	86
16	7	29	28	41	48	53	68	65	88
17	8	30	30	42	50	54	70	66	90
18	10	31	31	43	51	55	71	67	91
19	12	32	33	44	53	56	73	68	93
20	13	33	35	45	55	57	75	69	95
21	15	34	36	46	56	58	78	70	96
22	17	35	38	47	58	59	78	71	98
23	18	36	40	48	60	60	80	72	100
24	19								

5

Managerial Work-Values Scale

T. Venkateswara Rao

The term value has been defined as "the excellence or the degree of worth ascribed to an object. Though ascribed to the object and reacted to as if external or objective, value is a function of the valuing transaction, not of the object" (English & English, 1958). By this definition, work value means "the degree of worth ascribed to a particular type of work, activity, or aspect of the work." This definition of work value makes the term distinct from occupational (or job) preference, because it refers to the degree of worth that is ascribed to it. Whereas preference indicates a general attitude, value implies a stronger attitude or a positive evaluation.

REVIEW OF RESEARCH

From the 1920s through the 1980s, hundreds of investigations were conducted on the question of work values or job attitudes. Douglass (1922) studied 2,844 high school seniors, who gave the following reasons for preferring a job: (1) a general impression of the advantages and attractiveness of the job; (2) the respondent's own fitness for the job; (3) the job's financial returns; (4) opportunities for service; and (5) the respondent's knowledge of his or her fitness for the work based on personal experience. Kornhauser's 1936 study of 350 Chicago males indicated that security and independence were the most strongly desired aspects of a job by members of lower- and middle-income groups; this contrasted with members of wealthy and upper-income groups, who most desired social approval (Centers, 1949).

Centers (1961), whose many studies stimulated research in this particular field, conducted a nationwide survey of U.S. Americans. Centers found that the respondents desired independence, self-expression, security, the opportunity to serve others, and interesting experience, in that order. They placed less value on dimensions of power, fame, esteem, leadership, and profits.

Centers also found significant differences in value patterns for different occupational groups. Large business owners' preferences for self-expression, leadership, and interesting experiences were in marked contrast to those of unskilled laborers, who chose security more frequently than any other value.

Ginzberg (1951) theorized that choices made before seventeen years of age were only tentative and that real choices were made only after age seventeen.

Gray (1963) compared the work values of fifty secondary-school teachers, fifty accountants, and fifty engineers. Teachers scored highest on their preferences for social rewards, whereas accountants scored highest on the value of prestige.

Significant gender differences in the ranking of occupational values were reported by Thompson (1966). In this study women placed significantly less emphasis on leadership, pay, and recognition than men did. Men, in contrast, placed less emphasis on self-expression and social service than women did. High achievers valued jobs that encouraged individuality more than low achievers did. High pay, leadership, and interesting and challenging jobs were the other preferences of high achievers.

Domenichetti (1970) found that work values also change as a function of vocational maturity.

Schein (1990) identified the following eight categories of career anchors:

1. Technical/functional competence;

2. General managerial competence;

3. Autonomy/independence;

4. Security/stability;

5. Entrepreneurial creativity;

6. Service/dedication to a cause;

7. Pure challenge; and

8. Lifestyle.

According to Schein, a career anchor represents a person's self-image of what he or she excels in, wants, and values. Although a person can have only one career anchor, the categories can be arranged in a hierarchy according to what that person would be willing to give up if forced to choose between two anchors.

Managerial Work Values

Values often are considered to be organized into hierarchical structures. The concept of a value system suggests a rank ordering of values along a continuum of importance. Two distinct types of values—instrumental (means) and terminal (end) values—make possible two distinct value systems, each with a rank-ordered structure of its own. These value systems are functionally and cognitively connected with each other as well as connected with a person's attitudes toward other specific objects and situations.

Theoretically, with large numbers of values, a large number of variations in the rankings are possible. It is, however, unlikely that all possible value patterns will exist, because social factors (such as culture, social system, gender, occupation, education, religion, and political orientation) sharply restrict the number of actual variants.

Values impact managerial interactions in a variety of ways. Values influence managers' choices; choices, in turn, are important in determining managerial effectiveness because they influence outcomes. For example, the values that managers hold may influence their choices of subordinates, their likes and dislikes for given jobs, or the extent to which they involve themselves with certain tasks. A manager may value scientific and theoretical knowledge so much that he or she unconsciously may prefer a thinker or a theorizer for a routine job. Another manager's preference for a particular machine may be more a result of aesthetic values than an awareness of the efficiency of that machine. A research-and-development manager may try to economize unnecessarily because of personal economic values, thus limiting his or her ability to experiment with new products. The values an individual holds about different aspects of life constantly affect that person's choices. Managers are likely to make better decisions in all situations if they act with an awareness of their reasons and with the knowledge of the extent to which their values direct their decisions.

Dimensions of Work Values

Because work values are the degree of worth a person ascribes to particular aspects or dimensions of work, identifying the dimensions of work helps in understanding work values. Dimensions of work include the opportunities the work offers for a person to satisfy the following needs:

1. To be creative;
2. To earn money;
3. To be independent;
4. To enjoy prestige and status;
5. To serve others;
6. To do academic work;
7. To have a stable and secure job;
8. To enjoy one's colleagues; and
9. To have good working conditions.

Managers who prefer academic work may excel as trainers, whereas managers who want to be creative might be more resourceful in research-and-development departments. Managers who prefer service may do well in public services, whereas managers who prefer independence might better join organizations that offer autonomy and freedom. Knowledge of one's own work values helps a person to choose a job that is congruent with these values and/or to make career decisions that reflect these work values.

THE INSTRUMENT

The Managerial Work-Values Scale was first developed to measure the work values of medical doctors (Rao, 1976). Subsequently, the instrument was adapted to measure the work values of managers (Pareek, Rao, & Pestonjee, 1981).

The instrument has been further adapted here to focus more specifically on nine work values, using the paired comparison method to measure their relative strengths. The work dimensions included are creativity, economics, independence, status, service, academics, security, collegiality, and work conditions.

Of these dimensions, creativity, independence, service, and academics can be considered as *intrinsic* and the rest as *extrinsic* dimensions of work.

This instrument consists of thirty-six pairs of items. Each item in a pair represents one of the nine work dimensions. The respondent distributes three points between the items in each pair, based on personal preferences for that work dimension.

Because each work dimension is compared with eight other dimensions, the maximum possible score for any work value is 8 × 3, or 24 points. Thus, the score for any work value could range from 0 to 24.

Administration and Scoring

The Managerial Work-Values Scale can be self-administered. When the instrument is used in groups or for training programs, the administrator should have the respondents complete the instrument first, then discuss the concept of work values, and then help the respondents to score their own responses. Each respondent's scores on each item (1a, 1b, 2a, 2b, and so on) should be transferred to the scoring sheet. The score for each work-value dimension can be obtained by adding scores on all eight items of that dimension. The total of all scores on all work values is 108 points.

Interpretation

Because this scale uses the paired-comparison method and because it is intended to prepare the work-value profile of the respondent, no norms are necessary. On the basis of the scores obtained by a respondent, the corresponding work values can be ranked in descending order of the scores. Thus the highest-scored dimension is the dominant work value of the respondent, and the lowest-scored dimension is the least-valued dimension of work.

Normally, scores between eighteen and twenty-four indicate strongly valued work dimensions. A respondent can have more than one dominant work value. In fact, results for some respondents tend to demonstrate clusters of work values scored as high or low. Explanations for each dimension are provided on the interpretation sheet.

Validity and Reliability

Two types of validity have been established for this scale in its original version: content validity and validation with self-ratings. The scale items were given to eighteen research psychologists working in university departments of psychology and other institutes of education and administration. These psychologists were given the definitions of each of the work values and were asked to classify the scale items into work-value categories. Each item was correctly classified into its work-value category by 89 percent of the experts. Eighty-eight of the original ninety items were correctly classified by seventeen or eighteen of the judges, representing 95 to 100 percent agreement, indicating a high degree of content validity.

Coefficients of correlation were computed between the scores on this scale and self-rankings assigned to the work dimensions by 120 senior medical students as follows:

- Creativity = .86;

- Economics = .64;

- Independence = .39;

- Status = .51;

- Service = .73;

- Academics = .68;

- Security = .65;

- Collegiality = .35; and

- Work conditions = .47.

Given the limitations of self-rankings, these coefficients of correlation indicate a high degree of concurrent validity; all coefficients are significant at the .01 level.

Cluster analysis of the coefficients of correlation obtained on this scale (N = 309 senior medical students from seven medical schools) indicated that the original ten work values fell into four clusters. The first cluster consisted of status, security, economics, and work conditions; the second consisted of creativity and service values; the third consisted of academics and independence values; and the fourth consisted of collegiality and rural. The first cluster consists of extrinsic dimensions, and the next three are more intrinsic in nature.

Test-retest reliability was established by using twenty-six respondents. The test-retest coefficients of correlation obtained were as follows:

- Creativity = .81;

- Economics = .61;

- Independence = .87;

- Status = .81;

- Service = .75;

- Academics = .57;

- Security = .51;

- Collegiality = .57; and

- Work conditions = .29.

Except for work conditions, all coefficients are significant at the .01 level.

Suggested Uses

This instrument has been used in postgraduate programs of management as well as in management-development programs. It is particularly useful as a value-clarification activity, and it can be used in conjunction with any career-development program.

An action plan can be created for helping respondents to bring their careers more closely in line with their work values.

References

Centers, R. (1961). *The psychology of social classes: A study of class consciousness.* New York: Russell and Russell.

Domenichetti, M. (1970). Work-values in adolescence as a function of vocational maturity. *Dissertation Abstracts International, 21,* 4-A.

Douglass, A.A. (1922). Interests of high school seniors. *School & Society, 16,* 79–84.

English, H.B., & English, A.C. (1958). *A comprehensive dictionary of psychological and psychoanalytical terms: A guide to usage.* New York: McKay.

Ginzberg, E. (1951). Towards a theory of occupational choice. *Occupations, 30,* 491–494.

Gray, J.T. (1963). Needs and values in three occupations. *Personnel and Guidance Journal, 42,* 238–244.

Pareek, U., Rao, T.V., & Pestonjee, D.M. (1981). *Behavior processes in organizations.* New Delhi: Oxford & IBH.

Rao, T.V. (1976). *Doctors in making.* Ahmedabad, India: Sahitya Mudranalaya.

Schein, E.H. (1990). *Career anchors: Discovering your real values* (rev. ed.). San Francisco, CA: Pfeiffer.

Thompson, O.E. (1966). Occupational values of high school students. *Personnel and Guidance Journal, 44,* 850–853.

Originally published in The 1991 Annual: Developing Human Resources.

MANAGERIAL WORK-VALUES SCALE

T. Venkateswara Rao

Instructions: This questionnaire consists of pairs of statements related to work values. Read each pair of statements carefully and assess the relative values of the statements for you. Some alternatives may seem equally attractive or unattractive to you; nevertheless, you must choose between the alternatives. For each pair of statements, you have three points to distribute. For example, read the following pair of statements:

I prefer work in which:

_____ 1a. I develop new ideas.

_____ 1b. I am paid well.

In the blanks preceding items 1a and 1b, you would distribute points according to the explanations that follow.

- If you prefer "a" and do not prefer "b," mark the blanks as follows:

  ___*3*___ 1a.

  ___*0*___ 1b.

- If you have a slight preference for "a" over "b," mark the blanks as follows:

  ___*2*___ 1a.

  ___*1*___ 1b.

- If you have a slight preference for "b" over "a," mark the blanks as follows:

  ___*1*___ 1a.

  ___*2*___ 1b.

- If you prefer "b" and do not prefer "a," mark the blanks as follows:

  ___*0*___ 1a.

  ___*3*___ 1b.

Although you will see the same item more than once, proceed through the questionnaire and treat each pair of statements independently. Be sure to use only the combinations of numbers shown. Remember that first impressions are important.

I prefer work in which:

_____ 1a. I develop new ideas.

_____ 1b. I am paid well.

_____ 2a. I do not need to depend on others for help.

_____ 2b. I have a prestigious position.

_____ 3a. I solve others' problems.

_____ 3b. I have an opportunity to teach others what I know.

_____ 4a. I am paid enough that I can have all the things I want.

_____ 4b. I have a very secure position.

_____ 5a. People respect me.

_____ 5b. I teach and do research.

_____ 6a. I feel a sense of achievement.

_____ 6b. My colleagues and I get along well together.

_____ 7a. I have adequate freedom and independence.

_____ 7b. I solve others' problems.

_____ 8a. I have the opportunity to invent new things.

_____ 8b. I have no fear of losing my job.

_____ 9a. I do things the way I please.

_____ 9b. I do research.

_____ 10a. I can help others to be happy.

_____ 10b. I have all the physical facilities I need.

_____ 11a. I receive large financial rewards.

_____ 11b. I teach.

_____ 12a. I have high status.

_____ 12b. My physical surroundings are good.

I prefer work in which:

_____	13a. I help other people.
_____	13b. I am in no danger of being laid off.
_____	14a. I have a high salary.
_____	14b. I am respected by others.
_____	15a. I am an influential person.
_____	15b. Nothing can threaten my job.
_____	16a. I do unique things.
_____	16b. I do not need to depend on others for help.
_____	17a. I do things almost entirely by myself.
_____	17b. I do not fear losing my job.
_____	18a. I earn an adequate income.
_____	18b. I work in pleasant surroundings.
_____	19a. I solve the problems of others.
_____	19b. I have good associates.
_____	20a. I am respected by others.
_____	20b. My colleagues are people I like.
_____	21a. I invent new things and find new ways of doing things.
_____	21b. My surroundings are pleasant.
_____	22a. I have the freedom to do things the way I want to do them.
_____	22b. I am paid enough money.
_____	23a. I have the satisfaction of helping people.
_____	23b. I have good opportunities for salary increases.
_____	24a. I enjoy the company of my colleagues.
_____	24b. I can save money.
_____	25a. I use my great potential.
_____	25b. I have an influential position.
_____	26a. I do things independently.
_____	26b. My coworkers are my friends.

I prefer work in which:

_____ 27a. I can be creative and use my intellect.

_____ 27b. I have an opportunity to teach.

_____ 28a. I have the freedom to do things the way I want to do them.

_____ 28b. My physical surroundings are pleasant.

_____ 29a. I serve others.

_____ 29b. I have high status.

_____ 30a. I am secure in my job at all times.

_____ 30b. Superiors and subordinates get along well with each other.

_____ 31a. I teach and do research.

_____ 31b. I have adequate facilities.

_____ 32a. I can feel I did the job well.

_____ 32b. I satisfy a number of clients.

_____ 33a. My job is secure.

_____ 33b. I have adequate physical facilities.

_____ 34a. I have a steady job.

_____ 34b. I can be an academician.

_____ 35a. I get along well with others.

_____ 35b. I can explore theories of management.

_____ 36a. I like my superiors and subordinates.

_____ 36b. I have all the facilities I need.

MANAGERIAL WORK-VALUES SCALE SCORING SHEET

Instructions: Please transfer your scores from the questionnaire to this scoring sheet. Note that the blanks do not necessarily follow in order. Be sure to transfer your scores to the correct blank. When you have transferred all of your scores, total each of the nine columns.

Creativity	Economics	Independence
1a. _____	1b. _____	2a. _____
6a. _____	4a. _____	7a. _____
8a. _____	11a. _____	9a. _____
16a. _____	14a. _____	16b. _____
21a. _____	18a. _____	17a. _____
25a. _____	22b. _____	22a. _____
27a. _____	23b. _____	26a. _____
32a. _____	24b. _____	28a. _____
Total _____	*Total* _____	*Total* _____

Status	Service	Academics
2b. _____	3a. _____	3b. _____
5a. _____	7b. _____	5b. _____
12a. _____	10a. _____	9b. _____
14b. _____	13a. _____	11b. _____
15a. _____	19a. _____	27b. _____
20a. _____	23a. _____	31b. _____
25b. _____	29a. _____	34b. _____
29b. _____	32b. _____	35b. _____
Total _____	*Total* _____	*Total* _____

Security	Collegiality	Work Conditions
4b. _____	6b. _____	10b. _____
8b. _____	19b. _____	12b. _____
13b. _____	20b. _____	18b. _____
15b. _____	24a. _____	21b. _____
17b. _____	26b. _____	28b. _____
30a. _____	30b. _____	31b. _____
33a. _____	35a. _____	33b. _____
34a. _____	36a. _____	36b. _____
Total _____	*Total* _____	*Total* _____

Managerial Work-Values Scale Interpretation Sheet

Instructions: Transfer your total score from each of the nine dimensions on the preceding page to the chart below.

Work Value	Score
Creativity	_____
Economics	_____
Independence	_____
Status	_____
Service	_____
Academics	_____
Security	_____
Collegiality	_____
Work Conditions	_____

The higher your score for a particular dimension, the more value you place on that dimension. On the lines below, list your top-ranked work value (the one with the highest score) on line 1, the second-ranked work value on line 2, and so on through line 9.

	Work Value	Score
1.	_____	_____
2.	_____	_____
3.	_____	_____
4.	_____	_____
5.	_____	_____
6.	_____	_____
7.	_____	_____
8.	_____	_____
9.	_____	_____

The following list explains what each dimension indicates:

1. *Creativity* reflects the extent to which the respondent prefers a job that allows opportunities for achievement and creativity, one in which he or she can use original ideas and have a sense of accomplishment.

2. *Economics* correlates to how much a person values the financial or monetary aspects of a job.

3. *Independence* corresponds to the respondent's preference for a job in which he or she can work without interference from others and/or without depending on others in order to do a good job.

4. *Status* relates to a person's values regarding status, prestige, and the need to be respected by others.

5. *Service* refers to the respondent's desire for work in which he or she can be of service to others.

6. *Academics* indicates a preference for teaching and research-related work.

7. *Security* points to the extent to which a person prefers a secure and permanent job as protection from an uncertain future.

8. *Collegiality* shows the degree to which a person likes to have co-workers, superiors, and subordinates who are friendly and easy to work with.

9. *Work Conditions* refers to the person's concerns about physical facilities and other work conditions.

Managerial Work-Values Scale Action Plan

Instructions: Use the data from the interpretation sheet to evaluate your current job. The work-value dimensions you value most may or may not be present in your job. The following action plan will allow you to outline ways to get more of the dimensions you value most. List your work values in rank order and then assess the degree to which your current job satisfies these values, using a scale of high, medium, and low satisfaction. As an option, you may choose to retake the Managerial Work-Values Scale, responding to the statements from the frame of reference of your present job. The results of the second survey then can be compared with the results of the first survey and an action plan created from that point.

	My work values:	Degree to which my job satisfies these values:
1.	_____	_____
2.	_____	_____
3.	_____	_____
4.	_____	_____
5.	_____	_____
6.	_____	_____
7.	_____	_____
8.	_____	_____
9.	_____	_____

Action Plan

The outline on the next page allows you to look at the degree to which your job satisfies your work values and make action plans for maintaining the dimensions you like and for changing the dimensions you do not like. Perhaps you rated your job as "high" in satisfying most of your key work values; you might use the outline to make a plan for maintaining that satisfaction. If you rated your job as "low" or "medium" in its ability to satisfy certain work values, decide on the changes you desire and fill out the action plan accordingly.

Work Value	Change Desired	Assistance Needed	By Whom	Time Line

The Pfeiffer Book of Successful Leadership Development Tools © 2003 John Wiley & Sons, Inc. Published by Pfeiffer.

6

Patterns of Effective Supervisory Behavior

Henry P. Sims, Jr.

The purpose of the Supervisory Behavior Questionnaire is to identify patterns of leader behavior and to
describe them in terms of an operant theory of leadership (Mawhinney & Ford, 1977; Scott, 1977; Sims,
1977). This introduction to the instrument will present a conceptual approach to leadership theory that
is different from the traditional approaches of con-
sideration/initiating structure, managerial grid, and/
or contingency theory.

THEORY UNDERLYING THE INSTRUMENT

The instrument assumes a theory of leadership based on operant or reinforcement principles (Skinner, 1969). According to this theory, behavior within organizations is controlled by "contingencies of reinforcement." Figure 1
represents a positive reinforcement contingency, which consists of three parts.
The first part is a discriminative stimulus (S^D), which is an environmental cue
that provides an individual with information about how behavior will be reinforced. A discriminative stimulus is environmental information that comes before individual behavior. The second part is the response or behavior of the
individual. The behavior is followed by the administration of a reinforcer. A

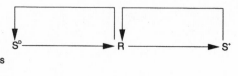

S⁰ = discriminative stimulus
R = response behavior
S⁺ = positive consequence

Figure 1. Contingency of Positive Reinforcement

positive reinforcer (the third part) is a reward that is administered following a desired behavior; it has the effect of increasing the frequency of the behavior.

Reinforcers are frequently thought of as material benefits, that is, pay or some extrinsic incentive. In the supervisor-subordinate relationship, however, interpersonal reinforcers frequently are more potent (at least in the short term). Compliments or statements of recognition that are contingent on desirable behavior at work can have reinforcing effects that serve to increase future performance.

Another type of reinforcement contingency is punishment[1]—the administration of an aversive stimulus contingent on a specific response. In leadership practice, punishment typically is used to decrease the frequency of an undesirable behavior. In work situations, leaders typically use oral reprimands or undesirable job assignments in an attempt to eliminate behavior that is undesirable or detrimental to job performance.

Both positive reinforcement and punishment are actions of the leader that *follow* subordinate behavior. Obviously, the behavior of the leader also can have a substantial impact on the subordinate's successive performance. Frequently, the type of behavior that occurs before subordinate behavior can be considered a discriminative stimulus (S^D)—a cue that informs the subordinate of what behavior is expected in order to be reinforced. An example of this is a goal or objective.

These three types of leader behavior (positive reinforcement, punishment, and discriminative stimulus or goal specification) are basic elements in a leader's behavioral repertoire. Although these classes of behavior are not exhaustive, they form the key foci for any operant-based theory of leadership.

---

1. "Punishment" is technically distinct from "negative reinforcement," which involves the removal of an aversive stimulus in order to increase a target behavior. However, punishment and negative reinforcement are both aversive control techniques.

Purpose of the Instrument

The Supervisory Behavior Questionnaire[2] was developed for training purposes. The instrument is designed to direct the participants' attention to three types of leader behavior: goal specification behavior (scale A), positive reward behavior (scale B), and punitive reward behavior (scale C).

The instrument is self-scored, and most participants can determine their own scores and derive a profile of the three scores with little or no assistance.

Procedure for Administering the Instrument

Each participant is instructed to think about a job that he or she now holds or has held in the past (and, more specifically, about the supervisor on that job) and then to complete the questionnaire. Participants may need to be reminded that the questions refer to the supervisor.

After completing the questionnaire, the participants are directed to complete the self-scoring procedure and then to draw a profile of the scores of all three scales on the graph.

Debriefing and Discussion

The facilitator begins the debriefing by initiating a process to name the three scales and, after this is done, reads the descriptive name most often used to designate the characteristics that were measured. These are supervisory goals and expectations (scale A), supervisory positive reward behavior (scale B), and supervisory punitive behavior (scale C).

A few volunteers go to the newsprint flip chart and write the names of the jobs they described and their scores for scales A, B, and C, for both the most effective and least effective supervisors. The facilitator directs each participant to briefly describe the aspects of the supervisor that prompted the

---

2. The roots of this instrument can be traced to a leadership instrument originated by Ronald Johnson, William E. Scott, and Joseph Reitz, and originally published in Johnson (1973). Other research using similar scales has been reported by Greene (1975), Reitz (1971), Sims (1977), and Sims and Szilagyi (1975). In general, these scales have been found to possess acceptable construct validity and reliability. People wishing to use these scales for research should not use the version reported here, which is intended to be a classroom exercise, but should consult the sources listed above.

scores reported (e.g., "He tells me what I will be doing next"). The facilitator then attempts to develop patterns of differentiation of scores between highly effective and highly ineffective supervisors and between conditions leading to highly satisfied and highly unsatisfied workers. The facilitator can calculate mean scores for both the most effective and the least effective supervisors.

Finally, the facilitator presents a lecturette on the theory underlying the instrument. Material from the literature of supervisory development can be assigned as backup reading or used as handouts (Hammer, 1974; Jablonsky & DeVries, 1972; Luthans & Kreitner, 1975; Mawhinney, 1975; Mawhinney & Ford, 1977; Nord, 1969; Scott, 1977; Sims, 1977; Skinner, 1969).

VARIATION

An alternative way to use the instrument is to direct the participants to provide two scores for each question: one for the supervisor and the second for how the participant would behave as a supervisor. This variation provides a self-description component.

VALUE OF THE INSTRUMENT

This instrument provides an experiential introduction to leadership theory and allows the participants to examine leadership behaviors from the perspective of their own past experiences. This personal aspect induces substantially greater interest and involvement and longer retention of the underlying theory. In addition, several opportunities exist during the debriefing phase to describe the underlying theoretical principles in terms of actual past behaviors. If accompanied by significant exposure to principles of behavior modification (Brown & Presbie, 1976; Luthans & Kreitner, 1975), the instrument offers a unique opportunity to demonstrate how leadership theory can be put into practice.

References

Brown, P.L., & Presbie, R.J. (1976). *Behavior modification in business, industry, and government*. New Paltz, NY: Behavior Improvement Associates.

Greene, C. (1975). Contingent relationships between instrumental leader behavior and subordinate satisfaction and performance. *Proceedings of the American Institute for Decision Sciences*.

Hamner, W.C. (1974). Reinforcement theory and contingency management in organization settings. In H.L. Tosi & W.C. Hamner (Eds.), *Organization behavior and management: A contingency approach.* Chicago: St. Clair Press.

Jablonsky, S.F., & DeVries, D.L. (1972). Operant conditioning principles extrapolated to the theory of management. *Organizational Behavior and Human Performance, 7,* 340–358.

Johnson, R.D. (1973). *An investigation of the interaction effects of ability and motivational variables on task performance.* Unpublished doctoral dissertation, Indiana University.

Luthans, F., & Kreitner, R. (1975). *Organizational behavior modification.* Glenview, IL: Scott, Foresman.

Mawhinney, T.C. (1975). Operant terms and concepts in the description of individual work behavior: Some problems of interpretation, application, and evaluation. *Journal of Applied Psychology, 60,* 704–714.

Mawhinney, T.C., & Ford, J.C. (1977). The path goal theory of leader effectiveness: An operant interpretation. *Academy of Management Review, 2,* 398–411.

Nord, W.R. (1969). Beyond the teaching machine: The neglected area of operant conditioning in the theory and practice of management. *Organizational Behavior and Human Performance, 4,* 375–401.

Reitz, H.J. (1971). Managerial attitudes and perceived contingencies between performance and organizational response. *Proceedings of the 31st Annual Meeting of the Academy of Management,* 227–238.

Scott, W.G. (1977). Leadership: A functional analysis. In J.G. Hunt & L. Larson (Eds.), *Leadership: The cutting edge.* Carbondale, IL: Southern Illinois University Press.

Sims, H.P. (1977). The leader as a manager of reinforcement contingencies: An empirical example and a model. In J.G. Hunt & L. Larson (Eds.), *Leadership: The cutting edge.* Carbondale, IL: Southern Illinois University Press.

Sims, H.P., & Szilagyi, A.D. (1975). Leader reward behavior and subordinate satisfaction and performance. *Organizational Behavior and Human Performance, 14,* 426–438.

Skinner, B.F. (1969). *The contingencies of reinforcement: A theoretical analysis.* New York: Appleton-Century-Crofts.

Originally published in The 1981 Annual Handbook for Group Facilitators,.

SUPERVISORY BEHAVIOR QUESTIONNAIRE

Henry P. Sims, Jr.

Instructions: This questionnaire is part of an activity designed to explore supervisory behaviors. It is not a test; there are no right or wrong answers.

Think about supervisors (managers) you have known or know now, and then select the most effective supervisor and the least effective supervisor (effective is defined as "being able to substantially influence the effort and performance of subordinates").

Read each of the following statements carefully. For the most effective supervisor, place an X over the number indicating how true or how untrue you believe the statement to be. For the least effective supervisor, place a circle around the number indicating how true you believe the statement to be.

Definitely Not True = 1   Not True = 2   Slightly Not True = 3   Uncertain = 4
Slightly True = 5   True = 6   Definitely True = 7

Most effective . . . X   Least effective . . . O

1. My supervisor would compliment me
   if I did outstanding work.   1   2   3   4   5   6   7

2. My supervisor maintains definite
   standards of performance.   1   2   3   4   5   6   7

3. My supervisor would reprimand me
   if my work were consistently below
   standards.   1   2   3   4   5   6   7

4. My supervisor defines clear goals and
   objectives for my job.   1   2   3   4   5   6   7

5. My supervisor would give me special
   recognition if my work performance
   were especially good.   1   2   3   4   5   6   7

6. My supervisor would "get on me" if
   my work were not as good as he or she
   thought it should be.   1   2   3   4   5   6   7

7. My supervisor would tell me if my work
   were outstanding.   1   2   3   4   5   6   7

Definitely Not True = 1   Not True = 2   Slightly Not True = 3   Uncertain = 4
Slightly True = 5   True = 6   Definitely True = 7

Most effective . . . X   Least effective . . . O

8. My supervisor establishes clear perfor-
   mance guidelines.   1   2   3   4   5   6   7

9. My supervisor would reprimand me if
   I were not making progress in my work. 1   2   3   4   5   6   7

SUPERVISORY BEHAVIOR QUESTIONNAIRE SCORING SHEET

Instructions: For each of the three scales (A, B, and C), compute a total score by summing the answers to the appropriate questions and then subtracting the number 12. Compute a score for both the most effective and the least effective supervisors.

Question Number	Most Effective	Least Effective	Question Number	Most Effective	Least Effective	Question Number	Most Effective	Least Effective
2.	+( )	+( )	1.	+( )	+( )	3.	+( )	+( )
4.	+( )	+( )	5.	+( )	+( )	6.	+( )	+( )
8.	+( )	+( )	7.	+( )	+( )	9.	+( )	+( )
Subtotal			Subtotal			Subtotal		
	( )	( )		( )	( )		( )	( )
	−12	−12		−12	−12		−12	−12
Total Score	___	___	Total Score	___	___	Total Score	___	___
	A	A		B	B		C	C

Next, on the following graph, write a large "X" to indicate the total score for scales A, B, and C for the most effective supervisor. Use a large "O" to indicate the scores for the least effective supervisor.

A. _____ | | | | | | | | | | | |
　　　　　　　　　　　−9 −7 −5 −3 −1 　　+1 +3 +5 +7 +9

B. _____ | | | | | | | | | | | |
　　　　　　　　　　　−9 −7 −5 −3 −1 　　+1 +3 +5 +7 +9

C. _____ | | | | | | | | | | | |
　　　　　　　　　　　−9 −7 −5 −3 −1 　　+1 +3 +5 +7 +9

7

The Leadership Dimensions Survey

Gerald V. Miller

Abstract: The Leadership Dimensions Survey is a tool to assist those on the odyssey of leadership. The survey is based on four leadership competencies: profound knowledge, profound strategy, purposeful direction, and purposeful behaviors. These four competencies, when paired on a grid, yield four leadership dimensions or "virtues": constancy of purpose, congruity of activity, competency of outcome, and compatibility of values. The four competencies, as measured by The Leadership Dimensions Survey, allow for the generation and sustenance of trust between leader and follower, which forms the basis for a work environment that is both productive and able to adapt to and thrive in a changing and complex business world.

The Leadership Dimensions Survey can be used for self-discovery, leadership development, coaching in human dimensions of leadership, and other leadership applications.

Reframing Leadership

In a world of unceasing change, downsizing, reinventing, reengineering, business process redesign, customer focus, and high-performance teams, the business leader of today must balance the tremendous demands of managing that change and complexity with work output and productivity. Those leaders who operate on the 19th Century model of bureaucracy, a model based on words and actions, of control and order, are not going to pass muster in the next millennium.

Successful business leaders have mastered a new set of knowledge, skills, and attitudes with which to face the challenges of corporate reality—in effect, a completely new form of leadership. This form of leadership is observable and learnable. Given the opportunity to learn, receive feedback, and practice, those who desire to lead and improve their ability to lead can do so.

Leadership Competencies and Dimensions

Today's leaders must think in terms of a leadership system, seeing a framework of patterns and interrelationships. Unfortunately, we usually focus on isolated parts instead of seeing the whole system of leadership, and then we wonder why our efforts at solving problems or perpetuating successes fail.

It is especially important to see the world of leadership as a whole system as it continues to grow more complex. Complexity can overwhelm and undermine our efforts if we do not have a model or a system to guide our efforts. A model helps us see the patterns that lie behind events and details, which can simplify the art of leadership.

The leadership systems model is based on four interrelated competencies:

- Profound knowledge,

- Profound strategy,

- Purposeful direction, and

- Purposeful behaviors.

These competencies can be visualized on an interconnecting axis, as shown in Figure 1.

The word "profound" connotes something deep-seated. To be profound is to go beyond the surface, beneath the veneer issues to what is the true essence of something. It requires an intellectual depth and insight. Perhaps you can remember a time when you were conversing with someone who said something profound. It took the conversation to a new depth.

Profound knowledge is a necessary competency that ensures a basis of information, experience, expertise, and data. To possess profound knowledge is to possess something beyond mere perceptions.

Profound strategy indicates a well-thought-out plan or course of action that goes beyond the status quo. It is the insightful art of development of the exceptional blueprint or scheme.

To be "purposeful" is to be, literally, full of purpose. To be purposeful is to be meaningful. It is acting with thoughtful intention, not out of convenience. It requires resolution and determination. When one is purposeful, one has an aim or goal, a reason for behaving in a particular manner.

Purposeful direction implies that there is a vision, goal, and mission that will result in a desired future state uniquely different from the present state.

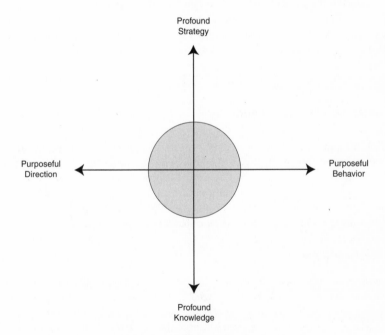

Figure 1. Competencies Axis

Purposeful behavior indicates that the leader's behaviors are, in fact, meaningful and are, on some level, inextricably attached to a vision or goal. The behaviors provide a role model for the values and skills needed to achieve a desired state.

THE ROLE OF TRUST IN LEADERSHIP

Leadership is not just about leaders; it is also about followers. Successful leadership depends far more on the followers' perception of the leader than on any other factor. It is a reciprocal process, occurring between people. Followers, not the leader, determine when someone possesses the qualities of leadership.

People would rather follow, and confer leadership on, individuals they can count on—even when they disagree with their viewpoints—rather than people they agree with but who shift positions frequently. Everything effective leaders do is congruent with their values, their viewpoints. The four leadership dimensions of constancy of purpose, congruity of activity, competency of outcome, and compatibility of values are realized through consistent behavior over time. This behavior is the basis of trust for followers who buy into the vision, the shared goals, and objectives and then confer leadership. Each of the four leadership dimensions takes time to generate and sustain. The result is trust.

DIMENSIONS OF LEADERSHIP

When we put the four competencies—profound knowledge, profound strategy, profound direction, and purposeful behavior—together, we form a grid with four quadrants, as seen in Figure 2. Each of these quadrants represents a leadership dimension: I: Constancy of purpose, II: Congruity of activity, III: Competency of outcome, and IV: Compatibility of values. It is these four dimensions that can be used to measure leadership proficiency.

I. Constancy of Purpose

Constancy of purpose is steadfastness, continued unwavering focus on the vision, "keeping one's eye on the prize." Purposeful direction and profound strategy make up this dimension of leadership, allowing for the development of basic trust between leader and follower, derived from a meaningfully communicated vision and strategy.

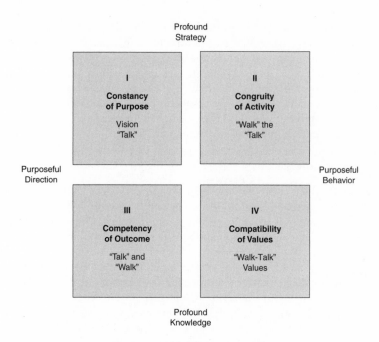

Profound
Strategy

I	II
Constancy of Purpose Vision "Talk"	**Congruity of Activity** "Walk" the "Talk"
III	IV
Competency of Outcome "Talk" and "Walk"	**Compatibility of Values** "Walk-Talk" Values

Purposeful
Direction

Purposeful
Behavior

Profound
Knowledge

Figure 2. Dimensions of Leadership

Trust requires repeated interactions between leaders and followers and begins with vision. In nurturing an environment in which people are aware of the vision, of what is important and why it is critical, the leader creates meaning. With meaning comes trust.

Meaning also emerges from concepts, words endowed with relevance and purpose. Words are powerful. The leader, therefore, must have a "talk" to nurture the vision-oriented environment. The leader must consistently state and restate the vision in a meaningful, purposeful way that encourages people to enroll for the duration. The vision must inspire. It must articulate passion. Speaking with passion, leaders light fires under others. When the leader is a "wet match," there are no sparks to ignite passion in others and the vision is set inside. It is the role of the leader to ensure that people know and buy in to the vision.

The leader helps define the vision (purposeful direction) and "talks the talk," laying the foundation for the development of trust between the leader and the followers. The fulfillment of the vision, by definition, implies a change from the state in which we are to the state in which we want to be.

This understanding on the part of the leader is the result of a well-thought-out plan and a course of action that goes beyond the status quo, the insightful art of developing the exceptional blueprint or scheme, the profound strategy.

Constancy of purpose occurs when followers believe that the leader has clear and specific reasons for initiating a change; has a clear and specific outcome in mind; understands the resources necessary to put changes into effect; understands the scope and organizational impact of a change; and understands the human impact of the change.

II. Congruity of Activity

Congruity of activity is the ability to match words and deeds, that is, to "practice what one preaches." Profound strategy and purposeful behaviors make up this dimension of leadership, promulgating the further development of trust between leader and follower and moving the organization and its people toward realization of the vision.

Saying one thing and doing another is perhaps the surest way to destroy trust. People are deeply concerned with congruity of word and deed. Congruity of activity is walking the talk and modeling the vision. What a leader does must be congruent with the vision. This dimension can generate a groundswell of trust from the foundation established through the first dimension, constancy of purpose.

Having established the vision and communicated a profound strategy, the leader must lead by example. If leaders ask followers to move toward a future state and observe certain values and standards in pursuit of that state, then the leaders must live by the same rules. That is exactly what we have been told countless times by exemplary leaders. Leadership does not sit in the stands and watch.

In order to fully commit themselves to the change process, members must believe that leaders themselves are fully committed. They should feel that the leaders are strongly convinced that the change must become a reality.

Congruity of activity ensures that followers will be committed to the change process. It shows that the leader will support the change, both publicly and privately; monitor change activities; reinforce the efforts of those who are to carry out the change effort; and make sacrifices to further the change effort.

III. Competency of Outcome

Competency of outcome is expressed in what one says, that is, "I've been there and I've done that." It occurs when a leader has profound knowledge and purposeful direction.

Dimensions I and II show how a leader must have a "talk" and a "walk"—constancy of purpose and congruity of activity. The next, dimension—competency of outcome—demands a "talk" and a "walk" backed up by substantive and demonstrable experience. This is leadership competence. To buy into leaders' visions, people must trust that leaders know what they are talking about and what they are doing. To instill trust, a leader must be seen as capable and effective. If people doubt the leader's abilities, they are unlikely to enlist in the change effort and pursue the vision.

Leadership competence does not necessarily refer to a leader's technical ability. Rather, people look for competency in the following areas:

- Systems thinking,

- Human side of management,

- Communication and interpersonal relationships,

- Giving and receiving feedback,

- Understanding and responding to needs of individual team members,

- One-on-one consultation (problems and individual needs),

- Team building and group dynamics,

- Employing informal power to influence team behavior and desired outcomes,

- Linking individuals, groups, and projects together across the organization, and

- Training and coaching in operational, administrative, and managerial functions.

Competency of outcome solidifies the trust developed thus far, setting the stage for the fourth dimension, compatibility of values.

IV. Compatibility of Values

Compatibility of values is the integration of what one believes, says, and does with the organizational value system, that is, "evidence of trust begets trust." It occurs when a leader has profound knowledge and purposeful behavior.

Compatibility of values manifests itself in interdependence, the necessarily shared value for effective leadership. Leaders must value and protect interdependence, rather than creating a climate of independence, dependence, or codependence. When held and employed unilaterally, interdependence

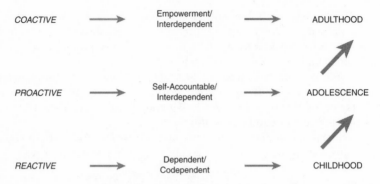

COACTIVE	→	Empowerment/ Interdependent	→	ADULTHOOD
PROACTIVE	→	Self-Accountable/ Interdependent	→	ADOLESCENCE
REACTIVE	→	Dependent/ Codependent	→	CHILDHOOD

Figure 3. The Development of Interdependence

creates a work environment of the highest efficiency, effectiveness, and professional and personal satisfaction.

Interdependence calls for coactive (synergistic) behaviors, consistent with the highest good of all concerned. Too often leaders encourage pure independence. Especially in the workplace, people must be interdependent. In the workplace, independence translates as adolescent, self-centered behavior. It is the role of the leader to believe in, value, and demonstrate the importance of interdependence. Figure 3 illustrates the developmental nature of interdependence.

The leader promotes an interdependent climate for team members and does not interfere unless it becomes necessary. The team members are trusted and given freedom (empowered and enabled) to plan their own ways of doing their work (the how) in accord with the leader's vision (the what and why). They are expected to solve problems and to ask for guidance only when it is needed. By providing freedom of work, encouraging initiative, and supporting experimentation and teamwork, leaders also help to satisfy the followers' needs for belonging, affection, and security.

SUMMARY

Although both management and leadership are necessary to the success of any effort in today's business world, change, complexity, and continued demands for productivity and efficiency require a greater emphasis on leading. The specific knowledge, behaviors, and skills that exceptional leaders have in common, all operating under the umbrella of human systems thinking, have been identified. They are embodied in the four dimensions of leadership: constancy of purpose, congruity of activity, competency of outcome, and compatibility of values.

Proper leadership empowers and enables the individuals and teams that constitute an organization. Good leaders make team members feel that they are at the very heart of things. Followers feel that they, interdependently, make a difference to the success of the organization. This sense of empowerment can lead to increased productivity and efficiency, keys to maintaining success in a changing business world.

The Instrument

The Leadership Dimensions Survey is designed to assess the leadership skills of aspiring, potential, or present leaders on four dimensions. The survey consists of a thirty-two-item questionnaire, a scoring sheet, an interpretation sheet that covers results on each of the four dimensions, and a Leadership Dimensions Map on which one can chart the results of his or her survey. In addition, a sample letter for participants to send to respondents and an action planning sheet are included here.

The survey is designed to be completed by five of the leader's peers, supervisors, or subordinates (the "respondents"). Each question presents a statement about the leader. Respondents are asked to mark whether they strongly agree, are inclined to agree, are inclined to disagree, or strongly disagree with the statement as it applies to the leader.

Validity and Reliability

No validity or reliability data are available on the Leadership Dimensions Survey. However, the instrument has face validity, as its purpose is to make participants more aware of their leadership behaviors through this feedback process.

Administration

The following process is suggested for facilitating a workshop on leadership with several participants. At least a week prior to working with the leaders, give each of them five copies of the Leadership Dimensions Survey and copies of the Leadership Dimensions Letter to Participants. Tell them to write letters on their own stationery similar to the sample letter to respondents, attach letters to the survey, and give them to five peers, supervisors, or subordinates, who are to follow the instructions to complete it and return it in a sealed envelope anonymously either to the leader or to you, the facilitator. (*Note:* Be sure to specify whether you are to receive the surveys or whether the leaders will collect them. An advantage of collecting them yourself is that they are less likely to be forgotten on the day of the workshop.) Anonymity allows for more candid responses. If the surveys are returned in time, they may be scored prior to the workshop, but it is important for leaders to do their own interpretation and mapping.

Scoring

The questionnaires can be scored either before or during the workshop. Both the Leadership Dimensions Scoring Sheet and Leadership Dimensions Interpretation Sheet sort the thirty-two statements by leadership dimension.

Hand out the completed Leadership Dimensions Scoring Sheets (or ask the leaders to score their own during the session) to the appropriate leader along with blank copies of the Leadership Dimensions Interpretation Sheet. If they are scoring their own surveys, tell the leaders to transfer the scores they received for each question to the A, B, C, D, and E columns on the Scoring Sheet. Each column represents one respondent. Be sure that they total the scores *horizontally* and divide by the number of responses to determine their average scores for each question, then write their scores in the "average" column. Next, tell leaders to add the averages *vertically* to obtain a total score for each dimension.

When they have finished filling out the Scoring Sheet, hand out the Leadership Dimensions Map and tell the leaders to plot their four totals in the appropriate quadrants. Draw a sample on the flip chart to show them how to map their leadership dimensions. Next, hand out Leadership Dimensions Interpretation Sheets to all leaders and ask them to study their scores. Discuss the meaning of various combinations of scores and have people share their maps and thoughts in small groups or in pairs. After everyone knows what his or her results say, hand out copies of the Leadership Dimensions Action Planning Sheet and ask leaders to make action plans to improve their leadership dimensions in the future. Ask everyone to share as appropriate.

The scoring, mapping, and interpretation of the Leadership Dimensions Survey usually requires thirty minutes to an hour to complete. The discussion phase and action planning will take another hour.

POTENTIAL USES OF THE INSTRUMENT

The Leadership Dimensions Survey is designed as a self-discovery and feedback tool. It has the following potential uses:

- As part of leadership training wherein participants have the survey completed by supervisors, peers, and subordinates prior to the training event. During the leadership training, the results can be discussed as the foundation for the workshop.

- As a coaching tool to be administered by the supervisor of someone who wishes to improve his or her leadership skills. The coach can review the results of the survey with the learner.

- As an assessment tool for future leaders. The results can form the basis of an individual leadership development plan.

- As a process intervention tool for consultants working with leaders. The results can show contributions the leaders make to the organization, point out potential pitfalls they have, and lead to suggestions for improvement and development.

- As a basis for discussion throughout an organization about the relationship between present and desired leadership styles.

- As a format for any organization that wishes to assess its readiness to implement a more effective style of leadership.

References

Bennis, W., & Nanus, B. (1986). *Leaders: The strategies for taking charge*. New York: Harper & Row.

Forkas, C.M,. & DeBacker, P. (1996). *Maximum leadership*. New York: Holt.

Hesselbein, F., Goldsmith, M., & Beckhard, R. (Eds.). (1996). *The leader of the future*. San Francisco, CA: Jossey-Bass.

Kotler, J.P. (1996). *Leading change*. Boston, MA: Harvard Business School Press.

Levine, S.P., & Crom, M.A. (1993). *The leader in you: How to win friends, influence people and succeed in a changing world*. New York: Dale Carnegie.

O'Toole, J. (1995). *Leading change: Overcoming the ideology of comfort and the tyranny of custom*. San Francisco, CA: Jossey-Bass.

Senge, P.M. (1990). *The fifth discipline*. New York: Currency Doubleday.

Originally published in The 1999 Annual: Volume 1, Training.

LEADERSHIP DIMENSIONS SURVEY LETTER TO PARTICIPANTS

To the Participant:

The Leadership Dimensions Survey is designed to assess your leadership skills on four dimensions by providing you with feedback about how others view the leadership practices you use.

Attached are five copies of the Leadership Dimensions Survey. Write your name on each as the person who is being evaluated. Distribute copies of the questionnaire to any five people (peers, subordinates, and/or supervisors) whom you believe know you well enough to comment on what you would do (and do not do) as a leader. *Please distribute all five, as this increases the reliability and validity of the results.*

Ask each respondent to complete the questionnaire anonymously and return it to you (or to the facilitator of your leadership training group) *in a sealed envelope.* A sample of a letter you can give to respondents explaining the purpose of the survey is shown below.

Sample Letter to Respondents Completing the Leadership Dimensions Survey

Dear Respondent:

Attached is one copy of the Leadership Dimensions Survey. I would appreciate it if you could fill out the survey about my own behavior as a leader. The purpose of this survey is to assist me in understanding my own behavior and the impact of that behavior on others in a work setting.

Your honest responses will help me to assess my leadership qualities. Please rate each behavior following the instructions at the top of the survey.

Do not write your name on the survey form. It is designed to be completed anonymously. Please return the completed survey in a sealed envelope marked to my attention [or to the facilitator].

Thank you for your time and honest feedback.

Sincerely,

[your name]

LEADERSHIP DIMENSIONS SURVEY

Gerald V. Miller

Person Being Assessed: _____

Instructions: Think of the person who gave this survey to you to complete, named above. To what extent do the following thirty-two statements apply to this person? For each statement, circle the response that best applies, using the following scale.

Strongly Agree = 3　　**Inclined to Agree = 2**　　**Inclined to Disagree = 1**　　**Strongly Disagree = 0**

This person:

1. Can describe the kind of future that he or she would like to create.	3	2	1	0
2. Has behavior that is congruent with his or her leadership philosophy.	3	2	1	0
3. Is aware of new developments in our field.	3	2	1	0
4. Is consistently an ethical and upstanding leader.	3	2	1	0
5. Can give a clear, specific outcome that would result from change.	3	2	1	0
6. Supports projects and changes, both publicly and privately.	3	2	1	0
7. Has experienced what he or she is talking about and knows what he or she is doing.	3	2	1	0
8. Practices principles of self-accountability.	3	2	1	0
9. Appeals to others to join in the vision of the future.	3	2	1	0
10. Is consistent in practicing what he or she preaches.	3	2	1	0
11. Seeks out challenging opportunities that test and stretch the organization's skills and abilities.	3	2	1	0
12. Encourages team members to be interdependent and empowered team members.	3	2	1	0

13. Has clear and specific reasons for initiating change.	3	2	1	0
14. Monitors projects and change activities with clear goals, plans, and established milestones.	3	2	1	0
15. Is consistently well-prepared for any project or change effort contingency.	3	2	1	0
16. Is sincere when asking for others' suggestions and opinions.	3	2	1	0
17. Clearly communicates a hopeful and inspiring outlook for the future of the organization.	3	2	1	0
18. Reinforces and rewards the efforts of those who carry out projects and change efforts.	3	2	1	0
19. Typically can provide team members with a thorough understanding of any project or change effort.	3	2	1	0
20. Creates an atmosphere of mutual trust during projects and change efforts.	3	2	1	0
21. Understands the resources necessary to put change into effect.	3	2	1	0
22. Experiments and takes risks with new approaches, regardless of the chance of failure.	3	2	1	0
23. Is capable and effective in both technical and leadership abilities.	3	2	1	0
24. Makes a concerted effort to tell the organization about the good work done by the team.	3	2	1	0
25. Shows others how their interests can be realized by joining a common vision.	3	2	1	0
26. Makes personal sacrifices in order to complete projects and to further change efforts.	3	2	1	0
27. Is competent in understanding how all the interacting parts of our organization come together.	3	2	1	0
28. Can always be believed about what he or she is saying.	3	2	1	0

29. Understands the scope of proposed changes and the impact of change on people and the organization.	3	2	1	0
30. Practices innovative leadership that fosters a sense of ownership in others.	3	2	1	0
31. Challenges the status quo regarding the way things are done.	3	2	1	0
32. Typically establishes open, trusting work relationships.	3	2	1	0

LEADERSHIP DIMENSIONS SCORING SHEET

Instructions: This scoring sheet is divided into four sections, each representing one dimension of leadership: constancy of purpose, congruity of activity, competency of outcome, or compatibility of values. Transfer the scores given to you by each respondent to the appropriate blanks below. Remember that items are not in numerical order, but are divided by quadrant. Each letter, A through E, represents a different respondent.

After you have filled in the scores for each question, add them horizontally and divide by the number of responses you received to determine your average score. Write your average scores for each question in the blank provided. Next add the eight average scores for each section and write the number in the blank marked "total."

I. Constancy of Purpose: Profound Strategy and Purposeful Direction

	Respondents					Average
	A	B	C	D	E	
1. Can describe the kind of future that he or she would like to create.	____	____	____	____	____	_____
5. Can give a clear, specific outcome that would result from change.	____	____	____	____	____	_____
9. Appeals to others to join in the vision of the future.	____	____	____	____	____	_____
13. Has clear and specific reasons for initiating change.	____	____	____	____	____	_____
17. Clearly communicates a hopeful and inspiring outlook for the future of the organization.	____	____	____	____	____	_____
21. Understands the resources necessary to put change into effect.	____	____	____	____	____	_____
25. Shows others how their interests can be realized by joining a common vision.	____	____	____	____	____	_____

	Respondents					Average
	A	**B**	**C**	**D**	**E**	
29. Understands the scope of proposed changes and the impact of change on people and the organization.	___	___	___	___	___	_____

					Total	_____

II. Congruity of Activity: Profound Strategy and Purposeful Behavior

	Respondents					Average
	A	**B**	**C**	**D**	**E**	
2. Has behavior that is congruent with his or her leadership philosophy.	___	___	___	___	___	_____
6. Supports projects and changes, both publicly and privately.	___	___	___	___	___	_____
10. Is consistent in practicing what he or she preaches.	___	___	___	___	___	_____
14. Monitors projects and change activities with clear goals, plans, and established milestones.	___	___	___	___	___	_____
18. Reinforces and rewards the efforts of those who carry out projects and change efforts.	___	___	___	___	___	_____
22. Experiments and takes risks with new approaches, regardless of the chance of failure.	___	___	___	___	___	_____
26. Makes personal sacrifices in order to complete projects and to further change efforts.	___	___	___	___	___	_____

	Respondents					Average
	A	**B**	**C**	**D**	**E**	
30. Practices innovative leadership that fosters a sense of ownership in others.	——	——	——	——	——	———

		Total	———

III. Competency of Outcome: Profound Knowledge and Purposeful Direction

	Respondents					Average
	A	**B**	**C**	**D**	**E**	
3. Is aware of new developments in our field.	——	——	——	——	——	———
7. Has experienced what he or she is talking about and knows what he or she is doing.	——	——	——	——	——	———
11. Seeks out challenging opportunities that test and stretch the organization's skills and abilities.	——	——	——	——	——	———
15. Is consistently well-prepared for any project or change effort contingency.	——	——	——	——	——	———
19. Typically can provide team members with a thorough understanding of any project or change effort.	——	——	——	——	——	———
23. Is capable and effective in both technical and leadership abilities.	——	——	——	——	——	———
27. Is competent in understanding how all the interacting parts of our organization come together.	——	——	——	——	——	———

	Respondents					Average
	A	B	C	D	E	
31. Challenges the status quo regarding the way things are done.	——	——	——	——	——	———

| | | Total | ——— |

IV. Compatibility of Values: Profound Knowledge and Purposeful Behavior

	Respondents					Average
	A	B	C	D	E	
4. Is consistently an ethical and upstanding leader.	——	——	——	——	——	———
8. Practices principles of self-accountability.	——	——	——	——	——	———
12. Encourages team members to be interdependent and empowered team members.	——	——	——	——	——	———
16. Is sincere when asking for others' suggestions and opinions.	——	——	——	——	——	———
20. Creates an atmosphere of mutual trust during projects and change efforts.	——	——	——	——	——	———
24. Makes a concerted effort to tell the organization about the good work done by the team.	——	——	——	——	——	———
28. Can always be believed about what he or she is saying.	——	——	——	——	——	———
32. Typically establishes open, trusting work relationships.	——	——	——	——	——	———

| | | Total | ——— |

LEADERSHIP DIMENSIONS MAP

Instructions: Plot your scores for each quadrant. For example, if you received a score of 19 for Quadrant I, Constancy of Purpose, mark the score on both the Profound Strategy and Purposeful Direction lines. Then draw a rule perpendicular to each line and make an X where the two lines meet in the quadrant. Do the same for your scores in each of the other quadrants as shown in the example.

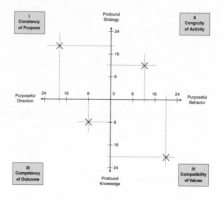

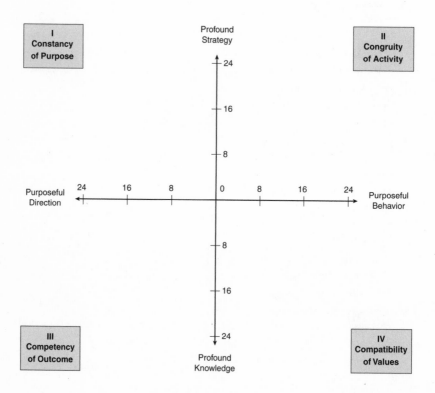

LEADERSHIP DIMENSIONS INTERPRETATION SHEET

Instructions: The most crucial step for learning is to answer the questions, "So what?" and "Now what?" Now that you have completed your Leadership Dimensions Scoring Sheet, you will want to interpret what the scores have to say and take action to improve your leadership skills. Utilizing what you have learned about how you behave in real-world leadership situations, you can make plans for your professional development.

The Leadership Dimensions Survey is interpreted on an item-by-item basis, as well as by comparison of total category scores. You will be able to determine the following information from your scores.

Individual Item Scores

Average scores for *individual items* of 2.0 and above reflect strengths, that is, respondents are telling you that they observe your use of this practice.

Average scores for items of 1.7 to 1.9 are questionable, that is, the total itself provides insufficient information on which to draw a conclusion. You must, instead, look at the spread of scores to determine whether the average score reflects a strength or a weakness. For example, you may receive a score of 1.8 because four people were "inclined to agree" about that item and one person was "inclined to disagree." This would not reflect a weakness. However, if you receive one "strongly agree," one "inclined to agree," and two "inclined to disagree," you may need to improve on that item.

Average scores of 1.6 or lower reflect weaknesses.

Category Scores

For each dimension, look at the total score (sum of all averages). Use the following scale to determine your skill level:

0 to 9 = Skills Need Significant Improvement
10 to 19 = Skills Are Adequate, but Could Be Improved
20 to 24 = Excellent Employment of the Skills

This will help you to apply what you have learned about yourself. For best results, focus on dimensions on which you scored between 10 and 19 (areas for improvement) and between 0 and 9 (areas requiring concerted effort).

Also address individual questions on which your average score was 1.6 or lower, which reflects a weakness, and between 1.7 and 1.9, which reflects a "wait and see" attitude on the part of the respondents.

What can you do to make improvements in each of the quadrants? Read all of the suggestions that follow the interpretation of your scores and then complete the Leadership Dimensions Action Planning Sheet.

Constancy of Purpose

Low (0 to 9) scores in this quadrant indicate that the following areas require improvement:

- Being able to describe the future toward which you are leading your team;
- Formulating clear, specific reasons and outcomes before initiating changes;
- Showing others how their interests can be realized by achieving a common vision and purpose and inspiring them to join you; and
- Showing your understanding of proposed changes and the impact they will have on people and the organization.

Suggestions for Improvement

- Take a course in public speaking or presentation skills.
- Read a book about motivating others and practice what you have learned.
- Develop your interpersonal skills in the areas of opening up and sharing your vision, purpose, and concerns with others.

Congruity of Activity

Low (0 to 9) scores in this quadrant indicate that the following areas require improvement:

- Backing up what you have said, both publicly and privately;
- Monitoring and reinforcing any project or change efforts;
- Fostering a sense of ownership in your team;
- Personally sacrificing to further any project or change; and
- Practicing innovative leadership.

Suggestions for Improvement

- Initiate third-party shadowing, for example, ask a trusted advisor to spend extensive time with you to observe your behavior and provide feedback to you.

- Begin daily "journaling" to note any behaviors that might lead others to believe that you are saying one thing and doing another.

Competency of Outcome

Low (0 to 9) scores in this quadrant indicate that the following areas require improvement:

- Keeping abreast of and ahead of any new developments in your field of expertise;

- Balancing your leadership skills with top-notch technical skills;

- Challenging the status quo and finding new ways of doing work; and

- Rolling up your sleeves and doing the actual work along with your team members.

Suggestions for Improvement

- Obtain just-in-time, experiential training that provides you with actual work skills.

- Request to be mentored by a trusted expert practitioner, someone who has a reputation for excellent application skills.

Compatibility of Values

Low (0 to 9) scores in this quadrant indicate that the following areas require improvement:

- Being responsible and accountable;

- Creating an atmosphere of mutual trust through open and direct communication;

- Communicating your personal and the organization's ethical standards of operation and values; and

- Encouraging team members to be empowered and interdependent.

Suggestions for Improvement

- Attend experiential business ethics training with emphasis on job satisfaction, cooperation, achievement, creativity, tolerance, dignity and respect, truth, honor, and loyalty.

- With the aid of a trusted consultant, conduct a values clarification activity with your team.

LEADERSHIP DIMENSIONS ACTION PLANNING SHEET

Summary

The quadrant in which I scored the lowest was _____.
List the questions on which you scored 1.6 or lower and 1.7 to 1.9 below. These
indicate areas for improvement.

_____

_____

_____

_____

      Statements in the other three quadrants for which I scored 1.6 or lower
include:

_____

_____

_____

_____

Planning

1. As a result of this survey I have learned:

   _____

   _____

   _____

2. The cost of not making changes would be:

   _____

   _____

   _____

3. In order to improve my leadership I must:

   Continue doing: _____

   _____

Start doing: _____

Stop doing: _____

4. My sources for help include:
   Mentors: _____

   Training: _____

   Readings and resources: _____

   Other: _____

5. To ensure success I will:

6. I will know I have been successful when:

7. I will improve by taking the following actions:

Action	Start Date	Complete By

Pfeiffer Publications Guide

This guide is designed to familiarize you with the various types of Pfeiffer publications. The formats section describes the various types of products that we publish; the methodologies section describes the many different ways that content might be provided within a product. We also provide a list of the topic areas in which we publish.

FORMATS

In addition to its extensive book-publishing program, Pfeiffer offers content in an array of formats, from fieldbooks for the practitioner to complete, ready-to-use training packages that support group learning.

FIELDBOOK Designed to provide information and guidance to practitioners in the midst of action. Most fieldbooks are companions to another, sometimes earlier, work, from which its ideas are derived; the fieldbook makes practical what was theoretical in the original text. Fieldbooks can certainly be read from cover to cover. More likely, though, you'll find yourself bouncing around following a particular theme, or dipping in as the mood, and the situation, dictate.

HANDBOOK A contributed volume of work on a single topic, comprising an eclectic mix of ideas, case studies, and best practices sourced by practitioners and experts in the field.

An editor or team of editors usually is appointed to seek out contributors and to evaluate content for relevance to the topic. Think of a handbook not as a ready-to-eat meal, but as a cookbook of ingredients that enables you to create the most fitting experience for the occasion.

RESOURCE Materials designed to support group learning. They come in many forms: a complete, ready-to-use exercise (such as a game); a comprehensive resource on one topic (such as conflict management) containing a variety of methods and approaches; or a collection of like-minded activities (such as icebreakers) on multiple subjects and situations.

TRAINING PACKAGE An entire, ready-to-use learning program that focuses on a particular topic or skill. All packages comprise a guide for the facilitator/trainer and a workbook for the participants. Some packages are supported with additional media—such as video—or learning aids, instruments, or other devices to help participants understand concepts or practice and develop skills.

- *Facilitator/trainer's guide* Contains an introduction to the program, advice on how to organize and facilitate the learning event, and step-by-step instructor notes. The guide also contains copies of presentation materials—handouts, presentations, and overhead designs, for example—used in the program.

- *Participant's workbook* Contains exercises and reading materials that support the learning goal and serves as a valuable reference and support guide for participants in the weeks and months that follow the learning event. Typically, each participant will require his or her own workbook.

ELECTRONIC CD-ROMs and web-based products transform static Pfeiffer content into dynamic, interactive experiences. Designed to take advantage of the searchability, automation, and ease-of-use that technology provides, our e-products bring convenience and immediate accessibility to your workspace.

METHODOLOGIES

CASE STUDY A presentation, in narrative form, of an actual event that has occurred inside an organization. Case studies are not prescriptive, nor are they used to prove a point; they are designed to develop critical analysis and decision-making skills. A case study has a specific time frame, specifies a sequence of events, is narrative in structure, and contains a plot structure—an issue (what should be/have been done?). Use case studies when the goal is to enable participants to apply previously learned theories to the circumstances in the case, decide what is pertinent, identify the real issues, decide what should have been done, and develop a plan of action.

ENERGIZER A short activity that develops readiness for the next session or learning event. Energizers are most commonly used after a break or lunch to stimulate or refocus the group. Many involve some form of physical activity, so they are a useful way to counter post-lunch lethargy. Other uses include transitioning from one topic to another, where "mental" distancing is important.

EXPERIENTIAL LEARNING ACTIVITY (ELA) A facilitator-led intervention that moves participants through the learning cycle from experience to application (also known as a Structured Experience). ELAs are carefully thought-out designs in which there is a definite learning purpose and intended outcome. Each step—everything that participants do during the activity—facilitates the accomplishment of the stated goal. Each ELA includes complete instructions for facilitating the intervention and a clear statement of goals, suggested group size and timing, materials required, an explanation of the process, and, where appropriate, possible variations to the activity. (For more detail on Experiential Learning Activities, see the Introduction to the *Reference Guide to Handbooks and Annuals*, 1999 edition, Pfeiffer, San Francisco.)

GAME A group activity that has the purpose of fostering team spirit and togetherness in addition to the achievement of a pre-stated goal. Usually contrived—undertaking a desert expedition, for example—this type of learning method offers an engaging means for participants to demonstrate and practice business and interpersonal skills. Games are effective for team-building and personal development mainly because the goal is subordinate to the process—the means through which participants reach decisions, collaborate, communicate, and generate trust and understanding. Games often engage teams in "friendly" competition.

ICEBREAKER A (usually) short activity designed to help participants overcome initial anxiety in a training session and/or to acquaint the participants with one another. An icebreaker can be a fun activity or can be tied to specific topics or training goals. While a useful tool in itself, the icebreaker comes into its own in situations where tension or resistance exists within a group.

INSTRUMENT A device used to assess, appraise, evaluate, describe, classify, and summarize various aspects of human behavior. The term used to describe an instrument depends primarily on its format and purpose. These terms include survey, questionnaire, inventory, diagnostic, survey, and poll. Some uses of instruments include providing instrumental feedback to group members, studying here-and-now processes or functioning within a group, manipulating group composition, and evaluating outcomes of training and other interventions.

Instruments are popular in the training and HR field because, in general, more growth can occur if an individual is provided with a method for focusing specifically on his or her own behavior. Instruments also are used to obtain information that will serve as a basis for change and to assist in workforce planning efforts.

Paper-and-pencil tests still dominate the instrument landscape with a typical package comprising a facilitator's guide, which offers advice on administering the instrument and interpreting the collected data, and an initial set of instruments. Additional instruments are available separately. Pfeiffer, though, is investing heavily in e-instruments. Electronic instrumentation provides effortless distribution and, for larger groups particularly, offers advantages over paper-and-pencil tests in the time it takes to analyze data and provide feedback.

LECTURETTE A short talk that provides an explanation of a principle, model, or process that is pertinent to the participants' current learning needs. A lecturette is intended to establish a common language bond between the trainer and the participants by providing a mutual frame of reference. Use a lecturette as an introduction to a group activity or event, as an interjection during an event, or as a handout.

MODEL A graphic depiction of a system or process and the relationship among its elements. Models provide a frame of reference and something more tangible, and more easily remembered, than a verbal explanation. They also give participants something to "go on," enabling them to track their own progress as they experience the dynamics, processes, and relationships being depicted in the model.

ROLE PLAY A technique in which people assume a role in a situation/scenario: a customer service rep in an angry-customer exchange, for example. The way in which the role is approached is then discussed and feedback is offered. The role play is often repeated using a different approach and/or incorporating changes made based on feedback received. In other words, role playing is a spontaneous interaction involving realistic behavior under artificial (and safe) conditions.

SIMULATION A methodology for understanding the interrelationships among components of a system or process. Simulations differ from games in that they test or use a model that depicts or mirrors some aspect of reality in form, if not necessarily in content. Learning occurs by studying the effects of change on one or more factors of the model. Simulations are commonly used to test hypotheses about what happens in a system—often referred to as "what if?" analysis—or to examine best-case/worst-case scenarios.

THEORY A presentation of an idea from a conjectural perspective. Theories are useful because they encourage us to examine behavior and phenomena through a different lens.

TOPICS

The twin goals of providing effective and practical solutions for workforce training and organization development and meeting the educational needs of training and human resource professionals shape Pfeiffer's publishing program. Core topics include the following:

Leadership & Management
Communication & Presentation
Coaching & Mentoring
Training & Development
E-Learning
Teams & Collaboration
OD & Strategic Planning
Human Resources
Consulting